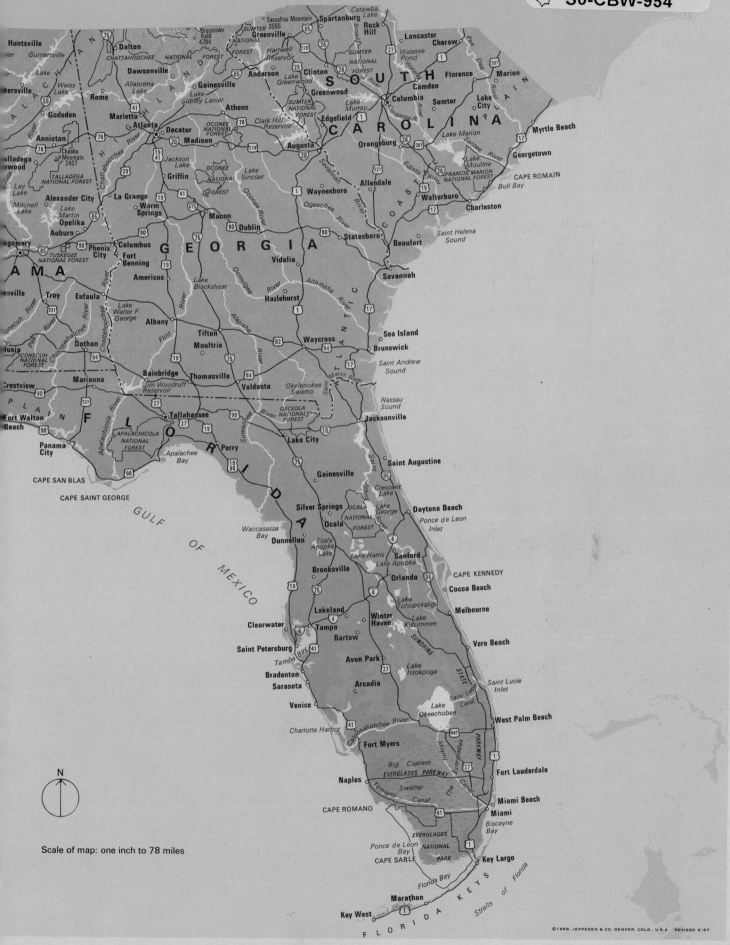

Scale of map: one inch to 78 miles

The Old South

TIME
LIFE
BOOKS ®

TIME-LIFE Library of America

The Old South

Alabama Florida Georgia Mississippi South Carolina

By John Osborne
and the Editors of
TIME-LIFE BOOKS

TIME-LIFE BOOKS, New York

The Author: John Osborne, a native of Mississippi, has established a distinguished reputation as a commentator on major social and political institutions. After serving as a TIME correspondent in London during and after World War II, he became foreign news editor and then chief editorial writer of LIFE, senior TIME-LIFE Far Eastern correspondent and a LIFE staff writer. He also contributed numerous articles to FORTUNE magazine and was the author of the LIFE World Library volume *Britain*. He now lives in Washington, D.C., devoting his energies to full-time freelance writing.

The Consulting Editor: Oscar Handlin, Charles Warren Professor of American History at Harvard University and director of the university's Charles Warren Center for Studies in American History, is one of America's foremost social historians. His work on U.S. immigrants, *The Uprooted*, won the Pulitzer Prize in 1952.

Old South Consultant: Bell Irvin Wiley, Professor of History at Emory University in Atlanta, has written and edited 22 books, including *Johnny Reb* and *Billy Yank,* accounts of soldier life in the Civil War.

The Cover: Framed by live oaks, the elegance of D'Evereux, a mansion near Natchez, Mississippi, recalls the romantic spirit of the antebellum Old South.

TIME-LIFE BOOKS

Editor
Maitland A. Edey

Executive Editor
Jerry Korn

Text Director   **Art Director**
Martin Mann   Sheldon Cotler

Chief of Research
Beatrice T. Dobie

Picture Editor
Robert G. Mason

Assistant Text Directors:
Harold C. Field, Ogden Tanner

Assistant Art Director:
Arnold C. Holeywell

Assistant Chief of Research:
Martha Turner

Publisher
Rhett Austell
General Manager: Joseph C. Hazen Jr.
Managing Director—International: Walter C. Rohrer
Planning Director: John P. Sousa III
Circulation Director: Joan D. Manley
Marketing Director: Carter Smith
Business Manager: John D. McSweeney
Publishing Board: Nicholas Benton,
Louis Bronzo, James Wendell Forbes

TIME-LIFE Library of America

Series Editor: Oliver E. Allen

Editorial Staff for *The Old South:*
Assistant Editor: James A. Maxwell
Picture Editor: Susan Rayfield
Designer: John Newcomb
Assistant Designer: Jean Lindsay
Staff Writers: Tony Chiu, Frank Kendig,
Victor Waldrop, Peter Wood
Chief Researcher: Clara E. Nicolai
Text Research: Terry Drucker, Vista Grayson
Picture Research: Ellen Youngblood, Toby Solovioff,
Rhea Finkelstein, Myra Mangan,
Marcia Gillespie, Margo Dryden, Joan Gerard
Art Assistant: Mervin Clay

Editorial Production
Color Director: Robert L. Young
Assistant: James J. Cox
Copy Staff: Marian Gordon Goldman, Patricia Miller,
Florence Keith
Picture Department: Dolores A. Littles,
Marquita Jones
Traffic: Arthur A. Goldberger
Studio: Jean Held

The text chapters of this book were written by John Osborne, the picture essays by the editorial staff. Valuable aid was provided by these individuals and departments of Time Inc.: LIFE staff photographers Bill Ray, Carl Mydans and Leonard McCombe; the Chief of the LIFE Picture Library, Doris O'Neil; the Chief of the Bureau of Editorial Reference, Peter Draz; the Chief of the TIME-LIFE News Service, Richard M. Clurman; Correspondents Jane Rieker (Miami), William Sartor (Greenville, Miss.), Joyce Leviton and Reg Murphy (Atlanta), Jack Bass (Columbia, S.C.), George Thurston (Tallahassee) and Sondra Hinson (Orlando).

Contents

Introduction 6

1 **A Sense of Difference** 9
Picture essay: Luxurious homes for a bygone aristocracy 15

2 **The Unique Experience** 33
Picture essay: Enthusiasm in war, rancor in defeat 41

3 **The Long-lived Racial Compact** 53
Picture essay: Negroes: moving up, with far to go 63

4 **Redeemers and Demagogues** 79
Picture essay: That oldtime religion 91

5 **The Southern Anomaly, Atlanta** 101
Picture essay: The fabled land called Florida 111

6 **The Drive for Growth and Change** 129
Picture essay: An industrial giant rejuvenated 137

7 **Great Writers in an Unlikely Setting** 149
Picture essay: A land honored by genius 161

Appendix
Suggested tours 174
Museums and galleries 180
Local festivals and events 181
Wildlife of the Old South 182
Statistical information 186
Pronunciation glossary 187
Credits and acknowledgments 187
Bibliography 188

Index 189

Introduction

It is an evocative phrase—"The Old South." Four of the five states that make up this old Cotton South were the heart of the old Confederacy, which also reached westward from Virginia to include Arkansas and far southward to bring in Florida, a teen-age state of 16 years when the Civil War began. Mr. Osborne eloquently and with fine clarity discusses the culture and economics of that Old South. It was a region compulsively preoccupied with agriculture in general and cotton in particular. While the East and New England were developing a skilled working force and an increasingly significant class of merchants and exporters, most of the South clung stubbornly to growing cotton. Slaves were its labor force. Moreover, planters, out of an expressed fear and concern about security, usually forbade any education to this labor force. With the same preoccupation with the "system," they rented out their slaves to work in the few factories that existed or to do carpentry or building. There was, therefore, no opportunity for a skilled artisan class to develop. The South was "different," as it felt itself to be.

But what the Old South was not is almost as important as what it was—and is. It never really was "a land of cavaliers and cotton." The thousands who poured into Alabama and Mississippi in the 1830s and early 1840s never became a class of goat-eed gentlemen in broad-brimmed black hats, sitting on the verandas of big pillared mansions, drinking juleps stirred with a silver spoon and served by adoring black servants. When the Civil War came, about 75 per cent of the Southern white people owned no slaves at all. A small planter class, by reason of its wealth and influence, managed to impress its politics and its legends on the Cotton South. The facts just now are catching up with the romantic myths of a luxurious civilization that was, the makers of myths said, like that of Greece, built on slave labor.

Mr. Osborne is at his forthright best in his analysis of the course of Southern political leadership after Appomattox. The leaders did bring down upon themselves a radical Reconstruction. This was the first postwar tragedy. The second was the abandonment of the Negro by the North. This immoral decision was part and parcel of the Hayes-Tilden election steal in 1876. The Confederate Democrats privately agreed to halt any serious opposition to Rutherford B. Hayes's receiving the disputed electoral votes that had been sent in from three Southern states—South Carolina, Florida and Louisiana. In return the Hayes government then removed remaining occupation troops and returned "states' rights" and the Negro problem to the several states.

"The New South" of the 1880s was the invention of an eloquent young editor, Henry Grady of *The Atlanta Constitution*. The antebellum South of slavery and secession was dead, he remarked. The South of union and freedom, however, was "living, breathing, growing every hour." Grady was an optimist with his eyes on the stars. He wanted industry and jobs for the South. In many ways he was ahead of his times. But on the critical issue of Negro voting rights, disregarded in spirit after 1876, and viciously denied after 1890, Grady was part of the consensus. He would not agree to such rights. Nor did he mention—nor did his audience ask about—the unconscionable violence in lynchings and other acts of physical repression that then disgraced the South and were to continue to do so until well into the 20th Century.

In the years since, many prophets from many and varied watchtowers have proclaimed a "New South." Still, the old past, the old convictions and the old attitudes remain. The agricultural revolution and the exodus of millions of uneducated and unskilled Southerners to the cities of northern America have helped provide the inflammatory material for urban riots, set off the flight to the homogenized suburbs and created a massive race problem throughout the country. But all this has paradoxically obscured the progress made in many areas of American life—and especially in the Old South. For despite the continued existence of old attitudes and prejudices, tremendous strides have been made in this region.

It is this presence of progress, I believe, that stimulates and continues my affection for the South. There is a mystique about the region, a feeling of attachment and warmth not easily translated into explanatory sentences. Even when one is frustrated by the many contradictions of the Old South, one feels this sense of moving on, of being a part of what is now, and what is ahead.

I remember some years ago, on a plane to Chicago, being seated beside a young Negro woman. She was, it developed, a teacher in a town near Atlanta. She was on her way to visit her parents in Chicago. They had migrated there years before, in the outflow of agricultural people that for so long has been a continuing chapter in the story of the South and the nation. She had come back to Georgia to teach. I asked her why.

"Well," she said, "I can tell you. Today I'm going back to Chicago. I'll see the girls who were in my class. They all have fairly good jobs. But, you know, their lives seem sterile to me. They go to the movies. They bowl. But, you know how it is in the South. That's where you are a part of what's going on! That's where the big change is taking place. You can be a part of it. You feel you are making a contribution. The South is alive—in motion. That's where I want to be." (She still is here. That conversation took place a decade ago. Her town has changed for the better. And she has been a part of the process of change.)

It is not the old myths, the legends or the roll of drums and the squeal of fifes as the bands strike up "Dixie" that hold one in the South. The Southerner in the Old South often muses about himself and his region. It is a pleasant place. There are flowers that grow the year around. In February the yellow jonquils bloom and in March clumps of yellow forsythia show richly golden in the hedges and along paths. The nights are deep-starred. In the piney woods of Georgia, Alabama, South Carolina, Mississippi and north Florida one rides for miles in a corridor between endless pines. They are best seen on a bright day with the myriad sun shafts shining through them. But even on rainy or foggy days they have a dark, ghostly beauty. The magnolias are like some antique, unbelievable beauty of ivory and carved jade leaves. In the Deep South summers one may turn off any of the interstate highways at dusk and quickly find side roads that smell heavily of honeysuckle. There are white-pillared mansions and poor farm cabins. There are manners, and there is arrogance.

But this is not "the South." The Southernism of the South is an arcane thing. It is not an agrarian civilization, as Vanderbilt University's "Fugitive" poets once dreamed and wrote. Nor is it the reek and rumble of an on-the-make bulldozer society.

The South is many Souths—many things. It is a region of white and black people, long separated and unknowing, groping painfully and arduously toward each other so that in good time they may clasp hands and together walk the glory road of the old hymn toward a time of jubilee.

"The South" is standing at night atop one of Atlanta's new towering buildings—with trees and fountain below—and looking out toward the distant, dark horizon. Yonder, the mind says, are the Big and Little Kennesaw Mountains around which red-bearded William Tecumseh Sherman fought his way into Atlanta. There ended the last meaningful resistance of the Old South. Once in the city, Sherman regrouped his forces, burned Atlanta and moved on, marching to the sea and up through the Carolinas to receive a surrender from Joe Johnston and to end the anguish of war in this region.

"The South" is driving through and seeing the miracle of Florida's growth and development, its beaches and citrus groves, and its industry. "The South" is coming up through Mississippi and remembering it 25 years ago—40 years ago—and seeing it now, moving away from cotton and isolation into the national future.

There is a New South, not yet here—but coming. One sees it in the faces of young Negro children in school singing lustily and confidently: "This land is your land/This land is my land. . . ." The New South is in the faces of students, white and black, and in the faces of the young executives, Southern trained and oriented. All these are a part of the new breed making a new South.

There is an excitement in the South. It is an excitement of the spirit and of reality. A recent Twentieth Century Fund study concludes that the South has a tremendous potential for growth and is undergoing "a slow-moving social revolution of significant proportions." The study emphasizes the need for improved education and upgrading the training of the work force.

That will be done—it is being done.

—RALPH MCGILL
Publisher, "The Atlanta Constitution"

1

A Sense
of Difference

Calling the five states with which this book deals the "Old South" is very Southern. It is an act of amiable arrogance, sentimental and imprecise in its evocation of the past to grace the present. It is done in awareness that professional spokesmen of those states would rather be known as exponents and builders of the "New South," a term Southern boosters have been using for more than a century. Less progressive natives of at least three Southern states outside the area could deem their exclusion cause for demanding satisfaction with pistols at dawn. But, as Southerners are prone to say when caught in tribal aberration, "Doing it suits us." And there is a case for applying the designation the "Old South," with all it connotes, to Alabama, Florida, Georgia, Mississippi and South Carolina.

These states were the first to secede from the Union in 1860 and 1861, and in one of them, South Carolina, the first battle of the Civil War was fought at Fort Sumter. In all of them, even in Florida to a greater extent than might be supposed, attitudes and characteristics that are associated

Reflecting the loyalty many people of the Old South feel for their institutions and traditions, a stern Confederate monument in the main square of Oxford, Mississippi, honors the "patriotism of the . . . soldiers" who "gave their lives in a just and holy cause."

with the traditional South persist to a remarkable and sometimes an embarrassing degree. At least two of the five, Mississippi and Alabama, behave on occasion as if they would still prefer to be affiliated with the Confederate States of America rather than with the United States.

The truth is, however, that the case for this particular Old South hardly needs making. The Old South is really an abstraction, having more to do with communal custom and posture than with geography, and subject by long practice to definition pretty much as the definer chooses.

If those who are defining the Old South are white Southerners, it is what they believe *their* South to have been at some misty point in the past —usually "before the war," meaning the Civil War: "the land of cotton," a land of gentle languors and gentle people, where everybody knew his place and was happy, or should have been happy, in that place. It also is what they, in dreamy moments, imagine their South still to be today, despite all the changes that have come upon it. If they are Negro Southerners, their image from the past is very dissimilar, considerably more accurate, and closer than they like to the present and known reality.

But in their recognition of a Southern "difference," Negro Southerners are at one with all other

9

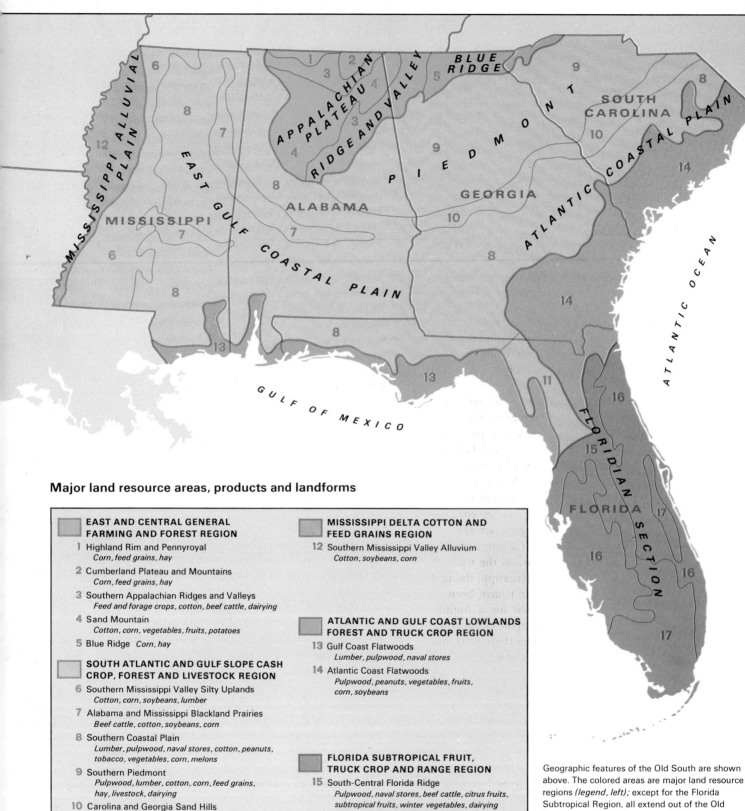

Major land resource areas, products and landforms

EAST AND CENTRAL GENERAL FARMING AND FOREST REGION

1 Highland Rim and Pennyroyal
  Corn, feed grains, hay

2 Cumberland Plateau and Mountains
  Corn, feed grains, hay

3 Southern Appalachian Ridges and Valleys
  Feed and forage crops, cotton, beef cattle, dairying

4 Sand Mountain
  Cotton, corn, vegetables, fruits, potatoes

5 Blue Ridge *Corn, hay*

SOUTH ATLANTIC AND GULF SLOPE CASH CROP, FOREST AND LIVESTOCK REGION

6 Southern Mississippi Valley Silty Uplands
  Cotton, corn, soybeans, lumber

7 Alabama and Mississippi Blackland Prairies
  Beef cattle, cotton, soybeans, corn

8 Southern Coastal Plain
  Lumber, pulpwood, naval stores, cotton, peanuts, tobacco, vegetables, corn, melons

9 Southern Piedmont
  Pulpwood, lumber, cotton, corn, feed grains, hay, livestock, dairying

10 Carolina and Georgia Sand Hills
  Pulpwood, lumber, corn, cotton

11 North-Central Florida Ridge
  Lumber, pulpwood, naval stores, corn, peanuts, tobacco, vegetables, melons, tung nuts, cattle

MISSISSIPPI DELTA COTTON AND FEED GRAINS REGION

12 Southern Mississippi Valley Alluvium
  Cotton, soybeans, corn

ATLANTIC AND GULF COAST LOWLANDS FOREST AND TRUCK CROP REGION

13 Gulf Coast Flatwoods
  Lumber, pulpwood, naval stores

14 Atlantic Coast Flatwoods
  Pulpwood, peanuts, vegetables, fruits, corn, soybeans

FLORIDA SUBTROPICAL FRUIT, TRUCK CROP AND RANGE REGION

15 South-Central Florida Ridge
  Pulpwood, naval stores, beef cattle, citrus fruits, subtropical fruits, winter vegetables, dairying

16 Southern Florida Flatwoods
  Winter vegetables, citrus fruits, subtropical fruits

17 Florida Everglades and Associated Areas
  Beef cattle, winter vegetables; sugar cane, dairying

Geographic features of the Old South are shown above. The colored areas are major land resource regions *(legend, left);* except for the Florida Subtropical Region, all extend out of the Old South into neighboring states. Within each region are numbered subregions, whose principal products are indicated in the legend. Prominent physical features are labeled on the map; some cover more than one land resource subregion.

Southerners. For the South and its people are profoundly marked by a sense of difference from the rest of the United States and, again if they are white Southerners, by a pride in that difference. In this age of diminishing sectional distinctions, an acceptable definition of the Old South could be that it is where the white man's Southern sense and pride of difference are most deeply ingrained.

Nowhere in the South are the sense and pride of difference more thoroughly imbedded and more stubbornly preserved than they are in South Carolina, Georgia, Alabama and Mississippi. The fifth of the states, Florida, is a phenomenon unto itself and is so described in the text and pictures on pages 111-127. Yet Florida, despite its hordes of vacationers and resident migrants and its increasing industrialization, also retains a Southern identity. Many areas of that state continue to display Southern traits, partially because the Old South influences its newcomers from other sections more than they influence the Old South. "You don't understand," a former New Hampshireman now living in Florida recently said to a bemused visitor. "*Our* Negroes are different."

Differences peculiar to the region do not imply sameness within the region. There are large variations of terrain, accent, manner, atmosphere and economic welfare between the states and between sections of each state. A reporter who went from one of the more somnolent parts of Mississippi into neighboring Alabama, gathering information for this book, felt as if he had entered another country. A north Mississippi hillbilly may be an alien in many counties of his own state, and one such was cut to the quick some years ago when the waitress at a resort hotel in southeastern Mississippi thought he was a New Yorker. "It wouldn't have been so painful if she'd just mistaken him for a fugitive bank robber," a sympathetic observer commented later. Northeastern Georgia, where there were few slaves or large plantations and where the people are relatively isolated from urban influences, has more in common with upland South Carolina than with Atlanta and south Georgia. Natives of Charleston and the adjacent Low Country regard birth and residence elsewhere in South Carolina as a pitiable misfortune. The Carolinians thus deprived retaliate by mocking the inimitable Charleston mode of speech—a slurred amalgam of idiom and accent that sounds rather like a muffled popgun emitting gobbets of molasses. "Garden," for example, comes out approximately as "gyarden" and "car" as "cyar."

But internal variations are minor by comparison with the melding Southern sense of shared, collective difference from the rest of the nation. With it goes a companion sense of alienation, lessening in some respects but intensifying in others, as national pressures, social and economic, bear upon the Old South. When William Faulkner, the Mississippi novelist, wrote "You can't understand it. You would have to be born there," he spoke for that South to non-Southerners. "Oh, you understand us," a Georgian or a Mississippian will say with obvious relief when he discovers that a stranger hails from Alabama or South Carolina, even though the visitor may have been so long away from the South that his origins are not instantly apparent and his attitudes have changed enormously.

Why the differences should seem so deep, why there should be so much to understand and to challenge understanding, are questions that have preoccupied myriad historians, sociologists, novelists and dabblers in regional psychology. Disagreeing in much, they generally attach great importance to "the influence of the southern physical world." It is typical that the Southern author of that phrase, Wilbur J. Cash, uses it in his classic study, *The Mind of the South*, as if there were a single "southern physical world"; there are, in fact, several.

The actual physical world may be the Appalachian ridges at the upper edges of South Carolina and Georgia. It may be the plateau of hills and red-dirt valleys called the Piedmont, which runs through South Carolina, Georgia and well into Alabama. Southerners in those three states may live along the geologic demarcation called the Fall Line, where the plateau slopes off into the Coastal Plain. That plain, variously flat and mildly rolling, reaches back into all five states from the Atlantic and the Gulf of Mexico and embraces such different terrains as the steamy Low Country of South Carolina, the pinewoods of Georgia and Alabama, and the swamps of Georgia and Florida. Or the Southern world may be the Black Belt—named not for its Negroes but for its soil—a loamy finger curving across central Alabama into eastern Mississippi. And it may be that very heartland and repository of all that is Southern, the Mississippi Delta, a fertile strip of flood silt beside the river and in the state that bear the same name.

Whichever of these or a hundred local variants the Southern eye may fall upon, the effect upon the Southerner is substantially the same. Cash noted that there was "a sort of cosmic conspiracy against reality" throughout the South. Wherever he may be, the Southerner sees Cash's country "of extravagant colors, of proliferating foliage and bloom, of flooding yellow sunlight, and, above all perhaps, of haze." No matter that the real colors and bloom may actually be those of back-road weeds; that the sunlight may be obscured in a latter-day haze of factory smoke; that suburban homes and supermarkets may sprawl through fields where Cash remembered in the 1930s "the far-away mourning of the hounds and the far-away crying of the doves." Even in today's busy and changing Old South, where bulldozer fumes compete with "such sweet and inexorable opiates as the rich odors of hot earth and pinewood and the perfume of the magnolia in bloom," the preferred if not always "the dominant" mood is still as Cash described it: "one of well-nigh drunken reverie . . . of soft languor . . . a mood, in sum, in which directed thinking is all but impossible."

The Southern *sense* of climate is more uniform and more influential than the real Southern climate. In the South, as it is perceived by natives —and in most writing about the South—it is always summer. From mid-spring through autumn the states of the Old South do enjoy the long spell of warm to hot weather for which they are celebrated. In lower Florida and along the Gulf Coasts of Alabama and Mississippi, the warmth may (or may not) endure through the winter. In the lowlands and the upland valleys, the summer heat becomes extreme and induces the renowned Southern languor. But cold weather does come to much of the Old South. The interesting point, however, is that the contrary aspects of the Southern climate are never considered to have a compensating effect upon Southern character. The Sartorises, Snopeses and Sutpens of William Faulkner's fictional Yoknapatawpha County are not affected by the chill that annually touches his home country around Oxford, Mississippi. On a February night in 1967, when a calamitous fire drew attention to Montgomery, Alabama, the reported temperature there was six degrees below freezing. During the previous winter, in the South Carolina Senate chamber at Columbia, a passionate defense of Southern institutions was briefly interrupted, but not otherwise affected, when one Senator threw a snowball at another. A woman who grew up in the 19th Century in Bainbridge, a Georgia town near the Florida border, used to recall with wry irritation the refusal of her family and neighbors to heat their houses. She said they simply declined to credit periodic evidence that the weather so far south could be uncomfortably cold.

That was a long time ago and things have changed in Bainbridge as elsewhere. But the chances are that Southerners there as elsewhere still view seasonal offenses against climatic tradition much as Cash did. "I know," he wrote, "that winter comes to the land, certainly. I know there are days when the color and the haze are stripped away and the real stands up in drab and depressing harshness. But these things pass and are forgotten."

They are rightly forgotten. It was the remembered summery norm, up to 300 mild days and frost-free nights in favored areas, and rarely fewer than 200 such days and nights each year in the more rigorous uplands, that made the Old South a region of farms and farmers, rural in life and spirit, slow to change, and kept it bound in rural attitudes long after they would have disappeared elsewhere.

The combination of terrain and climate, the sun-warmed land and its rich repayment for simple labor, brought the Negro and made the Old South the particular home of slavery. Almost half of the four million slaves in the United States in 1860 were in Georgia, Alabama, Mississippi and South Carolina. History proffers no greater irony than this, that the Negroes in their bondage indelibly marked and molded the society that we call the "white South." Almost every quality and attitude that have set that South apart during the two centuries of slavery and the following century of substitutes for slavery may be traced in some degree—and often wholly—to the presence of the Negro.

No aspect of the Southern myth is less credible than its insistence that white Southerners alone understand "their" Negroes. But the white South, in three centuries of life with Negroes in numbers unmatched in other American regions, came to grasp a fact of biracial existence that the country at large was still absorbing in 1967. This fact, riveted in the consciousness of the Old South, is that in a biracial society there is no practicable middle ground between complete equality and complete inequality of the two races.

Slavery assured the ascendancy of all Southern whites, whether they owned slaves or not. It also imposed the general racial peace, easily mistaken for general contentment, that prevailed during the slavery era and accustomed Southern whites to the notion that inequality is a natural prerequisite of biracial amity. Ever since slavery was abolished, the region has been preoccupied with the determination of white Southerners to maintain their ascendancy and, along with it, the only pattern of biracial life that they consider workable.

Under the pressure of national law and policy, and by dint of the Negroes' struggle, that pattern is now being smashed. Prejudice and hatred in their ugliest forms envenom the battle to preserve a remnant of the old order. But prejudice and hatred, as the nation has been compelled to recognize, are not Southern monopolies. What distinguishes the racial stance of the South and particularly of the Old South is a disbelief in halfway measures—an attitude that, surprising though the assertion may be, can be described as "racial realism."

This stance was until lately one of total and often ferocious resistance to racial concession. Many Southerners expressed this attitude by wearing buttons bearing the legend, "Never," a sentiment that now shares a "famous-last-words" crypt with the assertion, made by French generals in the 1930s, that the Maginot Line was an insurmountable barrier to the German Army. For despite continuing appearances to the contrary, the actual Southern stance is now one of enforced adjustment, of grimly anticipated surrender to full equality.

The rapid growth of industry in the Old South and the growing importance of the federal government to the region's economy have hastened the pace of the surrender. Northern firms, establishing plants in the area, often insist on maintaining a nondiscriminatory hiring policy. Companies fulfilling government contracts are compelled to adhere to federal fair-employment-practices laws. These same laws, of course, apply to the many installations wholly operated by the government.

In the face of these and the other powerful forces for change at work in the Old South, the ability of the region to retain so much of its traditional Southern character seems a paradox, a mystery. But the paradox fades and the mystery dissolves when the developments are viewed in their Southern context. The Old South, Florida excepted, is a region of *natives*, of people who live in the state where they were born. Just about the only statistical category, aside from the grimmer ones, in which Mississippi leads the nation is in the proportion of residents born in the state—nearly 90 per cent in 1960. Alabama, South Carolina and Georgia were all above 80 per cent in that year. Among native Americans generally, only about two thirds were living in their respective states of birth, and in the Western United States, only some 44 per cent. The high proportion of Negroes native to the four states (above 90 per cent) partly explains the contrast, but the equivalent figures for white residents—well over 75 per cent—are also far above the national level. The point is emphasized rather than contradicted by the massive flight of Negroes and the substantial migration of white natives from the same states in the past decades. Those who remain,

Down-South vittles

The *diet* of the South is one of its distinctive features. This is the only section of the nation in which people eat significant quantities of field corn. Some of the corn is ground into meal and baked into cornbread or fried as "hush puppies." Some is leached in lye and made into "hominy." The kernels of hominy may be fried whole, or they may be ground into flinty, pinhead-sized particles and boiled as "hominy grits" (or just plain "grits"), which is standard breakfast fare in many Southern homes and restaurants.

The diet is heavy on fats and fried foods, such as "Southern fried chicken." Chicken and pork, rather than beef, are the staple meats, and rice often supplants potatoes as a starch. Hot rolls or biscuits are considered a necessity with any meal, and iced tea is the standard summer beverage. Mayonnaise is often used where people in other parts of the country would use butter or margarine.

The Southern diet has a number of distinctive foods which are seldom eaten in other parts of the nation, including okra, black-eyed peas, sweet potatoes, and "salad greens," which means the leaves of plants such as pokeweed, collards, turnips, kale, rape or spinach; salad greens are prepared by lengthy boiling.

The Southeastern United States
by John Fraser Hart

whether by choice or from circumstance and inertia, are likely to be well set in habits of mind.

Viewed alone, the statistics of change—to be examined in detail in a later chapter—suggest that the region and its natives are caught up in a tumultuous and total revolution. Such national trends as the shift from rural life and farm labor to urban living and work in industry are evident even in laggard Mississippi, where the urban population rose from less than 20 per cent of the total in 1940 to an estimated 47 per cent in 1967. Although the economic bases of the Old South are admittedly lower than those of other areas, the region's *rates* of increase in personal income, urban expansion, capital investment and public spending for education are higher than the nation's as a whole. There is change within change: agriculture, although losing its primacy to industry and commerce, provides a higher return for fewer people on fewer and bigger farms. Cotton, correctly called "the passion" of an older South, takes up less and less of the region's land and energies as truck farming, citrus fruits, timber, soybeans and peanuts provide needed diversification. In the one-crop past, such diversification was thought to be not only visionary but against Southern nature. Industry, the new passion, also changes with improved technology that is more dependent upon human skills and machine techniques than upon sheer labor.

Yet viewed in the whole and on the scene, it is a curiously quiet and limited revolution. A visitor new to the South and coming to it from a raucous Northern or Western metropolis is likely to get an impression not of tumult and upheaval, but of the sleepy calm described in guidebooks a quarter century ago. Even a returning expatriate is likely to be comforted or disturbed (as the case may be) by the discovery that so much remains as it was amid so much that is new. Nor are these merely the superficial impressions of a wishful native or of a tourist bemused by the columned mansions of Natchez, the glorious gardens of lowland South Carolina, or the placid courtesy with which breakfast is served even in some new and raw motel. A team of university specialists, studying the South under the auspices of the Twentieth Century Fund, found in process "a slow-moving social revolution of significant proportions." The many changes of outlook and practice made them "optimistic" but less than certain about the future. "We can only hope," they wrote, "that the traditional values and beliefs of southern people have changed sufficiently in recent years to permit them . . . to develop the South's full potential."

"Traditional values and beliefs" remain strong, but they are not in themselves the restrictive factors they used to be. The Old South in revolution, striving toward economic parity and driven toward social parity with the nation, is no longer hobbled by conscious attachment to an idealized past. It is the region's heritage from the real past that slows the pace and obstructs the path of revolution.

In the bygone South of fact rather than legend, the most neglected resource was the population, and the region is paying for the neglect. In South Carolina, Georgia and Alabama, and to a beginning extent in Mississippi, the demand of both established and incoming industries for labor skills has forced state governments to recognize the human wastage characteristic of their societies. It is apparent in the hundreds of thousands of white and Negro adults who lack enough education to fit them for factory jobs and who, in rising numbers, must be trained, at enormous state and federal expense, in vocational and adult-education schools. The region's rate of draft rejection is the highest in the country, a galling indicator that holds good for white as well as Negro youths. The low levels of education, income, productive capacity and overall competence that have prevailed in the Old South make the accomplishment of recent years seem spectacular, especially when they are expressed in percentages. But the gloss dims when the achieved levels are seen to be usually below those of the rest of the nation and often at the very bottom.

Such comparisons should, but do not, chasten the regional ego, which remains in splendid shape. The impression elsewhere that residents of the Old South no longer consider their status as Southerners to be a distinction is in error. They do not permit all that remains to be achieved to cloud their pride in what has been done. The thought that in this flattening age their Old South may wind up more or less like everywhere else in the United States nags them at times, but it is not taken very seriously. They continue, in brief, to enjoy a conviction not only that their part of the country is different from all the other parts but that on the whole it is the best part and is going to stay that way. This is undoubtedly far more true of white than Negro Southerners, but it is not entirely untrue of the latter. Medgar Evers, the murdered leader of Mississippi Negroes, kept an answer ready for Yankee reporters who asked him why he stayed in his home state. His answer was, "I *like* Mississippi. This is the best state in the Union. The only thing is, I want to make it the best state for me and my people, too."

Luxurious homes for a bygone aristocracy

About the beginning of the 19th Century, cotton planters in the Old South began to amass huge fortunes and build mansions of great elegance. Some of the finest of these mansions crowned the high bluffs of the Mississippi River near Natchez, Mississippi; still inhabited and, for the most part, well maintained, they provide a glimpse of the grandeur and opulence of the antebellum South.

Surrounded by spacious grounds, these mansions were built in a variety of architectural styles ranging from Greek Revival to Moorish. The plantation owners filled their homes with fine furnishings— English tables, French mirrors, Italian arches —imported from Europe and brought up the Mississippi to Natchez by riverboat from New Orleans. In most of them this elegance can still be seen today, a reminder of a way of life that is gone forever.

Like most of the great antebellum mansions in Natchez, Longwood *(left)* has a gallery overlooking tree-shaded grounds. Such a porch served as a pleasant, cool retreat for the family on warm evenings as well as an ideal place to entertain guests.

Photographs by Alfred Eisenstaedt

Shaded by cedars, cooled by slaves

Guarded by tall cedars draped with Spanish moss, Linden *(above)* looks much as it did when the first shots were fired on Fort Sumter in 1861. The mansion's original owner is not known, but it is thought that this house was built about 1785. In 1818 the mansion was purchased by Thomas B. Reed, who was later to become a United States Senator from Mississippi. Reed added to each side of the house and built the upper and lower galleries, supported by Doric columns of cypress, that grace Linden's elegant façade. An ancestor of the present owner, Mrs. Frank Fauntleroy, bought the mansion in 1840, some years after Reed had sold it.

The interior of Linden, decorated with imported Empire and Victorian furnishings, reflects the aristocratic Southerners' love of comfort and opulence. Two of the earliest prints of the American naturalist painter John James Audubon can be seen in the dining room at right. Over the table, on which antique china is arranged, hangs a large, hand-carved punkah, or fan. During meals, a house servant created a breeze by pulling the fan back and forth with a long cord.

A regal setting for proper conversation

The parlor at left is one of the many elegant rooms of Melrose, a mansion built in 1845 by John T. McMurran, a lawyer. McMurran, who made his fortune investing in cotton plantations, furnished his home in splendor with imports from Europe and the Middle East. After losing his fortune in the Civil War, he sold Melrose to a friend and fellow lawyer, George M. Davis, in whose family it remains.

The parlor, one of the favorite spots of visitors to Melrose, is decorated with French brocade draperies and carved rosewood furniture. The gilded bronze chandelier, installed when the house was built, once burned oil but is now converted to electricity. The carpet is a copy of the one taken out of Melrose after the Civil War. At far left are twin rosewood swivel chairs and a low stool. The grouping shown was sometimes referred to as a courting set: a couple could chat decorously while separated by a chaperone watching over them from her place on the stool. The stool, though padded, was, according to legend, made hard to keep her from falling asleep.

Other furnishings in the mansion are of comparable distinction. There are fireplaces of Egyptian marble, huge mirrors framed with gold leaf, and a remarkable circular table decorated with inlaid marble birds whose eyes were once jewels. The jewels, it is said, were pried out by the bayonets of Union soldiers during the Civil War.

Gloucester, a magnificent Georgian mansion surrounded by beautiful grounds *(left)*, was the home of Winthrop Sargent, who came to Natchez in 1798 as the first territorial governor of Mississippi. A staunch Puritan of old New England stock, Sargent considered the town a "most abominable place." The Southerners' way of life clashed with his Puritanical concepts. Natchez, he said, was filled with "a refractory and turbulent spirit, with parties headed by men of perverseness and cunning."

Sargent would have found life in his post unsupportable had it not been for the David Williams family, particularly the recently widowed Maria McIntosh Williams. This respected Natchez family invited the newly appointed governor to their home, and it was here, relaxing on the front porch, that he found pleasure in living in the South. He soon married Maria Williams and later purchased the Williams house.

Sargent greatly expanded the mansion and gave it the name Gloucester, after his hometown in Massachusetts. The brass door knocker shown below is one of the decorative touches he added to the house. The French crystal liqueur set and wine decanters *(below left)* and the ornate picture frame of Florentine brass *(below right)* were imported from Europe by a later resident of Gloucester.

Although Sargent prospered in this region—he amassed a huge fortune that included a large number of slaves and more than 25,000 acres of land—he continued to object to the Southerners' frivolous way of life. In his will he asked that he be buried "speedily and without parade" and that "no mausoleum but some simple stone proclaim me dead." When he died in 1820, his widow sold the mansion, but a quarter of a century later one of her sons, George Washington Sargent, bought it back.

The younger Sargent met his death in Gloucester's doorway, shot during the Civil War by two Union soldiers. The soldiers were later apprehended, tried and then executed on the grounds of nearby D'Evereux *(cover)*.

A mansion haunted by ghostly music

Dunleith, an imposing mansion resembling a Greek temple, was completed in 1849 by Charles Dahlgren, son of the first Swedish consul to the United States. Born and brought up in Philadelphia, Dahlgren, a quick-tempered youth whose impetuous nature led him into duel after duel, traveled south to New Orleans, where the Southern code of honor blended perfectly with his temperament. Here he first admired the Neo-Grecian mansions of the Louisiana planters. When he moved upriver to Natchez he probably had pictured Dunleith in his mind.

In Natchez Dahlgren married into one of Mississippi's most respected families, the Rouths. A few years after the wedding the Dahlgren home—a brick house they had acquired from the Rouths—was struck by lightning and burned to the ground. On the site of this disaster Dahlgren erected Dunleith, his Greek temple.

Dahlgren had seven strapping boys by his wife, and since Mrs. Dahlgren already had four children by a former marriage, Dunleith was always filled with the sound of frolicking youngsters. Dahlgren's favorite was a bright-eyed, intelligent girl named Sarah Ann, who was to become an accomplished writer of scholarly essays, novels and poetry. But when Sarah Ann became a young woman she brought her stepfather great grief. The first serious rift occurred when, against her stepfather's wishes, she married a man many years her senior. The breach was widened during the Civil War, when Sarah Ann maintained her close friendship with Jefferson Davis, President of the Confederacy, after he had quarreled bitterly with Dahlgren, a brilliant Rebel officer, over the conduct of the war. The break between stepfather and daughter was never healed.

Despite the colorful careers of Dahlgren and Sarah Ann, the best-remembered resident of Dunleith was a wistful lady named Miss Percy. She was a relative of Mrs. Dahlgren's first husband and is said to have carried on an affair in France with a member of the court of Louis Philippe, the "Citizen King." Rejected by her noble suitor, she returned to Dunleith, where she acted as tutor to the Dahlgren children. There, supposedly stricken by her shattered love affair, Miss Percy kept mostly to herself, playing the harp at dusk. In the evenings, it is said, the sound of Miss Percy's harp can still be heard in the resplendent halls of Dunleith.

Spanish influence
on the Mississippi bluffs

In the heart of Natchez, two blocks from the main street, stands The Elms, one of the oldest of the city's mansions. Although the house, a large two-and-one-half-story structure with galleries on three sides, is now shaded by enormous oaks, it was probably once surrounded by elm trees that gave it its name. The Elms is thought to have been built around 1782, when Natchez was still a Spanish province. Its architecture shows a strong Spanish influence, and the mansion was furnished with European imports

like the Portuguese wrought-iron staircase *(below right)*.

The Spanish had come to Natchez for military reasons. Its high bluffs overlooking the vital Mississippi made the perfect spot for a fortified post, and the site was used at various times as a base for troops of three nations. In 1716 the French established a permanent settlement and military base there. Resenting this encroachment, the Natchez Indians massacred nearly 300 settlers in 1729. The French retaliated by wiping out most of the Natchez nation. In the early 1760s, with the end of the French and Indian Wars, the outpost was turned over to the British, who were happy to receive this bastion over the Mississippi. Occupied with the Revolutionary War, the British ceded Natchez to Spain in 1779. It was during this period that The Elms was built. Even after Natchez became part of the United States under the terms of a treaty with Spain in 1795, it retained much of its Spanish flavor, which continued to be reflected in its houses.

A romantic background for a life of gaiety

Arlington *(below right)*, a massive Georgian mansion of imported English brick, was built about 1816 by Jane Surget White, the daughter of the French colonist Pierre Surget and the widow of Captain James Hampton White. The scene of numerous gay parties attended by beautifully gowned women and their fashionably dressed escorts, Arlington became a major social center of Natchez. Competition for that title was severe; during the antebellum years, entertainment was almost continuous in the

town. A number of Northerners who came to visit are said to have become so engrossed with the social whirl that they simply stayed on and were finally buried in various family graveyards.

Arlington, like all the other Natchez mansions, was once surrounded by many acres of landscaped grounds, meticulously cared for by the slaves. On the way to a party at Arlington the elegant carriages of the Natchez gentry traveled up a long drive sheltered by enormous elms and oaks. Shrubbery and flowers were imported from all over the world; on the Arlington grounds there are still numerous pale pink azalea plants brought over from China in the 19th Century.

Arlington has been well kept since it was built, a happier fate than that of some of the Natchez mansions that fell into disrepair in the years after the Civil War. Several of these neglected mansions were restored by the late Mrs. Hubert Barnum, mother of Arlington's present owner, and a noted collector of dolls.

In a case-lined room in Arlington is the late Mrs. Hubert Barnum's collection of more than 1,000 antique dolls dating over several centuries.

Both the French fashion doll *(top right),* her dress trimmed in lace, and the French mechanical doll *(bottom right)* were made about 1870.

Nutt's Folly:
an unfulfilled dream

Perhaps the most remarkable mansion on the Natchez bluffs is an enormous, octagonal shell of Moorish design *(above)* named Longwood but more often referred to as "Nutt's Folly." The house, with its huge rotunda and onion-shaped dome, was the inspiration of Haller Nutt, a scientifically oriented planter possessed of boundless enthusiasm for Oriental and Moorish architecture. Intended to house the Nutts and their many children, Longwood was designed to Nutt's specifications by the Philadelphia architect Samuel Sloan. Slaves began construction, and in 1860 Sloan brought a small army of Pennsylvania craftsmen to Natchez to complete the work. But before the task was done the Civil War began and all the workmen left the job to return to the North. Believing the conflict would not last long, Nutt moved his family into the basement of the mansion. Unfortunately he died before the war ended and the house was never completed. It is still owned by Nutt's heirs, however, and the basement is occupied by a caretaker. On one of Longwood's porches *(right)*, tools, nail kegs and paint pots remain just where they were when the Pennsylvanians left to fight Johnny Reb.

2

The Unique Experience

"No other part of America lives so intimately with its past, or struggles so hard to survive its ruinous contradictions," wrote Harvard's Dr. Robert Coles in 1966 after an eight-year sociopsychiatric study of the people of the South. "The characteristic southerner," he concluded, "is the one American who really knows history because he lives constantly in its vengeful presence."

Southern historian C. Vann Woodward takes a similar view. The history of the South, he said, is to be found in "the collective experience of the southern people . . . their unique experience as Americans." It is an experience that touches every Southerner regardless of color or class.

That the Southern experience should be unique and that the region's history should be a "vengeful presence" seem as inevitable as the denouement of a Greek tragedy. From the days of the earliest English settlements, men, conditions and events conspired to set the Old South apart from the rest of America, to establish a provincial outlook, to spawn and nourish slavery, and to maintain the

lasting and tragic patterns that were its outgrowth.

The Old South's history can be divided into four distinct periods, the first of which is discussed in this chapter. In that period, lasting from 1607 until a few decades after the American Revolution, a core society based on a body of settled beliefs and on the institution of slavery became solidly entrenched. The 1820s marked the beginning of the second phase, during which slavery was defended not just as an economic necessity but as "a positive good"; at this time a militant separatism took hold and set the South on its course toward secession and defeat in the Civil War. The third period, postwar Reconstruction and its aftermath, marked the region's gradual recovery from its trauma and its return to the national Union on terms that permitted it to go right on being its Southern self, under a renewed system of white ascendancy and Negro submission. The fourth period, from 1930 to the present, has seen the first lasting encroachment of federal power and national standards on the social and economic structure of the Old South; it has been the first time in all of the Southern experience when national forces proved to be permanently stronger than the interior resistance to change.

In the late 1960s the Southerner old enough to remember the Old South of the past looked back

Seemingly unaffected by the conflict raging at the time, Negro slaves in 1862 prepare cotton for ginning on a South Carolina plantation. Three years later, along with some 1.8 million other slaves in the Old South, they would become free citizens.

St. Augustine, Florida, was already more than 100 years old when this sketch, showing the Spanish settlement as a thriving port, was published in Holland in 1671. There is considerable artistic license in the drawing. The area has no mountains, and only a few supply ships stopped there, for the town was primarily a military outpost and a headquarters for Catholic missions.

on a time and a way forever gone. And yet, whether he accepted or resisted change, he felt—he *knew* —that he was still involved in a special and continuing regional experience.

What is generally thought of as the "Southern experience" did not actually begin in the Old South until the 17th Century, when English settlers came to Virginia and the Carolinas and planted the roots of the society we know today. There were, however, earlier visitors and residents —though their effect on the region was purely transitory. In 1502, a decade after Christopher Columbus and his Spaniards blundered upon the New World, the Florida peninsula appeared on a Portuguese map. The Spaniards gave the thrust of land its name in 1513; because Ponce de León had first sighted the coastline during the Easter season, the land was called Florida, for *Pascua Florida,* their name for Easter. About half a century later other Spaniards were to found the town of St. Augustine, near the spot where Ponce de León first landed.

During the 16th Century, Roman Catholic Spaniards and Frenchmen, and Protestant French Huguenots in flight from Catholic persecution, vied with and occasionally shot and hanged each other as they explored the coasts of the Gulf of Mexico and the lower Atlantic. Some of them even settled briefly as far north as what later became Beaufort, in South Carolina. Spaniards led by Hernando de Soto trekked through much of Spanish Florida, which then extended well into today's Georgia, Alabama, Mississippi and Louisiana. The immense territory originally called Louisiana, alternately under French and Spanish sovereignty, stretched northward to the Great Lakes and westward to the Rocky Mountains. But, except in Louisiana proper, the impact of the French and Spanish on the region proved to be strangely fleeting. There are certain ancestral, architectural and atmospheric traces in such places as St. Augustine, Mobile and Charleston, but on the whole it was almost as if the French and Spanish had never come that way.

Much the same may be said for the original possessors of the Old South, the Indians; their cultures were simply eliminated. In the words of Henry Grady, a sanctimonious prophet of the "New South" in the 19th Century, they were "cut down as a weed" when they obstructed, actively or merely by their presence, the northern Europeans who principally settled and shaped the early South. There were probably no more than 100,000 Indians in the area of the Old South when the invaders first arrived; some 60,000 were involved when whole tribes were finally moved from Georgia,

Alabama, Mississippi and Florida to more open land west of the Mississippi River. Today there are only about 8,000 Indians in all of the Old South, and most of them are concentrated in Mississippi and Florida. The long process of Indian warfare, seizure and dispossession had no more effect upon the character of the South than its victims had upon the society that displaced them. Among the assets of the makers of America and the American South was a marked immunity from guilt. This, too, was part of the Southern experience.

The mold that shaped the experience was cast early in the colonial period. It was formed by the nature of the early immigrants, by the region's soil and climate, by its geographical isolation and even by the invention of a simple machine. Each of these factors tended to set the Old South on a course separate from that of the rest of America. Unlike the Puritans who came to New England to establish a permanent refuge from religious persecution, many of the Old South's first settlers were adventurers, men looking for quick fortunes, debtors released from prison and others to whom the doors of opportunity in Europe were closed. The land they found was unusual: the rich, well-watered soil and the prolonged growing season made farming highly profitable, particularly when slave labor was used. Its geographical separation from the other colonies created a provincialism, a sense of isolation from the rest of the country, which the Old South still has not overcome. Finally, the introduction of the cotton gin, by making cotton growing so enormously profitable that the Old South was converted into a single-crop area, greatly strengthened the institution of slavery and inexorably fixed the region on its special course.

The first true Southerners were about 100 men and four boys from, as it happened, southern England. The South they inaugurated at Jamestown, Virginia, in May of 1607 never recovered from the fact that most of the settlers ranked as gentry. Unhappily, their crude hamlet on the James River, the first permanent English settlement on the continent, almost succumbed to this superabundance of blue blood. Its inept founders abhorred routine work. Instead they searched for minerals, including gold, with some slight success, and lusted after Indian maidens with considerably more. Such limited activities were hardly conducive to the establishment of a stable settlement, and as every schoolboy learns, only the stern leadership of Captain John Smith saved these feckless colonists from extinction. But the captain was an effective promoter as well as a strong disciplinarian. His published

accounts of the new land, its opportunities and, of course, its diversions—"thirtie young women came naked out of the woods," he reported on one occasion—stimulated migration from England. A steady stream of farmers, artisans, paroled debtors, adventurous sons of upper-class families, indentured servants, religious dissenters and miscellaneous adventurers soon began to populate coastal Virginia.

A spillover of the human potpourri from Virginia into the northern part of Carolina resulted in that colony's first permanent settlement about 1654. Carolina was then a huge expanse encompassing all the land between Virginia and the Florida peninsula; it had no definite western boundary simply because no one knew exactly how much land lay in that direction. In granting Carolina to a group of favored subjects, King Charles II of England was transgressing on Spanish interests. At the time, Spain claimed all the land on the Eastern Seaboard from the southern tip of Florida to as far north as Virginia. Charles ignored the claim and assigned Carolina (named for him) to eight Lords Proprietors—none of whom ever laid an eye on his holdings.

While the northern part of Carolina was being settled by people from Virginia, a different breed of colonists came to the southern part of the territory. This second group of pioneers was composed mostly of Englishmen from the earlier established settlements in the West Indies. In 1670 they founded Charles Town on the Ashley River; a decade later they shifted the site of the community some 10 miles southeast to the present location of Charleston. The newcomers were largely men of substance and had little in common with the earlier settlers, the poor farmers, former indentured servants and bankrupts from Virginia who had moved into the northern part of Carolina.

The marked differences between the northern and southern settlements and the unwieldy size of Carolina led the Crown to establish two separate colonies, North and South Carolina, in 1729. Settling the boundary between them, however, proved a thorny problem that was not ironed out for nearly another century. It was not until 1819, after numerous survey commissions had attempted to settle the matter, that the present boundary line between North Carolina and South Carolina—roughly the 35th parallel—was set. It continues today to separate the Old South from the rest of the nation.

In 1732 King George II carved another colony out of the Carolina grant. Fearing an attack by the

Spanish in Florida, the English monarch decided to set up a separate colony in the southern section to act as a buffer against invasion. Called Georgia in his honor, the new colony was originally intended as a refuge for convicted debtors after their release from British jails. The plan was never carried out, however. The first group of settlers, some 120 men, women and children under the leadership of the English general and philanthropist James Oglethorpe, came to Georgia in 1733 and founded Savannah. As recent historians have demonstrated to the state's relief and joy, there were few, if any, convicted debtors in their number. The men in the group were a mixed lot of farmers, merchants, artisans (including two makers of men's wigs), bookkeepers, servants, a surgeon and an apothecary.

With the establishment of South Carolina and Georgia, the Old South came into being as a social phenomenon, "a state of mind." Only later was it fleshed out as the physical region we know today. Not until the late 18th Century did Mississippi become a territory, and only in the early 19th did Alabama achieve that status. Florida did not even become a part of the United States until 1819, and three years then passed before it was officially designated a territory. But by the time these new territories were brought into existence, there was an Old South for them to join, and they took their character, as well as many of their first settlers, from South Carolina and Georgia. In these two original states there was a distinctive posture, a body of implanted practices and attitudes already in existence for the new territories to adopt and share. Slavery and its attendant social and economic concepts, for example, spread as rapidly to the new territories as weeds between adjacent fields. So, too, did a crucially Southern attitude toward authority and property—and the distinctive flavor of the region's language.

The basic "Southern" accent and idiom, the slow drawl and elided "r" and altered vowels of common speech (*ain't; git* for get; *cote* for court) had been brought over intact from 17th Century southern England. These sounds were heard alike in mansions and backwoods hovels. Hence they were not the consequence of climate, languor and association with Negroes, as is supposed by Southerners who consider their way of talking to be among their distinguishing glories.

Far more significant than speech mannerisms were the Southerner's yearning and respect for property and his general accordance of leadership to those who owned it. This attitude was not unique to the early South. But the assumption of power as a matter of conceded right by the great landowners of Low Country South Carolina and Georgia set a precedent that endured long after their class had vanished as an acknowledged aristocracy. A Georgia guidebook noted in 1940 that "in this state the big man in a small town is so powerful that in certain communities he has the prerogatives of a patriarch and a dictator." The statement would have been valid in colonial times, and it is still valid today.

The feeling that ownership of land and political power went hand in hand was accompanied by another of the Southern settler's characteristic attitudes. This was his unwillingness to accept central authority over local affairs. In this attitude toward the firm exercise of control from London, the two colonies of South Carolina and Georgia did not differ greatly from the other parts of America. But after the Revolution the antipathy toward centralized government control over local matters survived in the South to a far greater degree than it did in the North. It remains the major political issue in the region today.

All the colonies, the Southern ones included, understood that they needed to be parts of some larger entity. Southerners valued their connection with Britain, and not solely because it was the mother country. What the Old South wanted from London in 1763—as from Washington in 1860 and today—was a maximum of support and protection and a minimum of interference. From the beginning to the end of its colonial status, Georgia got and welcomed a cash subsidy from Britain. A generous British bounty rewarded the cultivation and export of indigo, which was, after rice, South Carolina's leading crop. Other subsidies and preferments assuaged the requirement, galling only when it interfered with the normal flow of trade, that exports and imports be handled through British businessmen and ports in British ships. British troops were not only tolerated but welcomed, so long as they were stationed at the frontiers to protect the colony against hostile Indians, Spaniards and Frenchmen. Their presence was resented and became a cause of conflict with Britain only when, under the Quartering Act of 1765, they were billeted at local expense in such places as Charleston, where their principal use was to personify and enforce rule from the London center.

So long as that rule had been passive and negative—as it largely was until the 1760s—it was something to complain about and to mitigate with constant roiling for colonial autonomy, but never

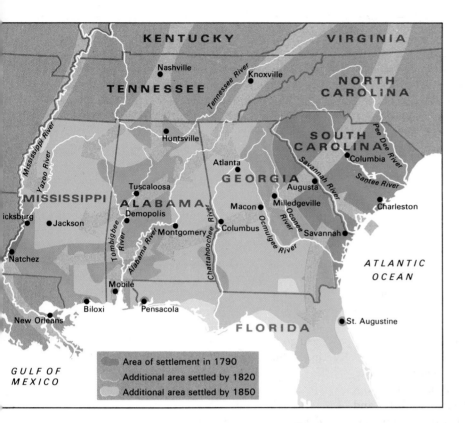

The progress of settlement of the Old South from 1790 to 1850 is shown at left, together with the general paths followed by the settlers *(arrows)*. By about 1790 the eastern part of the region had been settled by groups moving inland from Savannah and Charleston and down from North Carolina and Virginia; some settlers were American-born, but many were colonists from Europe—predominantly English, with, among others, French Huguenots, Welsh, Scotch-Irish, Germans and Swiss. Soon they occupied all of South Carolina, plus Georgia as far west as the Oconee River *(rust-colored area)*. By 1820 the rising demand for cotton was luring Georgians and South Carolinians into the fertile, newly opened lands of western Georgia, Alabama and Mississippi *(tan area)*. From the upper South, settlers were also moving south through Tennessee and down the Mississippi River. From the well-established city of New Orleans they reached western Mississippi by sailing up the Mississippi River, and from the town of Mobile many entered Alabama via the Alabama and Tombigbee Rivers. By 1850 the rest of the Old South *(beige area)* had been settled except for large areas of Florida and swampy parts of Georgia and Mississippi *(lightest areas)*.

to discard or reject. Sir James Wright, the last royal governor of Georgia and the owner of many acres and slaves, was perhaps the most popular man in the colony until he was required to impose taxes and regulations enacted in London. The famous cry against "taxation without representation" echoed a deep and genuine sentiment. The taxes voted without colonial representation in the British Parliament were particularly detested because they were a means of extending the central power through officials sent over from London to enforce the most offensive of the regulations. White Southerners reacted in much the same spirit two centuries later when voting registrars and other servants of expanding federal power came to enforce Constitutional rights for Negroes.

The differences with the mother country took on the special bitterness of a family quarrel simply because most of the settlers of the Old South were Englishmen who had transplanted as much as possible of English life to America. They brought with them their language, their religion, and their respect for property and for the authority that went with landowning. They also brought with them the social order they had known in England.

During the colonial period, patterns of life in the Old South bore many resemblances to those of contemporary England. As in England, there were clearly distinguished upper classes and lower ones, rich and poor. Yet the distinctions were not rigid, and the society was fluid and varied enough to allow lowly men to make their way up.

The early aristocracy of planters, along with town merchants and lawyers who were thought to be of the first quality only if they also owned land, was no less genuine because it was mostly home-grown and not, as gilded legend has it, straight from old England's upper reaches. In 18th Century South Carolina and Georgia, and later in Alabama and Mississippi, a man with a little capital or some credit, a few slaves and a lot of luck could clear cheap land and rise to eminence and wealth within a decade or two. Such, for the most part, were the Pinckneys, the Draytons, the Rutledges and the Izards in South Carolina, and the Noble Jones and Harris families in coastal Georgia, who grew rich and adorned their towns and lands with handsome mansions and splendid gardens.

The rich were, of course, a minority in the Old South, as they were and are everywhere in the world. The great majority of people were small farmers and poor whites. There were a number of these poorer folk in the generally wealthy lowlands along the coast, a neglected element of society that scratched a meager living from marginal land. But most of them lived in the hill country of South Carolina and the back country of Georgia. They were tillers of their own farms rather than masters of slave-worked plantations; in origin they were less likely to be pliant Anglicans than prickly Welsh and English Baptists and Methodists, German Lutherans, Scotch-Irish Presbyterians from northern Ireland and undiluted Scotch Presbyterians from their home Highlands. Religious differences were not taken lightly. In one backwoods community in South Carolina, the Presbyterians, offended by the intrusion of an Anglican missionary from the coast, corrupted one of the newcomer's congregations with free liquor and, on another occasion, brought 57 dogs to his church ("I counted them," the parson reported) and set them fighting during the sermon. Piety abounded, especially among the poorer whites, along with the familiar accompaniments to poverty: a fondness for whiskey and a high incidence of venereal disease, hookworm and pregnant brides.

All of these small farmers and poor whites came eventually to be portrayed as pious and sturdy yeomen, opposed to slavery and both resentful and contemptuous of the lowland aristocrats. There indeed were bitter variances of interest and outlook, of a kind that affect Southern politics and relationships to this day. But the stereotype is incomplete.

The owners of small farms and the backwoods poor forgot their differences with the landed gentry and made common cause with them whenever the North seemed to threaten Southern interests. Perhaps the most important pressure for unity came from the sense of "difference," almost of alienation, that all Southerners, regardless of class, felt between themselves and the rest of the country. When menaced by outsiders, they put internal struggles aside. Southern society also had its own inner strengths. It was just flexible enough to make the yeoman farmer feel ambivalent toward the slaveholding plantation owners. He resented their enormous economic advantage, but at the same time he longed to become one of their number, and often did, by acquiring sufficient land and slaves to qualify; a man was generally recognized as a "planter" if he owned 20 or more slaves.

This society of slavery, elegance and squalor, with its rapidly solidifying attitudes and customs, existed at the fringes of what was still a wilderness continent. In 1763, the landmark year from which colonial America's hesitant march toward revolution and independence is usually dated, inland South Carolina was thinly settled and the interior

of Georgia hardly at all. Florida, which Spain ceded to Great Britain in 1763, would be temporarily ceded back in 20 years, and it participated only marginally in the great events soon to come. There were perhaps 30,000 white colonists and 70,000 Negroes in South Carolina, in Georgia no more than 8,000 whites and 5,000 Negroes. The skins of wild deer ranked with rice and indigo dyes as South Carolina's major exports. But, in its social and political organization, the region was not as primitive as such facts suggest. Its royal governors had to deal with lively and fractious legislatures, and the dominance of the planter-aristocrats did not keep the lesser men of town and countryside from asserting their views.

The turbulence of the next three decades was to produce less fundamental change in the Old South than that which appeared on the surface. Both the white and the Negro populations increased enormously—by 1790 South Carolina would count an aggregate of 250,000 and in Georgia there were more than 80,000 persons in all; the great political events occurred that resulted in the mother country being forsaken, the Revolution won and the Constitution adopted. And yet through all these momentous happenings the Old South clung to its traditional ways.

Even the idea of independence itself was not immediately accepted by all Southerners. Many of Charleston's aristocrats, such as Henry Laurens, Edward and John Rutledge, William Henry Drayton and the Pinckney brothers, Thomas and Charles Cotesworth, opted for full independence only after events and passions had overwhelmed their hopes for an accommodation with England. There were pro-British "Tories" at every level in South Carolina and Georgia, and some historians doubt that most of the white colonists favored revolution. After British forces occupied Charleston and Savannah with relatively little trouble, the conflict degenerated largely into civil and guerrilla warfare of the kind that gave South Carolina's "Swamp Fox," General Francis Marion, his sobriquet. In both colonies the rapid growth of population throughout the war years demonstrated that far more people were engaged in taking new lands, clearing farms and raising families than in fighting.

By the time the Revolution ended there was general recognition throughout the new country that "The South" existed as a social and economic entity. Southerners had come to regard themselves as such and were regarded by people from Pennsylvania northward as different sorts of Americans with painfully different attitudes and concerns.

Having just thrown off the burden of a strong central government in England, the Old South was determined that the new federal authority would be powerless to interfere in what Southerners considered purely local matters. In the Constitutional Convention of 1787 most residents of the Old South believed that they had achieved both of their major objectives: a central government strong enough to assist and protect them but neither empowered nor inclined to intrude on the individual state's affairs; and a union of states linked in a constitutional compact freely entered and freely to be negated when any state, in its sovereign wisdom, so chose. This belief has survived nearly two centuries of steady correction by judges, Presidents (including some early Southern Presidents), a civil war and the remorseless federal interventions of today. The continuing disagreement between the South and the rest of the nation hinges only nominally on "states' rights," however. Everyone recognizes that the "states' right" almost always at issue is the right to determine the treatment of Negroes.

Slavery was, of course, the most important component of the Southern experience, and it was there almost from the beginning. Raising rice in South Carolina, like growing tobacco in Virginia, was hard, dull work requiring a large labor force but little skill, circumstances that encouraged the rapid importation of Negro slaves. The first had arrived on a Dutch frigate in 1619; soon they numbered in the thousands. By 1730 and through the remainder of the colonial period, for example, slaves outnumbered the white colonists in South Carolina by about 2 to 1. The royal trustees who ruled Georgia from London forbade slavery at first but in 1749 succumbed to the arguments of colonists, including George Whitefield, a pioneer Methodist missionary and evangelist, that "Negroes are as essentially necessary to the cultivation of Georgia as axes, hoes, or any other utensil of agriculture."

In the colonies, as always and everywhere in the South, the planters, farmers and townsmen who owned slaves were far fewer than the whites who did not. But this is deceptive. Owners hired out slaves to nonowners, and all white people, regardless of status, lived with slavery. The whites looked down upon the blacks and, with very few exceptions, considered enforced servitude to be the natural and proper lot of Negroes.

One of the corroding consequences of slavery, and thus one of the important additional elements in the Southern heritage, was white obsession with the danger of black rebellion. In South Carolina in 1720, slaves suspected of rebellious intent were

Tilting at a rope-held ring, a Southern equestrian displays his riding ability at an Alabama "tournament" held in 1858. Such events were patterned after the knightly jousting tournaments of the Middle Ages. The demonstrations of horsemanship, saber prowess and similar skills fitted the rich planter's romantic image of himself and his class as upholders of the chivalric tradition. The tournaments were held on large plantations and at state fairs.

burned alive just outside Charleston, and an actual uprising near the town in 1739 ended only after 30 whites and 44 Negroes had been killed. Rumors of plots to revolt were more frequent than actual outbreaks, but the facts had little connection with the results. At the slightest hint of slave rebellion, terrified whites beat and killed Negroes, tightened the "Black Codes," or controlling laws, and in general fell into a state approaching mass hysteria. Thus developed one of the many contradictions in the white view of Negroes that ever after would torment the South. It was believed with equal conviction that Negroes were docile by nature and therefore in no need of freedom, and at the same time intractable by nature and therefore a danger to society if they were freed.

The most human, the saddest and the most ironic of all the contradictions was soon evident in the ever-increasing numbers of mulatto slaves. Sexual intercourse between white men and Negro women and girls was frequent and condoned, though not formally approved. A white rake in Charleston, confessing in 1732 that he had a Negro mistress, made his affair the subject of doggerel poesy in one of the South's first newspapers, the *South-Carolina Gazette:* he rebuked those in the community who condemned his surrender to "the Monarch Passion of the Mind . . . by no Laws confin'd." Janet Schaw, a tolerant 18th Century diarist, seems to have been at once jesting and serious when she attributed the affinity of her planter friends for "their black wenches" to "no other desire or motive but that of adding to the number of their slaves." But the relationship was not limited to white males and black females. A Maryland statute of 1664 acknowledged that "divers freeborn English women . . . do intermarry with Negro slaves" and stipulated that the children of such unions "shall be slaves as their fathers were."

By the time the Old South entered the Union, slavery and its pathetic consequences troubled many minds. Public questioning of the institution was muted, but it did take place. Southerners, too, had heeded the ringing pronouncement in the Declaration of Independence that "all men are created equal." There were stirrings of interest in popular education and a gradual beginning of retreat from the proposition that only men of property were entitled to vote and hold office. The Church of England, that font of the colonial aristocracy, was deprived of its status as the "established" and official church, supported from public revenue. For the first time, slavery became embarrassing.

Some historians came to believe later that the South and the new nation had missed a historic chance to abandon slavery in those years. But events indicated that there was no real chance. Thomas Jefferson, the Virginia slaveowner who had written the Declaration of Independence, also helped draft a measure for gradual emancipation in his state, but because of the temper of the legislature the measure was never introduced. The delegates to the Constitutional Convention from South Carolina and Georgia stood with the great majority of their fellow Southerners in adamant opposition to any suggestion that the new Union should prohibit or limit slavery. They considered that they had made a sufficient concession in accepting the provision that the importation of slaves could be forbidden by federal law 20 years after the Constitution took effect.

But all the debates over the morality and the economic soundness of slavery became academic with an immensely significant event that occurred in the 1790s: the invention of the cotton gin. The effect of this simple machine upon the Old South was revolutionary—and in the end, catastrophic. It not only led to the Old South's becoming a one-crop region but so reinforced the institution of slavery that a civil war became virtually inevitable.

What set this train of events in motion was a friendship that developed aboard a ship bound from New York to Savannah in the fall of 1792. The two passengers involved were Mrs. Nathanael Greene, the widow of the famous Revolutionary War general, and Eli Whitney, an amateur inventor newly graduated from Yale and now en route to take a job as tutor in Savannah. Before the ship docked, Mrs. Greene invited the young man to visit her at her plantation, Mulberry Grove, which had been given to her late husband by the state of Georgia in recognition of his war services. Whitney proved to be no mere weekend guest; he came and remained for seven months. His would-be employer presumably hired another tutor.

There was a constant stream of visitors, many of them planters, at Mulberry Grove, and Whitney heard numerous complaints about the difficulties of separating cotton lint from the seed. The short-staple fiber suitable for general cultivation in the region clung so tightly to the seed that it took a slave a full day to prepare a single pound for the market. What was needed, everyone agreed, was a machine to do the job.

Whitney, who had minimal interest in cotton, paid little attention to the talk until his hostess suggested he try his hand at the project. Eager to repay her hospitality, he started to work. Ten days later he had completed a miniature of the machine. Within six months he was ready to demonstrate a working model of it; called a cotton gin, it consisted of a hand-turned roller mounted in a hopper and studded with wire teeth that pulled the fiber from the seed.

The improved versions of the gin (probably short for "engine") that soon followed made the Cotton South possible. Acreage devoted to cotton increased enormously now that fiber and seed could be quickly and easily separated. And there seemed no end to demand now that the power spinning machine and the power loom had also been invented. Picking cotton was still a hand job requiring a large work force, but importing more slaves was the simple and obvious answer to that problem. Given these circumstances, no one in the Old South wanted to grow anything else but cotton.

And so cotton—white and soft, enriching and smothering—spread from the Georgia and South Carolina lowlands to the back country and uplands, and across the cleared lands of Alabama and Mississippi, thus completing the shaping of the Old South. The "Southern experience" was far from over. But rooted as it was in the American past, it could hardly have been very different from what it was and continues to be.

Youthful Private Edwin Jennison was one of a host of early and enthusiastic volunteers for the Confederate Army; he was killed in battle in 1862.

Enthusiasm in war, rancor in defeat

From the five states of the Old South came much of the fervor that fanned secession and nourished the Confederate States of America. And when the Confederacy surrendered, it was the Old South that suffered most. South Carolina, Mississippi, Florida, Alabama and Georgia were the first states to leave the Union. Of all the Southern states, they were the most isolated from the rest of the country, and their plantation economy and society were more dependent upon slavery than were those of the other states. When the deeply felt cause was lost, the defeat was especially bitter. The trauma the Old South suffered during those years can still be sensed in old photographs, like the poignant portrait above. Their record of the exuberant secession, the destructive fighting and the humiliating Reconstruction offer a haunting chronicle of a region that suffered greatly and recovered slowly.

41

The jubilant beginning
of fraternal war

The Old South was in a festive mood when Jefferson Davis was inaugurated *(below left)* provisional President of the Confederacy in Montgomery, Alabama, on February 18, 1861. In the previous December South Carolina had become the first state to secede from the Union. By the time Davis took office there were seven states in the new government; four others were to join after hostilities began.

For a number of weeks after the inauguration both the North and South behaved cautiously; Abraham Lincoln, the new

A faded photograph shows Jefferson Davis' inauguration as provisional President of the Confederacy, "the grandest pageant ever witnessed in the South."

The Sumter Light Guards of Sumter County, Georgia, lines up in its home state in April 1861 before marching north to war.

President of the United States, hoped that forbearance would bring the recalcitrant states back into the Union; Southern leaders saw the possibility that the North would come to accept the secession as a *fait accompli*.

But in April Fort Sumter, in Charleston, was running low on supplies, and Lincoln notified the South Carolina authorities that ships were en route to restock the Union garrison. The Confederate government faced a crisis; if the ships were permitted to land, Fort Sumter could hold out indefinitely and a "foreign power" would control one of the South's principal ports. The Confederacy elected to demand the surrender of the fort and to open fire if the demand was not met.

There was an almost jubilant mood in the Old South now that the fraternal bloodletting was about to begin. A woman who was visiting Charleston wrote that on the eve of the bombardment she had attended "the merriest, maddest dinner we have had yet." The next day the war was joined and both the North and South began feverishly to assemble great armies.

Spit-and-polish officers, brave but shabby troops

The "Johnny Rebs"—as Confederate soldiers were commonly known—came from diverse backgrounds, but they had in common a zeal for their "just cause." Unlike the usually smartly dressed officers *(below right),* the enlisted men often looked less like disciplined troops than a ragtag posse *(below).* But they fought magnificently on the battlefield. "My men don't show to advantage in camp," General Robert E. Lee reportedly said, "and to tell the truth, I am a little ashamed to show them to visitors. But, sir, you should see them when they are fighing!

—then I would not mind if the whole world were looking on!"

Such fighting men swarmed from the backwoods, plantations and bayous alike to defend their beloved South. During the first nine months of recruiting, some 350,000 men joined the new army; before the war ended, a total of just under a million were to fight for the Confederacy. Many answered the call to arms as members of small, local units that boasted flamboyant names like Tallapoosa Thrashers, Cherokee Lincoln Killers, Chickasaw Desperadoes and Southern Rejectors of Old Abe—and wore homemade garb as individualistic as their names, although the official jacket of the Confederate troops was gray. Their varied dress caused trouble; sometimes Southern forces fired on one another.

Under the tutelage of an impressive corps of officers, many of whom were West Point graduates, this motley collection of men was molded into a tough, cohesive fighting force that was to win significant victories against great odds in such encounters as the Second Battle of Bull Run and Chancellorsville.

A look of bravado characterizes Lieutenant P. F. Thompson, who wears the typically jaunty cape of a Southern cavalry officer.

Company B of the Ninth Mississippi Regiment is hardly a parade-ground unit in camp, but it was praised for its valor at Corinth in 1862.

45

Breaking the South's will to fight

By 1864 the North's industrial superiority and greater manpower had made the South's defeat inevitable. But much bloodletting and destruction still lay ahead. There had been only limited fighting in the five states of the Old South, most of it in South Carolina and Mississippi; now the region was about to feel a much heavier impact. A new concept of war, a concept that foreshadowed some of the conflicts of the 20th Century, was about to be put into operation.

The architect of the new strategy was Union General William T. Sherman. After taking Atlanta in September 1864, he proposed to break the South's will to fight by bringing the war home to the civilians behind the lines and by destroying the economic resources on which the armies depended. That November, after burning much of Atlanta, Sherman and his men began their famous "march to the sea." They cut a huge 60-mile swath across Georgia, looting and destroying almost everything in their path. Savannah fell in December, and then Sherman started north through the Carolinas. Columbia, South Carolina, was captured and burned the following February.

The Old South was thoroughly humbled. With the Confederate armies largely destroyed, the region's economy disrupted and its way of life shattered, the South bitterly acknowledged that the war was lost.

Part of Charleston lies in ruins after Union bombardment.

Occupation of an impoverished but defiant land

Union soldiers take over a plantation owned by Confederate
General T. F. Drayton at Hilton Head, South Carolina.

In May 1865 the last of the Confederate forces surrendered and Northern troops occupied many of the Old South's towns and plantations *(below)*. The region was in desperate circumstances. Poverty was widespread; tools, horses and mules were scarce; most of the railroads were destroyed and few steamboats were running. In many instances the situation was aggravated by the victors. Ruinous taxes were imposed, and federal Treasury agents enriched themselves by seizing huge quantities of baled cotton.

Meanwhile, during a Congressional recess, President Andrew Johnson appointed supposedly less rabid Southerners as provisional governors of the various Confederate states and instructed them to call constitutional conventions to meet his mild requirements for rejoining the Union. But in the Old South especially, the conventions proved unregenerate and drew up constitutions that would re-establish white supremacy. The notorious Black Codes followed. Congress was outraged, and in 1867 it voted to impose Reconstruction.

Great expectations and profound disillusionment

Reconstruction was a traumatic experience for the whites of the Old South. Many of those who had supported the Confederacy were disfranchised, and political power was now in the hands of three groups: "carpetbaggers" from the North; white Southerners, called "scalawags," who collaborated with the carpetbaggers; and the recently freed Negroes.

For the Negroes, Reconstruction was a period of bewilderment, high hope and dashed expectations. Suddenly they had the right to accept or reject jobs *(right)*, to vote and even to hold office. As a people they saw that education was necessary to make their new freedom meaningful. From the North came teachers *(below)* to help remove the chains of ignorance.

But by 1880 the North had wearied of the South's problems, and the region's whites re-established their supremacy. Negroes were shorn of their political and social rights, and they became second-class citizens. The Old South paid a heavy economic price for this regressive step, but the whites were willing to pay almost anything to regain their racial superiority.

Teachers from the American Missionary Society of New York, in the South to educate former slaves, are photographed in South Carolina.

James McRea, the bearded man at right, explains the terms of a labor contract he is offering to ex-slaves on Grove Plantation in South Carolina.

3

The Long-lived
Racial Compact

Segregated public rest rooms in a rural area of South Carolina,
photographed a year after the U.S. Civil Rights Act of 1964 had
outlawed such discrimination, emphasize the firm and open
opposition to integration that remained outside the cities.

Almost one fourth of the nation's 21 million Negroes live in the five states of the Old South. Numbering five million, they share the region with some 13.5 million whites. But the proportion of Negroes varies considerably from state to state; despite a tripling of Florida's Negro population since 1910, they still constitute only about 18 per cent of the total, while in Mississippi they make up almost 40 per cent, the highest of any state in the Union. The proportions in Georgia, Alabama and South Carolina are between these extremes.

Except in Florida, these ratios of black to white have been dropping ever since the early part of the 20th Century, thanks to the heavy migration of Negroes to the Northern states. This migration became a mass exodus during World War II and in the decades that followed. But the decreasing proportion of Negroes in the Old South has not diminished their psychological effect upon the white majority. If anything, the sense of massive and potentially overwhelming Negro presence has been sharpened and magnified by the mounting pressures exerted both by and on behalf of those Negroes who have remained in the region.

These pressures have also been felt in the North, especially in the big cities, as huge numbers of Negroes have moved in and expressed, often violently, their demand for full equality. Racial segregation and discrimination have never been confined to the South, and the response of many white Northerners to large and militant concentrations of Negroes has been, in many ways, similar to that of white

Southerners. Yet until recently there was one fundamental difference between the positions of the Negro in the South and the Negro living elsewhere.

That fundamental difference had to do with the relationship between white Southerners and Negro Southerners. One way of defining it is to say that there *was* a relationship, an unwritten and unspoken social compact, that did not exist elsewhere. Three centuries of Southern history had gone into the making of it and Negroes neither could nor wished to take it with them when they moved out of the South. The essence of it was expressed in the cruel but long-accepted requirement that Negroes "stay in their place." In that place they could own homes, farms or even businesses (as some did), develop an elite of sorts, hold jobs of sorts, get an education of sorts and lead their own lives within their own world.

The terms of the compact did not debar contacts with the white world. In fact they *required* contacts. There was none of the isolation that Negroes usually experienced elsewhere in the country. Negroes worked as servants in white homes and often lived in them; they bought at white men's stores, rented land from white owners, and worked for and with white men in the fields and factories. In rural areas on Saturday nights, when everybody "went to town," the streets were studies in mingled black and white. Negroes had, or tried to have, their white protectors, and white men took pride in looking after "their" Negroes.

The intimacy of these contacts was exaggerated, especially by Southerners living in the larger towns and cities. They deluded themselves in the fashion of a McComb, Mississippi, merchant who assured a visitor in 1958 that his Negro customers "tell me things they would never tell you." Some of them had just been telling the visitor that they loathed the town's ruling whites, including the merchant, with a passion that in a few years was to break into open rioting. Deceptive to whites and galling to Negroes as the association was, it did exist. And it made the South distinctly different from the North. Well into the 1950s it was possible for a white New Yorker, working in mid-Manhattan and living there or in a suburb, to be almost unaware of Negroes. This was impossible in the South, even in areas and localities where there were few Negroes. Seen and unseen by white Southerners, Negroes were never out of mind.

For such satisfactions and amenities as they could enjoy within their world, Negroes were entirely dependent upon white Southerners and on the whites' willingness to honor their obligation under the compact, which was no more and no less than to sustain, protect and respect the Negro "in his place." The Negro in turn was obligated to be compliant. Very few white Southerners met their obligation, but most of them believed that they did, even when they were agreeing with the view, expressed in the early 20th Century by Mississippi's Senator James K. Vardaman, that "the way to control the nigger is to whip him when he does not obey without it."

There is reason to write of the compact as a thing of the past and to describe it as it stood, eroded but still intact, in 1960. That census year was pivotal in the nation's racial and social history. It was the year of the sit-ins, when thousands of young Southern Negroes plunked themselves down at "white" lunch counters and refused to leave until they were hauled out, often to jail, or were served the way white customers were. They demonstrated the power of ordered disorder, pioneered techniques of protest that later went beyond region and race, and led the nationwide Negro revolution into its aggressive phase. And, with their spectacular refusal to stay in the Negroes' assigned place, they demolished the compact.

The amorphous understanding had been viable only so long as white Southerners could believe that Negroes consented to it. Whether the consent was voluntary or mandatory was immaterial, but the appearance of consent was vital. It enabled white Southerners to convince themselves and to assure others that Negroes preferred their prescribed status of consenting inferiors and were not fitted for any other.

The show of consent was not altogether false. Southern Negroes in the mass knew no other way of life and had every reason to suppose that any effort to change it would compound their troubles. Even middle-class Negroes—farm owners, public-school teachers, doctors, a few lawyers, undertakers, ministers, the heads and faculties of impoverished Negro colleges—usually went along with the compact. They were no braver as a group than white Southerners who abhorred the meaner aspects of the system but dared not move or speak against it.

So strong was this compact that as late as the 1960s it survived a series of revolutionary court decisions and localized Negro protests. When the United States Supreme Court ruled in 1954 that racially segregated public schooling was "inherently unequal" and therefore unconstitutional, the unanimous decision clearly implied that all other forms of legalized segregation and discrimination were sure to be outlawed. The high court and lower federal courts soon rendered scores of subsequent decisions to support this concept. There were a good many Negro protests and some Negro victories, notably the 1955-1956 bus boycott in Montgomery, Alabama, which set the Reverend Martin Luther King Jr. on his way to national influence and world fame.

But the assumption of assent and the way of biracial life pillowed upon it were not to be so readily abandoned in the Old South. There the frequently proved capacity of white Southerners to believe what they wanted to believe was demonstrated anew. Upon the advice of eminent politicians, judges and lawyers, ordinary white Southerners refused to believe that the Supreme Court's current interpretations of the Constitution were constitutional. They similarly refused to believe that Negro complainants who brought suit after suit for integrated schooling, and who demanded such concessions as nonsegregated buses and equal access to public libraries and parks, spoke for the mass of still quiescent Negroes. Given that quiescence, the Old South's white majority continued to believe with unique tenacity that in clinging to segregation and all that went with it they served not only their preference but the preference of most Negroes. During the 1960-1961 school year, the only states in the entire Southern U.S. that did not have a single integrated public-school district were South Carolina, Georgia, Alabama and Mississippi. In Florida, the least "Southern" state of the Old South, only one of 67 school districts had been desegregated, and it was in metropolitan Miami.

Later on, when tensions mounted and racial conflict erupted from New York City to Los Angeles, this stubborn adherence to the Southern way did not seem as remarkable as it had in 1960. Many observers concluded that there was no significant difference in racial attitudes between the most recalcitrant portions of the white South and the whole of white America: in effect, that white Southerners were just doing what other white Americans would do if they could get by with it. But there *was* a quality in the Old South's denial of racial equity that was not found elsewhere, and it was a key element in the racial compact. The characteristic white people of the region acted from a depth of conviction, a sense of total rightness, that white Americans elsewhere did not bring to the struggle to debar Negroes from full parity. For an understanding of how this could be so, of how so many people could hold themselves to be in the right in their maintenance and defense of manifest

wrong we must turn back to the Southern past.

The belief that racial segregation and discrimination were right—not merely convenient or desirable or preferable to racial equality, but morally and socially *right*—descended from an earlier belief that slavery was right. This antecedent belief in the rightness of slavery developed into consensus very late, in the last 30 years before the Civil War. It was never as complete and firm as the successor belief in segregation was to become. Always there were Southerners who felt with Mary Boykin Chesnut, a South Carolina aristocrat, that slavery was "a monstrous system, a wrong and an iniquity!" Others maintained no more than that it was essential to the Southern economy, a necessary evil, admittedly debasing to slave and master, but less dangerous to society than millions of illiterate and vengeful Negroes would be if they were freed. Still others, in the lower orders of small farmers and landless whites, perceived that slavery was a prop of class privilege. But from about 1830 on, such dissenters were always a bullied and repressed minority, certain to be harried as Yankee-lovin' enemies of the South if they questioned in the slightest the revised proposition that slavery was "instead of an evil, a good—a positive good."

The man who spoke these words, John C. Calhoun of South Carolina, personified the processes by which the white South arrived at and adopted this preposterous stance. Calhoun, a Presidential aspirant who served as Vice President, Secretary of War, Secretary of State and United States Senator, merited the title "Father of Confederate Secession," although that event occurred 11 years after his death. No public man of his time considered himself, or was thought by others, to be more honorable, more righteous. He came of Scotch-Irish Presbyterians who had settled in upland South Carolina. His father was a farmer who later acquired slaves and planter status in Abbeville County on the Georgia border. John Calhoun was well educated—in boyhood by his brother-in-law, Moses Waddel, a pedagogue and stern disciplinarian; later at Yale; and then at the best law school of the day, Tapping Reeve's in Connecticut.

Though an owner of plantations and slaves—by inheritance and by marriage into a family of Low Country planters—he detested the elegant aristocrats who graced old Charleston and sneered that they were given to "intemperance and debaucheries." He wrote of himself that he was a kind "master and guardian" of slaves, but with him as with others, mastery sometimes involved considerable cruelty. In 1831, when he was Vice President

Two Negro men go to the highest bidder in this 1861 sketch of a slave auction in Montgomery, Alabama, one of the principal slave markets in the Old South. Slave trading was a profitable business in the region. The price of a slave, ranging from less than $100 to as much as $5,000, depended on such factors as the condition of the cotton market and the qualities of the slave. Buyers carefully examined the offerings, evaluating age, health, physique, skills, estimated intelligence and sex—young female slaves were often costly because of their breeding potential. Healthy young field hands were in the greatest demand at most auctions, but craftsmen and experienced house servants usually brought higher prices.

of the United States, he asked a friend in Abbeville to have a runaway servant jailed for a week on bread and water and to "employ some one for me to give him 30 lashes well laid on."

The qualms about slavery that had troubled such other Southerners as George Washington and Thomas Jefferson never bothered Calhoun. But he was a national figure for 26 years before he went so far as to say in a Senate debate in 1837 that slavery was "a positive good." That statement and its timing reflected a fateful change in his and the South's attitudes. In his early career and for a time after 1820, the critical year of the Missouri Compromise, when Congress drew a line beyond which slavery was not to be extended into new territories and states, Calhoun remained confident that the South could hold its own in the expanding national Union. He advocated national measures "to advance the general interest" and denounced the paranoid tendency of Southerners to see "a conspiracy" against them in the accelerating growth of other sections. For despite everything that he later said and did, it must be remembered that Calhoun cherished the Union. Nevertheless he believed with overriding passion that the rightness of slavery and the right of the slave states to preserve it had to be recognized above all else. In the end his belief in

slavery triumphed over his love for the Union, and he succumbed, with his region, to the defensive frights, illusions and extremes that led to secession and the Civil War.

Thus it was that he took South Carolina to the brink of rebellion in 1832 with the doctrine that any state had a Constitutional right to "nullify" federal acts that it disliked. The immediate issue was a high tariff, but the underlying issue was slavery and the possibility that the federal government might someday claim the power to abolish it. In 1844, when he was Secretary of State, Calhoun interwove the moral argument for slavery with the Constitutional and practical arguments. "With us," he told the antislavery British government, "it is a question to be decided not by the Federal Government, but by each member of this Union, for itself, according to its own views of its domestic policy, and without any right on the part of the Federal Government to interfere in any manner whatever." Then he shifted to practical grounds: "What is called slavery is in reality a political institution, essential to the peace, safety and prosperity of those states of the Union in which it exists." And, he said, it was good for the slaves: ". . . in no other condition, or in any other age or country, has the Negro race ever attained so high an elevation in morals, intelligence, or civilization." In 1849, when he was dying, Calhoun completed the matrix of Southern reasoning and apprehensions with the assertion that whites and Negroes "cannot live together in peace . . . except in their present relation." It followed that "political and social equality" was unattainable and unthinkable.

Southerners drenched themselves with such views in their newspapers and periodicals, in books, in oratory, in letters to each other, in the common talk of every day. In what a modern historian calls "a striking victory of mass propaganda—one of the greatest in human history," they swept aside, ignored and arbitrarily denied the obvious wrongs of slavery and the principles of equality and freedom set forth in the Declaration of Independence and the Bill of Rights. In the upper, or border, states of the South—North Carolina, Virginia, Kentucky and Tennessee—a certain amount of humanitarian dissent remained possible—although the penalties were often heavy—up to and even beyond the time of secession. But in the states of the Old South, where slaves were most numerous and passions were highest, slavery itself came to be virtually unopposed. Ostracism was certain and worse was likely for any who dared to doubt in public that it was "a positive good." Abraham Lincoln, assuming the Presidency in 1861, sadly measured the grip of moral fantasy upon the South when he said in his inaugural address: "One section of our country believes that slavery is *right* and ought to be extended, while the other believes it is wrong and ought not to be extended."

The fantasy and its grip upon the Old South survived the abolition of slavery for a reason so obvious that it is easily overlooked. What the South justified, what Southerners persuaded themselves to believe to be morally right, was *Negro* slavery. Others had been enslaved—white bondsmen and bondswomen in effect, Indians in fact—in early America. Some of the first South Carolinians made a business of enslaving Indians and selling them in the West Indies. But slavery in America endured only for Negroes. This notion was only a part, though the basic part, of a social system designed to keep Negroes, whether slave or free, in a subordinate status for which they were believed to be naturally suited and, as many Southerners held in all seriousness, ordained by God.

Southern laws and judges expressed and enforced the prevailing view of Negroes, not as slaves but as Negroes. From the beginning some Negroes had been freed by their owners, others had purchased their freedom, and some had been born of free parents. By 1860 there were about 250,000 free Negroes in the South. Most of them were in the upper South and relatively few in the Old South (for example, 84,000 in Maryland versus 773 in Mississippi). But there were some everywhere, and the white South's view of them took early and lasting form. A Southern appellate court remarked in 1824 that "nobody has ever questioned the power of the [Virginia] Legislature, to deny to free blacks and mulattoes, one of the first privileges of a citizen; that of voting at elections, although they might in every particular, except color, be in precisely the same condition as those qualified to vote."

In their conviction that Negroes were natural inferiors and that it therefore was right to treat them as such, white Southerners were fortified by abundant evidence of similar prejudice in the North. By 1860 only five states outside the South granted Negroes a full right to vote, 27 denied it altogether, and one qualified it with restrictions. The Northern abolitionists who demanded immediate emancipation of the slaves were a disliked and often ostracized minority in their own region. During a tour of New England and other Northern states in 1831, abolitionist leader William Lloyd Garrison encountered "contempt more bitter, opposition more active, detraction more relentless, prejudice more stubborn, and apathy more frozen, than among slave owners themselves." One of the most savage race riots in American history occurred in New York City in 1863 when mobs of white objectors to the wartime draft tortured or lynched Negro men, women and children in numbers never precisely determined. Abraham Lincoln, the Great Emancipator, understood that Northern opposition to slavery was far from unanimous and unqualified and that it did not connote Northern affection for Negroes.

But there was a profound difference between North and South in matters of race. Most Northerners who opposed the abolition of slavery and later were against Negro equality were motivated largely by economic considerations, especially the fear of competition for jobs. Rarely did Northerners defend this position as just. On the other hand, Southerners, both before and after the Civil War, insisted that the superior-inferior relationship was morally right. Seemingly they had to believe it in a way that other white Americans did not.

The Civil War changed everything for the South—everything except the rigid racial convictions of white Southerners. More than 250,000 deaths in the Confederate cause, the only experience of final defeat in war that Americans have known, the social cataclysm involved in the abolition of slavery, the widespread devastation and immense economic loss, the will and power of the victorious North—together they were not enough to alter those convictions. Their strength and durability are illustrated by the behavior of the first state governments set up in the Old South after the guns were stilled in 1865.

Lincoln, before his assassination, and Andrew Johnson, the Tennessean who succeeded him, had offered the defeated states such lenient political terms for re-entry into the Union that Congress was already in uproar. Elemental prudence dictated that the provisional governors appointed by Johnson and the constitutional conventions summoned by them meet his mild requirements without fuss or quibble before more onerous conditions were imposed. The temporary governors and most of the all-white convention delegates were moderates, men known to have opposed or at least regretted secession. Such men, it was thought, could make the minimal show of humility and repentance required in the North without alienating their white constituents in the South. Johnson, a firm believer in states' rights, had suggested token grants of the voting franchise to the newly freed Negroes but had left that touchy decision to the conventions. But moderation did not become the order of the day.

South Carolina's provisional Governor Benjamin F. Perry sounded the general tone of defiance when he announced that "this is a white man's government, and intended for white men only." The South Carolina convention went along with emancipation of the state's slaves but denied them the vote, refused to fly the United States flag and managed to repeal the Confederacy's first act of secession without declaring it void. The Mississippi, Alabama and Georgia conventions declared that slavery had been abolished by events, thus evading the requirement that they specifically outlaw it; they ignored the President's pacific suggestion that the few Negroes who knew how to read and how to write their names and who owned a little property or money be allowed to vote. Florida also refused to extend suffrage to Negroes. Many actions of the conventions and the subsequent state governments had no direct connection with race. But the driving purpose was to insure that the states of the dead Confederacy could re-enter the Union as they had left it, under governments for "white men only."

The circumstances impelled white Southerners to believe then, as always, that they did only what was right and necessary. Their society, their whole system of government and commerce and daily life, was in ruins and had to be pulled together and made to function again. Their major assets were land and labor—and now the labor did not appear very reliable. The Negroes on whom they depended for labor had known only the utter dependence of slavery. Now they were free to go where they pleased and to work or not as they pleased, and many of them pleased not to work for a spell. Most of them were illiterates and, as one of their Northern friends in Congress said, unaccustomed to "managing the ordinary business of life." Part of what was considered their indolent behavior may have been deliberate. Negro writers in a later time would report the skill with which Negro slaves had skimped their work in order to lighten their lot and get back at their masters, doing as little as possible and doing that little as badly as possible. There was enough truth in this to encourage the view that Negroes were innately lazy and would work only under compulsion.

Meanwhile, the North's attitude toward the vanquished South was hardening. This toughness aroused the region's chronic sense of injury and with it the special righteousness of people who feel abused. There was a note of sheer vengeance, of a desire to punish for punishment's sake, in the warning of Pennsylvania Representative Thaddeus Stevens that the Southern states must accept any conditions laid down by Congress or "remain as conquered provinces." Stevens, a leader of the reformist Radical Republicans, made it brutally clear that simple justice and Negro welfare were not his faction's only reasons for insisting that freed slaves be given the vote and otherwise raised to full equality. He said that "the blacks" and white Southerners willing to vote Republican "would act in a body, form a majority, control the States" and "insure the ascendancy of the Union party"—i.e., the Republican Party. Here, not in Southern fantasy but in threatened fact, was something near fulfillment of old John Calhoun's prophecy that if the Negroes were ever given the chance they would combine with Yankee supporters to keep white Southerners "in complete subjection." Here, too, were the roots of the white South's long identification of the Republican Party as the enemy, the party in the wrong, and of the Democratic Party as the party for Southerners, standing with and for them in their concept of racial right.

The Southerners' belief that they alone knew the requirements of a biracial society led, in 1865, to the state laws known as the Black Codes. How even the blindest Southerner could have failed to see that they would surely bring down the wrath of the Northern conquerors is hard to understand now, but the fact is that the white South believed it was acting both rationally and righteously. The laws varied, but they had in common definitions of vagrancy that enabled the authorities to force idle Negroes to work for employers—often their former owners—who would pay fines and "costs." An Alabama Negro could be convicted and jailed or hired out for no other reason than that he was "stubborn." In South Carolina, Negroes had to be specially licensed to do anything except farm or domestic work. Mississippi's code included the standard compulsions to work, forbade Negroes to own or rent farmland, and made all interracial association "on terms of equality" punishable. White people found in such association were classed as vagrants. "Living in adultery or fornication with a freedwoman, free Negro, or mulatto" was defined as an act of vagrancy, no worse than any other "equal" association. But racial intermarriage was made a felony, and upon conviction both parties were subject to life imprisonment.

With the Black Codes, and with the accompanying show of unrepentant pride dramatized by the white-robed riders of the Ku Klux Klan and similar bands of thuggish vigilantes, the South brought mandatory Reconstruction upon itself in 1867. Between then and 1877 the North (actually the Northern states plus the expanding West) sought to "reconstruct"—reform and transform from top to bottom—the white South's social and political system and practices. For periods varying from two years in Georgia to nine in South Carolina and Florida, the states of the Old South were first under military rule and then under mixed white and Negro Republican rule supported by the military. This was the gaudy and searing time of the "carpetbaggers," Northerners accused fairly and unfairly of flocking down with empty suitcases to be filled with loot; of the "scalawags," a term of scorn applied to white Southerners, rascals and honest men alike, who collaborated with and sometimes headed the imposed regimes; and of Negroes voting and in public office, having their first and, until very recently, their only experience of something near full participation in the American adventure.

People in the Old South have been saying for a century that Reconstruction left a permanent mark. So it did, but the mark was largely of Southern making. Nothing is more revealing of the Old South then and as it is today than a comparison of

John C. Calhoun of South Carolina, who spent almost a half century in national office, stands by his Senate seat in this 1850 portrait. Calhoun formulated the South's fateful position that a state retained the power to veto federal laws that the state believed to be unconstitutional, as well as the right to secede from the Union.

Reconstruction as it was with Reconstruction as it survived in the regional memory.

It is true, as the orthodox Southern version has it, that white men who had served the Confederacy were excluded from voting and public office, that Negroes were welcomed to citizenship and office regardless of literacy or other qualification, and that they outnumbered the eligible white electorate in Mississippi, Alabama, South Carolina and Florida. In the performance of some former slaves who served as magistrates, jurors, legislators and state officials there was much that was outrageous and ludicrous. Only 22 of 87 Negroes elected to the South Carolina legislature in 1868 could read and write. Negro militiamen in South Carolina and Mississippi lorded over whites, and in Mississippi federal troops had to suppress imminent racial warfare. Some ignorant Negro magistrates and jurors treated white defendants as rudely as Negroes had been, and as they would again be, treated in white courts. Inefficiency, graft, confiscatory taxes, wasted revenues and inflated public debts all but bankrupted some of the states, and thousands of individuals fell into actual bankruptcy. A fifth of Mississippi's farmland was sold for unpaid taxes.

Such were the circumstances Southerners at the time observed without understanding, remembered

Fighting segregation

After generations of submission to rigid segregation laws and practices, the Old South's Negroes began a massive counterattack in the 1950s and 1960s. Their weapons were nonviolent, but within a decade many of the Old South's most entrenched social patterns were being changed.

The boycott was first used in Montgomery, Alabama, to end segregation on city buses. Other communities employed the boycott on such fronts as the fight against discriminatory hiring policies. The sit-in to desegregate public eating places began in North Carolina and was soon adopted elsewhere in the South. In time, both forms of segregation were outlawed by Congress and the Supreme Court. The Court also re-enforced its rule that such institutions as the University of Mississippi could not bar Negro students.

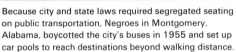

Because city and state laws required segregated seating on public transportation, Negroes in Montgomery, Alabama, boycotted the city's buses in 1955 and set up car pools to reach destinations beyond walking distance.

with grim satisfaction and told to their children as the sum of the experience. But the Reconstruction era was not without positive benefits—a fact that Southerners refused to credit, or dismissed as irrelevant. The new constitutions adopted by Negro and white Republican conventions laid progressive foundations that the South, at the peak of its later reaction, never entirely discarded: inclusive male suffrage, widened popular elections, some power to regulate private activity in the public interest and free public schools. Federal and private funds, the latter mostly from churches, financed new schools and colleges for Negroes and so initiated the slow emergence of the Negro masses from illiteracy—a development that would sooner or later bring immense benefits to the South.

Many of the newly elected black leaders, furthermore, were capable men. As if by a miracle, scores of literate and able Negroes appeared out of slavery and from among free Negroes who had been educated in the North. Notable among them were two men named Hiram R. Revels and Blanche K. Bruce, who sat for Mississippi in the United States Senate, and such state legislators as Robert Smalls of South Carolina, who had led other Negroes in the seizure of a Confederate steamer during the war and commanded it in the Union Navy. Many

Negroes of this stamp pleaded, usually in vain, for the understanding and cooperation of "our white friends in the South" and tried to protect them from rapacious white officials.

But the caricatured buffoon in top hat and cutaway tail coat, carousing and grafting at the public trough, was the remembered Reconstruction Negro in office. One lasting tragedy of Reconstruction was that the whites could neither perceive nor admit that there was good along with the bad. The bad they attributed to the elevation of the Negro, and in the bad they saw only proof that they had always been right about the Negro and his proper place in a biracial society.

The other tragedy had to do with the white North. It gave up. It wearied of the Negro and his problems; of the white South and its problems with the Negro; of the whole Reconstruction effort. In 1889, just 12 years after the last Reconstruction government fell in Louisiana and the last federal occupation troops were withdrawn, a famous Atlanta editor and spokesman for what he indelibly labeled the "New South" was applauded in Boston when he argued that Negro rights were not important enough for white Americans to differ about. "Never before in this Republic," Henry W. Grady said, "has the white man divided on the rights of

Sit-ins, like the one above at a lunch counter in Tampa, Florida, in 1960, were designed to break the bar against serving Negroes. Black customers took seats and refused to leave until they were served or carried out.

James Meredith *(forefront, center)*, accompanied by U.S. marshals under orders to enforce a federal-court mandate, was enrolled at the University of Mississippi in 1962. Rioting on the campus preceded his admission.

an alien race." In any case, he added, there was no cause for concern about the black man. Grady assured Northerners that the Southern Negro enjoyed "the fullest protection of our laws and the friendship of our people," and advised that his fate be left "to those among whom his lot is cast." Despite systematic segregation and such glaring facts as the numbers of lynched Negroes (534 in Mississippi, 491 in Georgia, 299 in Alabama between 1882 and 1952), white America took Grady's advice and left the Old South much to its own racial ways and convictions through the next 70 years.

Then, in February of 1960, four Negro college students at Greensboro, North Carolina, launched the sit-ins at a chain-store lunch counter. Hundreds of others, mostly Negro students, did the same in South Carolina, Alabama and Georgia (but not then in hard-core Mississippi). Counters and restaurants in some 200 towns and cities throughout the South were opened to Negroes that year and the next. Although this was a momentous change in itself, it was only the surface consequence of Negro audacity. They accomplished what a century of civil warfare, defeat, abortive reconstruction and manifold change in all other respects had not accomplished. They destroyed the basis of the Old South's belief in the rightness of

discrimination. The sense of rightness remained, but its sustaining power was gone. After the sit-ins, through which the Southern Negro dramatically rejected his lot, formal segregation and the accompanying patterns of discrimination could no longer be justified in the old way with the old confidence by white Southerners. "Their" Negroes were inexplicably—to the whites—in rebellion against the old pattern. They no longer assented to segregation; they courageously attacked it. The defense of the "southern way" continued after 1960, but with steadily waning conviction and effect.

The turmoil of the next years, and the extremes of white reaction, obscured the extensive erosion of white resistance. Especially in Alabama and Mississippi, the white populace as a whole submitted to upheavals and intrusions that in times past would have aroused reprisals more vicious and more extensive than actually took place. The Freedom Riders of 1961 were beaten in Alabama and arrested by the hundreds in Mississippi, but white Alabamans and Mississippians eventually resigned themselves to Negroes sitting where they pleased in buses and eating at desegregated terminal restaurants. A Mississippi Negro, James Meredith, was able to enter the state university only under guard of federal marshals and the U.S. Army in 1962, but afterward Negroes were admitted almost without incident. Birmingham in 1963 lived up to its reputation as the most rigidly segregated city in the South; there was brutal repression of Negro demonstrators and four Negro children died in the bombing of a church, but later there were some positive results. Communication was established between the Negro community and city officials, a few Negroes were permitted to join the formerly lily-white police force, and a few others were appointed to various municipal boards. There was some integration of pupils in the public schools, a handful of Negroes found employment in downtown stores, and some were given better jobs in local industrial plants. Perhaps these gains in Birmingham and at the University of Mississippi—where, in 1967, there were still only 70 Negroes in a student body of 6,800—may be dismissed as mere tokenism. But it would be wrong to say that the victories were without value. A seemingly impenetrable wall had been breached; the defenders of that wall, sworn to remain fast, had retreated.

Not that the struggle for racial equality had ended in the Old South or would be likely to end in the foreseeable future. Upward of 500 assorted racial activists from other sections swarmed through Mississippi in the "Freedom Summer" of 1964, working with militant Negroes to promote voter registration and general protest. Two young white men from the North and a young Mississippi Negro were murdered in Neshoba County with the clear connivance of local authority, numerous Negro churches were burned, and white and Negro agitators were arrested, beaten, bullied. In Alabama's Black Belt in 1965, in the old cotton town of Selma and in rural Lowndes County, white men murdered a Unitarian minister from Boston, a white woman from Detroit and a theological student from New Hampshire and shot down a Catholic priest from Chicago.

But perhaps the posture of Southern Senators and Congressmen during the enactment of the Civil Rights Act of 1965 told more about the white South than the violence did. It was the posture of recognized defeat, of politicians who knew that the cause of legalized white ascendancy and Negro subordination was now lost. They talked and voted against the bill, but with none of the fire and assurance of the period when any measure seriously offensive to the Southern sense of racial propriety could be smothered in committee or filibustered down in the Senate. This one, the second major civil rights statute in two years, passed in short order, and soon federal registrars were enrolling

Negro voters in a number of hitherto implacable counties of the Old South.

No specific index of change, of what the Negro revolution had accomplished by 1967, adequately reflected the extent of what might be called the White revolution. It was a negative and inglorious revolution, a slow process of surrender to reforms that many Southerners still believed to be deeply wrong. The measure of it was in what they accepted, unhappily and under duress, but still accepted, and what a gradually growing white minority welcomed with a quiet sense of relief from the racist burden of the past. A Negro sheriff in Alabama, 11 Negro legislators in Georgia, Negroes standing for office in Mississippi, Negroes registered and voting in numbers sufficient to decide state-wide elections when the white majority was divided, Negroes in factory and clerical and even in some executive jobs long closed to them—such were the indicators.

In South Carolina, Georgia, Alabama and Mississippi, where not one Negro child attended a public school with white children in 1960, thousands did in 1966-1967, the numbers and proportions of enrolled Negro youngsters varying from about 8,500 and 3.2 per cent in Mississippi to more than 34,000 and 9.9 per cent in Georgia. In Florida 20.8 per cent of enrolled Negroes were at school with white children. The five states were on irresistible federal notice that they would soon have to abandon their separate school systems and, despite real difficulties, accept the mingling of Negro and white children and teachers in the same schools.

Incredibly but surely, the condition of legal and formal equality, long known by Southerners to be the only alternative to full inequality, was at hand. Now the looming problem was how to live in that condition, in racial amity. But that is a national problem, not just a problem of the Old South. Some knowledgeable observers believe that the South's "racial realism" may bring about a faster and more solid rapprochement between the races in the Southern states than in the Northern. Explaining why he had moved back to the South after living many years in the North, Negro writer Arna Bontemps said, "I was . . . betting that progress toward this objective [racial equality] in the Southern region would be more rapid, the results more satisfying, than could be expected in the metropolitan center of the North . . . ." A similar attitude was expressed by Whitney M. Young Jr., Executive Director of the National Urban League: "If most of the South has a farther way to go than the rest of America, I believe that it is at least going there quicker." History has recorded few greater ironies.

Before going to work in his fields, Robert Lee Heard carries water from the back-yard well to his small house. Until 1948, when his landlord built Heard's present home, the family lived in a shack much like the storage shed at right.

Negroes: moving up, with far to go

The lives of three black men reveal the paradox of hope and discouragement that tantalizes the Negro in the Old South today. Herman J. Russell is rich, a respected force in the business community; Paul Bray has worked his way into the substantial and growing black middle class; Robert Lee Heard *(above)* is a poor sharecropper.

Both Russell and Bray are products of the economic and social revolution that is transforming the South. Industrialization, the prosperity it brings, and the hard-won gains of the civil rights struggle have given these men a way of life undreamed of by earlier generations of black men. But Heard is also representative. He is part of a huge segment of the Negro population whose financial lot has been only marginally improved by the thriving economy and whose social existence remains almost wholly unchanged by the partial lowering of racial bars.

Photographs by Burk Uzzle

A hard life
with little reward

Robert Lee Heard *(above)*, a sharecropper outside Coldwater, Mississippi, lives with his wife and seven of his 15 children in a small five-room house covered with asphalt-sheet siding. The house has electricity but no modern heating or running water. With the exception of the kitchen, all of the rooms in the house are bedrooms, drably decorated with torn flower-print wallpaper. Heard has been a poor man all of his life, and he harbors no expectation of being anything else. To stretch his meager income, he must grow most of his own food. He has no money saved and no land to sell when age forces him to give up farming. At best, he will receive a few dollars from Social Security and a pittance from the state old-age fund.

Yet to the black sharecropper of the 1930s Heard would seem well off already. He owns a tractor, a serviceable pickup truck, two dozen chickens, a few pigs and 10 cows. On 20 of the 250 acres he tends for the white landowner, Heard raises cotton and peanuts and receives three fourths of the profits. The remainder of the farm is used as pastureland for Heard's and the owner's cattle. From his various activities Heard nets about $3,000 per year, a cash income that would have seemed prodigal to his father's generation but that is still below modern subsistence levels.

The measure of the change in the sharecropper's lot is the prospects for at least some of Heard's children. Five of the 15 have gone to college, mostly earning their own way but getting some help from Heard. A few of the younger children have also shown an interest in continuing their education; others, however, have dropped out of school.

For Robert Heard there is likely to be little improvement in the hard life he has always known. But a few doors are beginning to open, slowly but inevitably, for his children.

Robert Lee Heard and his family gather for the evening meal in the kitchen of their modest house. The electric range in the background, a refrigerator and a television set are the Heards' only modern conveniences.

Two of the Heard children take a short break from their farm chores. When not in school, they all work on the farm.

After completing her household duties, Cordelia Heard helps her husband pick and sort peanuts.

Thelma Heard *(above)*, 23 years old, unemployed, a high-school dropout, muses on his front porch.

Youngsters hurry out of the Heard house to catch the bus that takes them to the segregated school, 15 miles away.

A skilled workman
and active citizen

Paul Bray *(left)*, a 33-year-old, 230-pound former fullback with Miles College, is a member of the Old South's rapidly growing Negro middle class, enjoying its comforts and suffering its tensions. He holds a good job, lives in a modern apartment, owns a new car, and likes literature and music. And, most important to him, he commands respect from whites and Negroes alike.

Bray is a skilled worker at the Conner Steel Company in Birmingham, Alabama, and has been promoted to successively more responsible tasks. On his former job as ladleman *(right)* Bray had assistants; often they were white. When asked if he had experienced any racial difficulties working with white subordinates, he replied, "You've got to talk to people intelligently, respect them and act like you want to be respected. If you do that, you'll get respect."

In his off-duty time Bray is active in the civil rights movement. He is a tireless worker for the Office of Economic Opportunity—he was directly responsible for opening up 600 jobs in Birmingham—and for the National Association for the Advancement of Colored People. Commenting on black power and militant civil disobedience, Bray says, "I think we're past all that." He prefers the kind of results being obtained by such groups as the powerful Birmingham Downtown Action Committee, a biracial group of influential business leaders who devote their efforts to creating new economic opportunities in Birmingham.

Recently divorced, Bray spends what little free time he has with his two daughters. "I got into civil rights because of my children," he says. "I wanted things to be better for them and I knew somebody had to do it."

Bray discusses Negro employment with Amelia Boykins, executive director of the Jefferson County Office for Economic Development.

Clad in helmet, goggles and asbestos coat, Bray maneuvers a ladle of molten steel.

Enjoying a day with his children, Bray prepares his charcoal grill while Yvonne *(leaning on railing)* and her sister, Jan *(seated second from left)*, look on.

Jan Bray gazes out the large picture window of her father's apartment in a pleasant—but segregated—neighborhood. Jan and her sister live with their mother, but they often visit their father after school and on weekends.

The rarefied air
at the top

Herman J. Russell *(left)* is a member of a tiny minority in the Old South: he is a wealthy Negro. In 1955 his plastering firm in Atlanta, Georgia, employed three men; today, H. J. Russell and Company has more than 200 employees. While plastering is still a major part of the business—his firm contracted to plaster, insulate and partition the new Equitable Life Assurance Building in Atlanta, one of the largest buildings in the South—the company has also become an important real-estate operator, building and retaining ownership of luxury apartment buildings in Atlanta.

Russell's way of life reflects his wealth and prominence. He and his wife, Otelia, and their three children occupy a large ranch-type house, complete with indoor swimming pool, in a fashionable, all-Negro suburb of Atlanta. He takes a leading role in community affairs. A friend of such prominent Negro leaders as the late Dr. Martin Luther King Jr. and acutely aware of the plight of the Negro in the Old South, Russell is sympathetic to the civil rights movement. But he normally exerts his influence from the top, rather than from the picket lines. Despite his efforts to remain behind the scenes, Russell received public attention for his singlehanded—and accidental—integration of the Atlanta Chamber of Commerce in 1962. Not realizing that Russell was a Negro, the 3,000-member all-white group unwittingly sent him a cordial invitation to join. Russell promptly accepted the invitation, to become the first of several Negro businessmen to join.

Herman Russell inspects his employees' work on the new Equitable Life Assurance Building in Atlanta.

The Russells and their son, Michael *(right)*, are welcome guests at one of Atlanta's posh restaurants.

In the living room of their 12-room house, Mrs. Otelia Russell reads from a storybook to Michael, aged three, her youngest child.

Russell frolics with his daughter Donata, aged nine, and his son Jerome, aged five, in his indoor glass-enclosed swimming pool.

Shadows of a white grillwork, one of the decorative touches that embellish the Russells' home, hold the attention of young Jerome.

President, Lieut Gov Boozer   40 Acres and a Mule.

Judas Moses who raised the Confederate Flag on Fort Sumter !!

RADICAL MEMBERS
OF THE So. Ca. LEGISLATURE.

4

Redeemers
and Demagogues

The politics and political institutions of the Old South changed greatly during the 1960s. Federal money supported and federal power dominated more and more of the business of government within the five states. Having no recourse, the state legislatures submitted like fretful lambs to the requirement of the U.S. Supreme Court that they reapportion their election districts themselves or suffer reapportionment by federal judges. As this realignment of voters began to curtail the traditional power of the rural counties, the people of the towns and cities won representation more in scale with their rising numbers. Two-party politics emerged.

Multitudes of white southerners found that they could call themselves Republicans and vote Republican without consigning themselves to the chilly hell once reserved for apostates from the Democratic Party. Florida chose a Republican Governor in 1966 and Georgia almost did, too; the same choice ceased to be a fantastic impossibility in South Carolina, Alabama and Mississippi.

Radicals in South Carolina's Reconstruction legislature are shown in a composite picture made in 1868 by James Gibbes, an "unreconstructed" Southerner. He is probably the one who labeled ex-Confederate officer Franklin Moses *(right center)* a "Judas."

Nearly 1.3 million Negroes were registered to vote in the five states by 1967, compared with fewer than 400,000 in 1952. In the 1967 primaries and general election in Mississippi, more than 100 Negroes ran for public office, and enough of them won to shatter the state's claim to being the last bastion of lily-white politics and government.

Here was a political revolution. But there was something odd and, for the literal-minded, rather baffling about it. Proper revolutions are expected to have revolutionary effects, and this one appeared to be having strangely few. The changed South of the latter years, with rural dominance of the state legislatures broken, with Negroes voting and winning office as a matter of right, and with born-Democrats voting Republican, was still recognizably and distinctively Southern.

This strange situation had many aspects and many causes, some immediate and some rooted in that Southern past, that now as always condition the present. The reapportioned legislatures were more responsive to urban needs and less hostile to moderately progressive measures than their predecessors had been, but in overall performance and attitude they remained essentially conservative. The new Republican state parties tended to be even more conservative, even more "Southern," than the established Democrats, and they attracted support for that reason. The enlarged Negro electorates still found themselves in a minority within their states as a whole and therefore—with local exceptions—were confined to choices offered them by the white majority. Mississippi Negroes, slow to break the habits of subservience, hesitated to exert their new potential even in counties where they outnumbered white voters. Some of the Negroes were frightened by the whites' threats of reprisal if they supported an aggressively reformist "Black Power" party, while other Negroes were repelled by that party's emphasis on "separatism" of the races, the very condition many blacks had been fighting. To be sure, the black vote could at times be crucial. In South Carolina it saved the incumbent Democratic Governor and a Democratic candidate for the United States Senate from defeat by Republicans in 1966.

But on the whole the political revolution has been conservative, partly because federal funds and programs have worked to enhance, rather than diminish, the power and influence of those guardians of the existing order, the state governors. The state executives have a say in how the money is spent on such projects as the poverty program and how such programs are to be administered. Naturally they seek to minimize a process of change that they cannot prevent. Federal administrators, for their part, often are hesitant about rigorously enforcing projects that they feel the societies involved may be unable to tolerate and absorb in a given period.

The political and social patterns that the governors try to protect from erosion—and that the federal authorities are reluctant to undermine too rapidly—were formed and written into the state constitutions during the years immediately following the Yankee-imposed Reconstruction. It was the period when white Southerners regained control of their states and set about undoing the impositions of the victorious North. Its span differed from state to state, but it may be generally dated from 1875 through 1910. It was a time of political, social and economic ferment, of turbulent adjustment to the new conditions brought about by defeat in the Civil War, the abolition of slavery, and the stresses of reunion with victorious states that themselves were in rapid and straining transition. For the South generally, and especially for the states of the Old South, it was above all a time of intense and shared awareness, a time of regional decision and choice, when Southerners understood more clearly than people usually do that they were shaping a society for the future. The society they shaped reflected their own Southern past and, in part, the pressures of national change from rural and mercantile America to the raw beginnings of today's urban and industrial America. It did not become in all respects what the dominant Southerners of the time wanted it to become; instead of achieving the sound and enriching economy they sought, they doomed the region to persistent poverty. In the respect that mattered most to them, however, the Old South emerged into the 20th Century with a political system deliberately designed to accomplish their overriding aim.

In the words of a delegate to the Mississippi constitutional convention of 1890, that aim was "to secure the supremacy of the white race." The purpose was as old as slavery, and ironically the effort had been strengthened by the galling attempt to elevate Negroes to political parity during Reconstruction. The whites had tried political coexistence with the Negro, in their fashion, and the experience convinced them that the desired "supremacy of the white race" could be satisfactorily assured only if Negroes were excluded from effective participation in politics and government. The whites soon found that political exclusion was possible despite the Constitutional and statutory protections that the North had provided for Negroes during Reconstruction.

It is commonly forgotten now, even in the South, that for a time after the end of Reconstruction the imposed protections continued to have some effect. As late as 1890 more Negroes than whites were registered to vote in Mississippi, and Negroes sat in the South Carolina legislature until 1896. For the moment, Southerners did not ignore the 14th amendment to the national Constitution, which entitled Negroes to "the equal protection of the laws"; the 15th amendment, which forbade denial of the right to vote because of race; and the comprehensive civil rights laws, federal and state, that remained on the books. Overt repression was deterred by fears of renewed national intervention and difficulty in believing that the North actually had ceased to care about the blacks whom it had so recently liberated. Many Southerners, including the most eminent leaders of the day, thought that white ascendancy could be reasserted and preserved without utterly proscribing and degrading the Negro. In the slavery era, arbitrary segregation had been neither wanted nor practicable. The proposal to apply it to schools and every area of the common life introduced a new and strange idea. In short, the meaning of the period is distorted if it is assumed that the measures finally taken "to secure the supremacy of the white race" represented nothing more than a blind and instinctive reversion to Southern nature. The new laws developed from the experience of a paradoxical time, when inherited attitudes and current circumstances seemed to conspire against all hope that the Old South might choose another course.

Some of the most interesting figures in American political history guided the region out of Reconstruction and helped shape the new mood. Called "Redeemers" by their supporters because they sought to redeem the South from the rule of carpetbaggers and Negroes, and "Bourbons" by their detractors because, like the archconservative monarchs of France, they were hostile to popular government, these leaders were a new breed on the Southern political scene. Most of them were businessmen, entrepreneurs and corporation lawyers, not the landed gentry who had ruled the South before the Civil War. Profoundly conservative, the new leaders were attracted politically to the business-oriented Republican Party, but because that party was anathema in the South, they proceeded to mold the Southern wing of the relatively more liberal Democratic Party into a model of reaction.

The most notable of the Bourbons and Redeemers was the least typical of them. General Wade Hampton of South Carolina was a true aristocrat, the third Wade Hampton of his line. The onetime owner of eight plantations and 3,000 slaves, a commander of Confederate cavalry and one of the last rebel effectives in the field at the end of the Civil War, he had been among the first to urge Southerners to accept defeat with submissive grace. After a postwar bankruptcy proceeding had relieved him of debts totaling more than one million dollars, he became one of the few solvent survivors of his ruined class. The upper ranks of post-Reconstruction politics teemed with such ex-Confederate generals; there was Georgia's valorous John B. Gordon, famous for his flowing hair; and Hampton's chief supporter, United States Senator Matthew C. Butler, who had lost a foot in battle. But the Bourbons as a group, including the sometime warriors, were deeply conservative men interested above all in business and finance; many of them were lawyers who placed their power and their "redeemed" regimes at the service of their business and industrial clients.

One such leader was Mississippi's munificently named and talented Lucius Quintus Cincinnatus Lamar. Born a Georgian, he had been a professor of mathematics, metaphysics and law at the University of Mississippi; a Congressman before and after the war; a reluctant secessionist who had nevertheless drafted his adopted state's act of secession; a leader in its overthrow of a Reconstruction government in 1875; a United States Senator, Secretary of the Interior and U.S. Supreme Court Justice. He was an eloquent pleader for reunion of "the common country" on Southern terms and, at the peak of his power in Mississippi, attorney for sundry Southern and Northern financial interests. He and his fellows, Hampton included, labored to draw desperately needed Northern capital to the gutted South. In the process they managed to draw substantial amounts of it to themselves by means that may have been questionable but were never proved illegal. Hampton invested with some of his Georgia friends in an insurance company that received remarkably generous treatment from the state. Gordon followed his Georgia crony, Governor and Senator Joseph E. Brown—an agile turncoat who was in sequence a secessionist Democrat, a scalawag Republican and a Redeemer-Democrat —from high political office into the presidency of a subsidized railroad. At the same time, he served as general counsel for the Northern-owned Louisville & Nashville Railroad, whose officers practically ran Alabama.

Hampton, Gordon, Lamar and others were allied in various shadowy deals, political and financial. Their biggest negotiation made Southern and national history. Democrats all—though some of them still preferred to be known as old-style Whigs —they gave decisive support to Rutherford B. Hayes, the Republican candidate for President in the close and corrupt election of 1876, in return for his promises to support Southern railroad interests and to withdraw the last federal troops of occupation from South Carolina, Florida and Louisiana. As President, Hayes did little about railroads in the South, but he did keep the second pledge. When Hayes removed the soldiers in 1877, Hampton in South Carolina and George F. "Millionaire" Drew, a merchant and lumberman in Florida, were able to shove aside Yankee-Republican claimants to victory in the disputed elections of the previous year and become the first Redemption governors of their states. Georgia, Alabama and Mississippi had already discarded their Reconstruction masters, and the Old South of the 20th Century was about to come into being.

Two legends that came to be adopted as truth in the Bourbon era powerfully affected the political process in the years that followed. These were the legends of the original, or the antebellum, "Old South" and of its "Lost Cause." They transformed

The Redeemers

After the Civil War, Southern politics were dominated by men like Wade Hampton *(left)* of South Carolina and Lucius Lamar *(right)* of Mississippi, leaders of the "Redeemers," who claimed to have "redeemed" the South from Northern rule. Their concept of white supremacy is still a political factor in many areas of the Old South.

Hampton, who served two terms as governor and two as U.S. Senator, was largely responsible for the return of self-government to his state. During the bitterly contested Presidential election of 1876, Hampton, a Democrat, swung his support to Rutherford B. Hayes, the Republican candidate, in return for Hayes's promise to remove the remaining federal troops from the South. Hayes was elected and kept his promise, leaving Hampton in firm control of South Carolina.

Lamar, like Hampton, went to unusual lengths to end Reconstruction rule. In 1874 he delivered a warm eulogy of Massachusetts' Senator Charles Sumner, a supporter of those Northerners who wanted to impose harsh conditions on the defeated South. Demonstrating the South's reconciliation with the rest of the nation, his gesture gained much Northern support for his regime.

the Southern time before the war into an impossibly golden age, invested the Confederacy's defeat with the glories and comfort of spiritual victory, and provided generation after generation of postwar leaders with an inexhaustible reservoir of sentiment and tradition, valid and contrived, upon which to draw. Every conceivable form of political and social behavior, from the most arrant abuse of power to the advocacy of "popular" rule through direct (white-only) primaries, from paternal solicitude for Negroes to lynching, was justified in the name of a South not really gone, a Cause never really lost. There was progress of a kind during this period. But it was grossly exaggerated, it was achieved at enormous social cost, and it was marred by inequities that had important political consequences.

The inequities bore hardest upon Negroes and rural whites. However much the two groups differed in status, they were in the same economic plight. Most of them were farmers, farm workers or dwellers in small towns dependent upon farming. Most of them lived from cotton, which had increasingly become the one crop that farmers knew how to grow and were allowed to grow by the bankers and merchant-lenders to whom they looked for indispensable credit. About a third of the region's

farms were tenant-operated by 1880. Most owners, especially of small farms, suffered with the tenants from low prices for their cotton, high rates for their loans and high prices for tariff-protected manufactured items that the South imported from the North.

Just under half of the 5.2 million inhabitants of the Old South region were Negroes. They were the majority only in South Carolina and Mississippi, and throughout the region they were in effective subjection. Although crude schooling was now provided for some of them, most were still illiterate. Migration from the countryside was beginning, but most Negroes were still on the land. A few owned farms, and some owned mules and tools and paid cash rent, but three of four Negro farmers were bound to the plow by labor contracts or by sharecrop arrangements amounting to peonage. Conditions for whites were also worsening. More and more white farmers were falling from ownership into tenancy, and the economic gap between the races in rural areas was not as wide as the whites wished to believe. Negroes, disappointed by the meager rewards of freedom, had their unique causes for resentment. But the majority of rural white Southerners also had cause to doubt the Bourbon gospel that they, one and all, had "found the hills of gold in the energies of an imperishable race."

If the Southern course had been determined mainly by economic circumstances, the history of the region might have been far less tragic. But other factors were at work, and one of them was the distribution of the black and white populations. Most Negroes lived where the prewar plantation system had placed them, in the coastal lowlands, plains country and the river deltas. There were more Negroes than whites in such areas—the local proportions ran as high as 5 to 1—and white residents of these "black belts" were accustomed to the presence of Negroes in large numbers. Most of the rural white population was in the uplands and back country, where there were likely to be comparatively few Negroes—in some counties, none at all. Here were the poorest of the poor whites; here were the smallest farms, the poorest land, the hardest living. Like every Southern circumstance, this one had a racial aspect. It was the same in 1880 as it was to be in 1933, when a north Alabama hillbilly told Carl Carmer, the author of *Stars Fell on Alabama:* "We don't like niggers in this neck o' the woods. We ain't ever liked 'em. I can remember my father standin' on the mountain where you can look off down toward the Black Belt an' the flat country an' sayin': 'Them black bastards is takin' the food out'n our mouths. We oughta be down there workin' that black land but we got too much pride to work for nothin'. They're down there sharin' the good things with the rich while good white folks in the hills have to starve."

And they were down there providing superior political power for the lowland whites, the Bourbon magnificoes who mostly came from, and relied upon, the "black counties." Here we have the great irony of the time, the circumstance fatal beyond all others to any prospect there may have been for racial equity. The technical enfranchisement of Negroes had not given them a real voice in the government of the South, but it had made them pawns in the struggle to control that government. And the importance of this role meant that to the ancient prejudice against the black man was added the full heat of the contentions arising among white Southerners. As differences of interest and welfare developed between townsmen and farmers, rich and poor, the red-necks in the hills and the postwar pretenders to lowland aristocracy, the conflicts created new political divisions and intensified political warfare. Whether the Negroes did or did not vote, they were caught in the cross fire.

Before Emancipation and Reconstruction, they had figured in politics only as so many digits: three fifths of the slave population was counted with the white population for purposes of allotting each state's Congressional quota. After Reconstruction, Negroes were counted equally with whites in apportioning representation in state legislatures and party conventions as well as in Congress. The "black counties" consequently had more legislators, convention delegates and Congressmen than the "white counties" did, a situation the Bourbon leaders exploited. The rural whites who suffered from it tended to place the blame on the hapless Negroes.

Nor was this all. Negroes were not merely allowed to vote; they were begged and bribed and forced to vote when it suited white contenders. Dependably compliant Negroes were occasionally rewarded with public offices, usually minor but in some cases including even seats in Congress. By whatever means Negro support was won or compelled, it inevitably embittered the whites. Most political groups sought and found black support, but the losers in a contest could always charge their defeat to Negro voters. In the end, the "black county" politicians, although in many instances they owed their dominance to the margin provided by black voters, turned upon them and became as anxious as the most vengeful back-country whites to eliminate Negroes from politics. Some historians have suggested that it was the syndrome of white superiority rather than Negro enfranchisement as such that proved to be the intolerable factor. Whites were humiliated by the need to compete with one another for Negro favor, and by the extremes of violence and corruption to which they let this necessity drive them.

Briefly and with sad result, some white and Negro Southerners did stand together for what they saw to be their common interests and rights. They were mostly small farmers, farm workers and politicians who joined "the agrarian revolt" of the 1880s and 1890s. This was a complex economic and political rebellion, national in scope, that resulted in the People's Party, or Populist movement, of the 1890s. The party was to disappear from the national scene in less than a decade, in part because many of its principles were adopted by the Democrats. But in the Old South the movement's demise was caused largely by the racial question.

In the South, as elsewhere, the energizing force of the movement was the angry belief of rural Americans that the industrialists and financiers of the cities were hogging the rewards of the erratic but ever-growing national economy. Militant farm "alliances" recruited three million white and one and a quarter million Negro members in the South. In a few instances aggrieved agrarians of both races united in integrated groups, but generally they tried to make common cause through racially separate organizations. Yet even this attempt at arms-length collaboration failed—"stoned, shot and niggered to death," in social historian Vera Rony's vivid phrase, by conservative white Democrats who were frightened by the movement and used violence and the old specter of "Negro domination" to combat it. Populist sentiment did not immediately die, but the People's Party gradually lost its political effectiveness.

The conservative Democrats who revived the cry of "Negro domination" were the same Bourbons who professed to evoke all that was good and gentle and paternal in the Southern tradition. Wade Hampton, the South Carolina patrician, and Lucius Lamar, the revered Mississippi statesman from Georgia, performed with typical ambivalence. They simultaneously courted Negro support, tolerated the night-riding thugs of the Ku Klux Klan, set their own gangs of red-shirted floggers and killers upon Negroes who failed to vote as ordered or showed a disposition to vote when and where they were not supposed to, and shouted to the Dixie heavens that Negroes would attain a decisive balance of political power if white voters divided among themselves and supported opponents of Bourbon rule and policies.

But this specious argument was losing its effectiveness with the poor whites. Even the appeal to racism could not obscure the fact that their economic interests and those of the rich were usually at odds. The times were propitious for the entrance of a new group of leaders, the demagogues, who by riding the wave of Populist sentiment would largely replace the Bourbons in the starring political roles. Hostility to large corporate and financial power was common to all the demagogues, although most of them continued to use the Negro as a secondary whipping boy. "Their election," says historian John S. Ezell, "resulted from great promises on behalf of the electorate, and while their achievements rank low historically, they often seemed large to the voter in comparison with the do-nothing attitudes of their [Bourbon] predecessors."

Two early challengers of Bourbon power who deeply influenced their states and region were Tom Watson of Georgia and Benjamin R. "Pitchfork Ben" Tillman of South Carolina. Both were demagogues. A minor but interesting difference in physical characteristics between the two pioneers of the line and their Bourbon foes probably had something to do with their magnetic appeal for the poor and ill-used of the rural South. Hampton, Lamar and their ilk were generally ample and imposing men, with a look of having been born in Prince Albert tail coats. Watson and Tillman were screechy of voice and grubby in manner and appearance, looking as if they were always hungry for a country meal of pork, pone and turnip greens. The "man of the people" image they fostered was to be copied by later demagogues. A number of these figures did come from the ranks of the poor and therefore knew the language, aspirations and mores of the masses of voters in the Old South. Those who were born of rich families and had good educations carefully hid their backgrounds and dressed, behaved and spoke like yokels when they were with their constituents.

Tom (for Thomas Edward) Watson was one of the Southerners who dared to breach the racial wall, with consequences for him and for his people that tempt the historian to say that his career typified the region's dilemma and tragedy. Dilemma there was, tragedy there was, but in Tom Watson's case there also was a personal sickness of the mind.

During his early rise in the 1880s and his campaigns for Congress in 1890 and 1892, Watson appeared in company with Negro supporters and risked his life to save them from infuriated Georgia yokels. On one occasion townspeople threatened to lynch a young Negro preacher because of the speeches he was making in behalf of Watson's candidacy. Watson hid the man and then rallied some 2,000 armed Populists from the surrounding farms and brought them to town. The lynching never took place. "After that," the preacher said, "Mr. Watson was held almost as a savior by the Negroes." Watson urged impoverished whites and Negroes in mixed audiences not to let "the accident of color" divide them and said they were "kept apart" only so that they might be separately cheated. Elected with biracial backing in 1890, he quit the Democratic Party, declared himself a Populist and rose to the top rank of the new People's Party. He ran for U.S. Vice President in 1896 and for President in 1904 and 1908 on Populist tickets, and he is still a noteworthy figure in the history of radical politics in America.

But his 1890 victory with black support had frightened white Georgians. His Bourbon enemies altered the boundaries of his Congressional district, intensified their warnings of "Negro domination," and at the same time used their usual combination of cajolery, bribery and intimidation to draw many Negroes away from Watson when he stood for re-election. He was twice defeated, in 1892 and again in 1894. Finally, he broke under the strain. Out of office but still a power in Georgia, he became an outspoken bigot. Striving with vindictive frenzy to isolate Negroes politically, he justified their repression by any means, including lynching. With speeches and writings, he also fomented prejudice against Catholics and Jews and was in part responsible for the barbarous lynching of a Jew from New York, Leo Frank, in Atlanta in 1915. At the last, when he was old and steeped in racist guilt, Tom Watson tried to reclaim his repute as a progressive idealist. Georgians who had applauded his pandering to their darkest traits elected him as a liberal to the United States Senate by an enormous majority in 1920. When he died in 1922, he was defending the civil liberties and minority rights that he had long traduced.

Benjamin R. Tillman was a simpler man. His agrarian sentiments and, in matters apart from race, his genuine progressivism developed from his troubles as a debt-ridden farmer in upcountry South Carolina. He received Populist support but he remained a more or less loyal Democrat, even when he was earning his nickname of "Pitchfork Ben" by promising to jab the conservative Democratic President, Grover Cleveland, with a pitchfork. His appeal was to white farmers and farm workers, never to Negroes. But with all of his "nigger-baiting" he never catered to what he called the "damned factory class" of venomously anti-Negro "lint heads," the poor whites who had left the land for work at pittance wages in the state's multiplying textile mills.

Tillman's chosen enemies were the merchants, lawyers and industrialists who had kept Wade Hampton and his Bourbon clique in power. Tillman pretended no love for the lowland Negroes, who, in South Carolina as elsewhere, usually voted Bourbon when they were allowed to vote at all. But he regarded them less as enemies than as benighted pawns of the "white scoundrels" who mobilized them against him. He told white voters in effect that they were fools to let their fear of "Negro domination" deter them from supporting him against the incumbent Bourbons, and in this sense he usefully questioned one of the region's paralyzing shibboleths. Once he was in power himself, first as governor and then as a United States Senator, he decided that the way to deal with the problem of Negroes in politics was, as he said, to "take from them every ballot that we can under the laws of our national government." Total exclusion of Negroes

from political life would not only end the possibility of "black domination" but would also undercut the Negro aspect of Bourbon power. White supremacy, demagogue-style, would be assured.

To achieve this purpose, Tillman arranged a convention in 1895 to revise the state's constitution. He and his followers did not have to be very inventive. They had only to heed the example of Mississippi, where the standard Southern model of a constitution designed to bar Negroes from politics and government had been adopted in 1890.

Backward in all else, Mississippi had been showing the region how to stay "Southern" and "white" since 1875. The first "Mississippi Plan" had been devoted to minimizing the effects of Negro enfranchisement and ending Reconstruction. It had been widely admired and copied in the South. The 1890 Mississippi constitution, replacing the one adopted under Yankee compulsion in 1868, embodied the second "Mississippi Plan." It was to set the pattern of politics and government in the Old South for the next 70 years.

Oddly enough, this Mississippi pattern was established by Bourbons who had nothing to gain, in political terms, by opting for a new constitution. After the state had been "redeemed" in 1875 and Negro rights had become little more than a shoddy joke, the Bourbons had taken complete political control. Negroes comprised nearly 60 per cent of the population, but they were concentrated in some 30 "black counties." By virtue of their population, these counties dominated the state legislature. Conservative Democrats led by Lamar and two other wealthy lawyers, James Z. George and Edward C. Walthall, permitted a certain amount of Negro voting in the "black counties," but it was fully controlled through intimidation, fraud and minimal rewards. In the poorer "white counties" these same leaders played on the "Negro domination" theme and thus thwarted every effort to develop effective agrarian protest. On the face of things, Mississippi seemed to have worked out political arrangements that should have satisfied the Bourbon beneficiaries and, at the same time, kept the less favored elements of the white population reasonably quiescent.

Yet all white factions and classes were unhappy with the constitution established during Reconstruction. Apart from its egalitarian provisions, which could be ignored, it was a standing affront to Mississippi pride. But there were practical reasons as well. Large numbers of the white minority were illiterate, but their politicians could count and they figured that they might wrest control from the

"A man of mighty power"

In a political career that spanned four decades, Georgia's Thomas E. Watson *(right)* ran the gamut from militant liberalism to violent bigotry and back to liberalism. His Jekyll-Hyde politics bewildered some of his followers and disgusted others, but in a folk song still heard in the backwoods of Georgia, he is called "a man of mighty power."

In 1882, when he was 25 years old, Watson was elected to the Georgia State Assembly, where he carried on his fight against the powerful industrialists. Then, in 1890, he was elected to Congress and soon became a leader of the rising Populist movement, a political alliance composed mainly of small farmers of both races. By the turn of

the century the People's Party was collapsing and Watson, having suffered a string of political defeats, retired to private life. But he was greatly affected by his political frustration. From his Georgia plantation he bitterly attacked Catholics, Socialists, Negroes and Jews. Later he reversed his field again and ran for the U.S. Senate in 1920 as a liberal Democrat. He was elected and championed organized labor and oppressed minorities until his death in 1922. A statue of this volatile politician *(below)* now stands on the lawn of the Georgia State Capitol.

THOMAS E. WATSON
BORN SEPT. 5ᵗʰ 1856
DIED SEPT. 26ᵗʰ 1922
HONOR'S PATH HE TROD

EDITOR, LAWYER, HISTORIAN, AUTHOR, ORATOR, STATESMAN. AUTHOR OF RURAL FREE DELIVERY A CHAMPION OF RIGHT WHO NEVER FALTERED IN THE CAUSE

"black counties" if the Negroes massed there could somehow be eliminated from the political equation. With due recognition of these and related factors, however, an interesting question remains. Why were the entrenched Bourbons, who were doing very well, at least as eager as the deprived rural poor of back-country Mississippi were to change the system?

Did they believe their propaganda about "Negro domination"? Men like Lamar, who in 1890 was an Associate Justice of the U.S. Supreme Court, must have known that there was not the slightest possibility of it. Nearly all of the 150,000 male Negroes then of voting age were former slaves or sons of slaves. Only about a quarter of them were even nominally literate, and all were in what amounted to economic shackles. It is difficult to conceive of a less likely threat to a well-organized, solidly entrenched ruling class. The composition of the elected constitutional convention of 1890 demonstrated the extent to which Negroes already could be and were excluded from power: there were 133 white delegates and just one Negro delegate, a former slave who had belonged to a brother of Confederate President Jefferson Davis. But what men "knew" did not determine what they feared. The frightening cry of "black domination" dated back to slavery. Memories ranging from the prewar prophecies of old John Calhoun to all-Negro militia patrolling Mississippi towns and counties after the war were much alive. There can be no doubt that delegate W. S. Eskridge of Tallahatchie County spoke for the run of white Mississippians when he said to the 1890 convention: "The white people of the State want to feel and know that they are protected not only against the probability but the possibility of negro rule and negro domination." (Most right-thinking Mississippians, including those who reported the proceedings, made a point of spelling "Negro" with a lower-case "n.")

Some delegates to the Mississippi convention bespoke a consideration that is, in our day, perhaps the most difficult to comprehend. This was the desire, the impelling need, of white citizens to repair the damage recently done to their sense of "southern rightness." The profound conviction that they were *right* in resisting any move toward equality of the two races *(Chapter 3)* was as strong as ever. But the means of resistance to which they had fallen during and since Reconstruction troubled and alarmed the thoughtful among them. In describing to the U.S. Senate the brutalities and frauds practiced on Negroes in order to deny them political power, Ben Tillman of South Carolina said, "We are not ashamed of it." Tillman was wrong. Many Southerners were ashamed, and many shared the concern expressed by Judge J. B. Chrisman in a frequently quoted statement to the Mississippi convention: "Sir," he said, "it is no secret that there has not been a full vote and a fair count in Mississippi since 1875—that we have been preserving the ascendancy of the white people by revolutionary methods. In plain words, we have been stuffing ballot boxes, committing perjury and here and there in the state carrying the elections by fraud and violence until the whole machinery for elections was about to rot down." The convention president, S. S. Calhoon, observed with sorrow that white men had taken to cheating one another as well as Negroes in the ballot counts. And he echoed the moral justification of slavery when he said that measures assuring that Negroes "shall be practically excluded from the government control" were required alike for "their own good and our own."

The desired exclusion took a lot of doing. Back-country politicians suspected with reason that the lowland Bourbons would have been happy to bar poor and illiterate rural whites from the voting rolls along with Negroes. But a way around that obstacle was found and the route was described by the Mississippi Supreme Court in 1896. "Restrained by the federal constitution from discriminating against the negro race," the court said, "the convention discriminated against its characteristics."

The vulnerable characteristics were assumed to be poverty, a tendency to roam, a proclivity for certain crimes, and ignorance. A two-dollar poll tax, to be paid months in advance of each election, was, a delegate said, "tantamount to the State of Mississippi, saying to the Negro: 'We will give you two dollars not to vote.'" In requiring residence in the state for two years and in the voter's election district for one year, the convention had in mind a "disposition of young Negroes . . . to change their homes and precincts every year." The inclusion of burglary, theft, arson and the like, and the omission of murder, rape and felonious assault, in a list of crimes that would disqualify applicants for registration were explained in a striking way by the state Supreme Court. Negro miscreants, it said, were "given rather to furtive offenses than to the robust crimes of the whites." But the major bar to Negro voters was the complexity and obtuse language of the new constitution itself—a document, Senator Theodore Bilbo boasted 56 years later, "that damn few white men and no niggers at all can explain."

The terms of a literacy test for prospective voters made the muddily written constitution an instrument of the very discrimination that it imposed. After much haggling between "black county" and "white county" delegates, the convention produced a test that was a masterpiece of electoral chicanery, based upon the supposition, somewhat flattering to the favored race, that "at least 10 per cent of the white, and 60 per cent of the colored population can neither read nor write." This test, in use until the national Civil Rights Act of 1965 was passed and enforced, required citizens undertaking to register as voters to satisfy a county registrar (white, of course) that they could read any section of the constitution chosen by the registrar, or understand it when it was read to them, or "give a reasonable interpretation" of it. The intent and effect were to make the registrars the sole judges of voter qualification. They were in a position to overlook the deficiencies of white illiterates and to reject, on one pretext or another, any among the literate minority of Negroes who were so imprudent as to show that they could read and interpret the murky passages usually thrust at them. Very few tried: the total of registered Negroes fell from around 100,000 in 1890 to 8,600 in 1892 and in 1955 was estimated at only 21,500, less than 5 per cent of the black voting-age population.

The "Mississippi Plan," modified somewhat in the various states, swept most of the South. Only Florida in the Old South continued to find ordinary repression and the restrictions in its constitution of 1885 sufficient for its purposes. Versions of the Mississippi formula were written into new constitutions by South Carolina in 1895 and by Alabama in 1901. In Georgia Tom Watson argued that this type of legalized political exclusion of Negroes would free "every white man" to vote "according to his own conscience and judgment." Watson got his way by constitutional amendment in 1908.

A few Southerners perceived the fallacy in such arguments as Watson's and foresaw the consequences. Alabama-born author William Garrott Brown wrote in 1903 that the Old South was weakening instead of strengthening its political processes through its preoccupation with the Negro and its determination "to get rid of him politically, and to do so by law, once and for all." An Alabama churchman and social reformer, the Reverend Edgar Gardiner Murphy, begged Southerners in 1904 to abandon their obsession with "the old benumbing and baffling error . . . the crude fiction of negro power." He told the whites that instead of freeing themselves for rational political choice and action they were bringing upon themselves "a form of negro domination which we have least suspected." He compared them with "the soldier of old who bound his wretched captive to his wrist," and thereby bound himself to the captive.

But the whites persisted. Most of them were willing to pay any price—including the price of "Negro domination" in the form discerned by Murphy—for the desired result: the exclusion of the Negro from meaningful participation in the politics and governments of the region. The situation suited most white Southerners very well. However blind they were to their true interest and to what they were doing to themselves, they acted in these years from conscious choice and preference in their political and other dealings with the Negro. Even in the late 1960s very few white people in the region saw a connection between political freedom for themselves and political freedom for the Negro. Sufficient evidence that most of them would have preferred to continue the denial of political freedom to the Negro is the fact that it was granted to him only under federal compulsion and, once granted, was still widely and fiercely resented.

Long before federal intervention doomed the system of legalized exclusion and segregation, maintaining it had proved to be a never-ending and ever-degrading task. For instance, some Negroes continued to vote in every state. Mississippi politicians bought votes of Negroes, whether registered or not, with a dollar or two, a pint of corn whiskey, perhaps a vague promise of intercession in time of trouble. The practice scandalized newspaper editors now and then, but it did not disturb the electorate so long as it did not endanger white supremacy. A U.S. Supreme Court decision in 1944, prohibiting the restriction of Democratic primaries to white voters, spurred a revival of legitimate Negro registration and voting in the border states and in a few cities of the lower South. On the whole, however, voting came to be a dreary status symbol for compliant Negroes—a signal to the black community that these individuals were accepted by the whites, and, to the white community, a token of submission. In most of the Old South there was no significant change before the 1960s.

The effect on white voters was perhaps more subtle, but equally depressing. Many white citizens neglected the franchise that they had so insistently reserved for themselves. The proportions of eligible voters who turned out for nominating primaries and general elections fell far below the national averages. Poll taxes, literacy tests and other devices aimed at Negroes served to bar or discourage some whites. But, more significant, voting itself no longer seemed to be as important as it once had been. Negroes were out of the picture, save as occasional pawns and as lurking menaces to be denounced with mandatory vigor at political rallies. Except in the Border States and in a few upland areas, Republicans did not figure either, the Grand Old Party having been deprived of its Negro support and fatally identified as an instrument of Yankee meddlers and racial egalitarians. In states where a Republican candidate for President could not conceivably win a majority, there was no compelling urge to vote for the Democrat.

The elections that mattered were the primaries in which the Democrats nominated their local, state and Congressional candidates. Rivals might differ on important issues, or claim to, but all of them were Democrats and there was a comfortable feeling that the differences were minimal. Local contests turned on myriad communal and personal considerations, such as whether one man needed the job more than another or had been in office so long that keeping him there was a ritual duty. All of this made for a low level of serious political concern and often for a low level of performance in office. At the same time, politics as a matter of diversion, as a kind of team sport, never ceased to be of intense interest and incessant talk among the citizenry. The reason for this paradox was simple enough: Southern politicians tended to be splendid showmen and their oratory provided a welcome form of public entertainment.

Such was the "solid South" of former years where, it has been justly said, the tie with the Democratic Party was "all but a religious affiliation." The bond was stronger in the lower South than in such marginal states as Kentucky and Tennessee, and stronger in four states of the Old South—Georgia, South Carolina, Alabama and Mississippi—than in Florida. Although the Presidential election of 1928 put the Old South's Protestant fundamentalism to a major test—Alfred E. Smith, the Democratic nominee, was both Catholic and anti-Prohibitionist—only Florida broke ranks and gave a majority to the Republican candidate, Herbert Hoover. In 1948, when Democratic President Harry Truman's advocacy of civil rights legislation and other threats of federal intrusion again strained Southern loyalties, a defiant "Dixiecrat" ticket headed by the Governors of South Carolina and Mississippi carried those two states plus Alabama and Louisiana. In order to do it, however, the Dixiecrats had to run as Democrats—in rebellion

"Big Jim" Folsom, a six-foot-eight giant who was one of the most colorful politicians in Alabama's history, is shown at left holding a "suds bucket," a trademark of his successful campaign for governor in 1946. "You furnish the suds [campaign contributions] and I'll do the scrubbin'," he said in promising to clean up corruption in state politics. Folsom also became known as "Kissin' Jim." Shown above embracing an Alabama beauty, Folsom claimed to have kissed more than 50,000 girls during his 1946 campaign. He served a second term as governor from 1955 to 1959. He later retired from politics.

against the national party, but still Democrats.

In 1952 and 1956, despite General Dwight D. Eisenhower's great attraction, the majority in South Carolina, Georgia, Alabama and Mississippi still could not bring themselves to vote for a Republican President. The same was true in 1960. When they finally did vote Republican, in 1964, for Barry Goldwater of Arizona in preference to a Texas Southerner, Lyndon B. Johnson, the determining reason was clear. Goldwater as a United States Senator had voted against the civil rights bill of that year; Johnson had favored the measure and had declared for the relentless federal enforcement of civil rights for Negroes. Federal intrusion in other forms was also at issue, but the racial issue was paramount in the Old South. Nothing else would have caused 87 per cent of Mississippi voters to reject a Democratic Southern President for a notably mediocre Republican. In Florida, where majorities had voted Republican in the three previous national elections, the racial factor worked the other way. Florida Negroes, who by 1964 were registered in significant numbers, voted massively for Johnson and enabled him to win the state.

Although the 1964 Presidential vote showed beyond doubt that the Old South's "religious affiliation" to the Democratic Party belonged to the past, the outcome of lesser races then and afterward was even more indicative of the permanent political change. One-party politics had plainly approached its end when, in 1967, three Congressmen from Alabama, three from Florida and one from South Carolina were Republicans. The dominant political figure in South Carolina was United States Senator and former Governor Strom Thurmond, a sometime Democrat turned Republican. The Governor of Florida, 20 of its 48 state Senators and 39 of its 119 state Representatives were also Republicans. There were smaller Republican minorities in the Georgia and South Carolina legislatures, and Alabama had a Republican state Senator. The election of Republicans to local office had become unremarkable, if not as yet commonplace, in South Carolina, Georgia, Alabama and Florida and was beginning to occur without bloodshed in Mississippi. Republicans in all five states were giving lessons in political organization to the Democrats, who after years of sanctified monopoly were lazy, split into factions and poorly prepared for the rigors of partisan competition.

But it was still competition between Southerners, reflecting Southern peculiarities and tensions. Most of the new Republicans were former Democrats for whom the change of party was a form of protest. The politics of the region had to a considerable extent become the politics of illusion, a kind of charade. There was little of the process of healthy debate and division over authentic issues that in theory should have developed with the passing of one-party stagnation.

The case of George Corley Wallace Jr. of Alabama, the most interesting politician produced by the Old South in the 1960s, illustrates the point. Although the state constitution forbids a governor from succeeding himself, Wallace continued to govern Alabama after his term as governor ended in early 1967. This was what the voters expected him to do when, at his bidding, they elected his wife, Lurleen, to succeed him. They had also expected him to go on playing out, as he had done during his official tenure, a comforting fantasy of resistance to the irresistible tides of change and reform sweeping Alabama and the region. The ultimate irony lay in the fact that Wallace in many respects had been one of the Old South's more progressive and efficient governors. He was rated a "liberal" by most knowledgeable observers in matters other than his two corroding preoccupations—race and what he denounced as federal dictation of state affairs. He knew that federal regulations and federal court orders requiring Alabama to integrate its public schools had to be obeyed. And in truth they were being obeyed more widely than Wallace and the white Alabamans to whom he catered liked to admit. Yet he called upon the subservient legislature to respond in 1967, as it had been doing for years, with segregationist laws of a kind that had been consistently invalidated by the federal courts and would surely be ruled out once more. A good many Alabamans were asking whether there was any point to this futility. But there was a point: it was still an unforgivable political sin to appear to submit willingly and openly to federal demands, particularly when submission had to do with racial reform.

Figures published by the U.S. Treasury in 1967 put the Wallace posture of resistance to federal intrusion in a somewhat comic perspective. Federal grants in fiscal 1966 to state and local governments in Alabama totaled well over $300 million. Including payments to individuals and private institutions, but excluding outlays for federal agencies and installations in Alabama, the total was almost $400 million—only some $26 million less than the state's total tax revenue in the previous fiscal year. In the Old South only Georgia received more (about $410 million), and only 12 other states in the whole country got as much or more. However,

the Wallace administrations put up a vigorous show of battle against the federal requirements that came with the money.

At one time Alabama appeared ready to sacrifice nearly $100 million for welfare purposes rather than comply with federal integration requirements. But the federal administrators concerned understood from experience that it was more show than substance. Frank Sloane, a South Carolina politician who had been placed in Atlanta to ease poverty-program relationships with state governments, remarked in 1966 that he would *never* say out loud that behind all the public fussing the Wallace administration was among the more cooperative in his area. And with Paul Johnson, who was then the governor of Mississippi, Sloane had a smoother working relationship than either man cared to acknowledge publicly.

An aide to Governor Robert E. McNair of South Carolina, a moderate Democrat, touched on a lighter aspect of federal-state actualities in the region. South Carolina had in Washington a Democratic Senator, Ernest F. Hollings, and a turncoat Republican Senator, Strom Thurmond. "I'd say we have it made," Governor McNair's man said. "We got our Democrat up there, getting all that federal money for us. And we got ol' Strom, kicking Lyndon Johnson in the tail to make us feel good about taking it."

Fantasy remains a major ingredient of politics in the Old South. But the cold realities of law and contemporary economics are penetrating the magnolia-scented dreams of the region. The awakening is slow and unwilling, but it is taking place. Mississippi, the hardest of the hard-core states, has provided one example. Rubel Phillips preached the straight segregationist line when he was the Republican candidate for governor in 1963. Four years later, when he was again the GOP nominee for that office, his words had a strangely different import. "It is painfully clear," he said, "that the race issue has retarded the development of our human resources. The white cannot keep the Negro down without paying the awesome penalty of restricting his own development."

The fact that he was defeated by an archsegregationist was not unexpected; the centuries-old determination to maintain white dominance does not end quickly. But for a serious candidate in Mississippi to voice such realities is, in itself, a monumental and portentous advance. The conflict between fantasy and reality will undoubtedly continue for a long time in the Old South, but it is already obvious that the latter's victory is inevitable.

That oldtime religion

In much of the world today laymen and clergy alike are questioning centuries-old religious doctrines and practices, and theologians are attempting to reconcile established faiths with the realities of modern life. This trend is less apparent in the South, and especially in the Old South. There the evangelical Protestant denominations remain strongly entrenched and are growing rapidly. "Nowhere else, almost surely," says historian Kenneth K. Bailey, "is there a Protestant population of equal size so renowned for its piety." For these believers, the church is the central structure of their lives. Emotional in their religious expression *(left),* bound to one another by a shared certainty, members of such denominations as the Pentecostal Holiness Church and the Church of God form cohesive brotherhoods that are increasingly rare in the modern world.

This frontier-style faith had grown strong in the rural society that for so long dominated the Old South. In recent decades, there has been a considerable migration from the rural areas to the cities, and the people have brought their religion with them. It continues to preserve a simpler way of life and to fulfill the spiritual needs of a devout people.

Photographs by Bruce Roberts

A feeling of warmth through shared experiences

Southern evangelical congregations probably spend more time in their churches and become more deeply involved in their activities than most Americans in other parts of the country. Devout members attend not only Sunday services but Sunday school and mid-week prayer meetings as well. Services are unstructured and warmly human. Visitors are recognized and

Members arrive for the evening services at a small church located in northwestern Georgia.

introduced—before, after and even during worship—with a heartiness that suggests a family gathering. Warm personal relationships inevitably develop from these shared experiences. Perhaps it is the unselfconscious expression of this kind of "fellowship" *(below)*—members greet one another enthusiastically, like devoted members of a family—that most distinguishes Southern churches. The Southerner's dedication to religion is manifest even to the visitor who never attends a church. Signs like "Jesus is coming. Be ready." dot highways throughout the region, and advertisements for hymn-singing events are commonplace. Whatever other faults the Southerner may have, he is no mere "Sunday-morning" Christian.

Close friends as well as fellow parishioners, two members of a Southern congregation show their mutual regard.

"Make a joyful noise unto the Lord"

A marked trait of a Southern evangelical congregation is its fervor during services. Although some denominations in the Old South have become more restrained in recent decades, there are still some churches where members deliver their own emotion-charged sermons; "speak in tongues," i.e., in unintelligible utterances *(below left);* and tremble and swoon

Filled with religious ecstasy, a young Southern girl "speaks in tongues."

in religious ecstasy. Even in the more conventional churches, the "hell-fire-and-damnation" sermon is still heard, and the need for "oldtime Bible preaching" is often stressed at meetings of the clergy.

Emotionalism was characteristic of many Protestant churches in the Old South from the earliest days. The majority of people were uneducated and felt the need for a religion of uncomplicated theology, a faith that could bring emotional release, color and drama to their harsh, dull lives. The preachers frequently had no more education than their followers and therefore there was no tendency to intellectualize religion or to question the precepts handed down by earlier generations. Religious fervor and dedication were enough.

Clapping their hands joyfully, members of the Tremont Avenue Church of God in Greenville, South Carolina, sing an oldtime gospel song.

"and, lo, the heavens were opened"

The doctrines of the evangelical Southern churches are simple and few. There is a firm belief in a literal interpretation of the Bible—an insistence, for example, that human life as we know it began in the way the Bible said it did, with the creation of Adam and Eve. Whenever there is a conflict between a Biblical statement and scientific fact, these Southern churchmen rely on the Bible as final truth.

Such undeviating acceptance of the words of the Bible has made baptism by total immersion one of the most strongly held tenets of the Southern evangelical churches. Matthew 3:16 indicates that Christ was baptized in this way: "And Jesus, when he was baptized, went up straightway out of the water; and, lo, the heavens were opened unto him." Furthermore, because the Bible in its Greek version describes Jesus' baptism in words that imply total immersion, it is believed that the ordinance must follow this practice. Although most baptisms now take place inside a church, a few parishioners still ask to be baptized outdoors, in a river or lake, to adhere more closely to tradition.

Parishioners gather beside a pond in Lakeland, Florida, to witness the baptism of a new member of the Lake Wire Church of God. The minister *(left)* and his assistant lead the woman into the water while the congregation sings a traditional baptismal hymn.

97

Marshaling soldiers for Christ

At the climax of a tent revival in Birmingham, Alabama, young people raise their clasped hands skyward as they rededicate themselves to God and pledge to continue their efforts to be good witnesses for Christ.

For the ardent Southern churchgoer, religious faith must be constantly renewed, and the revival, which enables the faithful to reaffirm their belief and brings sinners into the fold, is among the most dramatic customs of the evangelical churches in the Old South. Usually held in summer, revivals often take place in tents, although today most are held in churches. Sometimes an auditorium or even a football stadium is used to accommodate the large crowd. Since the revival is the high point of the Southerner's religious life, the churches try to obtain such inspiring preachers as Billy Graham, E. J. Daniels and T. F. Lowery. But even when led by a relatively unknown preacher *(below)*, the event stirs its participants markedly.

5

The Southern Anomaly, Atlanta

So far in this account we have tried mainly to define and explain the differences that have set the Old South and its people apart from the rest of America and its citizens, and indeed from other sections and people of the geographic South. We have noted a pervasive languor, an attachment to the past, a habit of mind that historians have identified—perhaps too sweepingly—with a tradition not so much of failure as of positive pride in the differences associated with failure. Of course these are not and never have been the region's only qualities. It may even be argued that they are not and never have been the Old South's predominant qualities. But the shortcomings are too many, too glaring and—even now, after some years of relative economic and social advancement—too persistent for that argument to be sustained. Nevertheless, over the years there have been a number of notable Southern departures from the Southern pattern in the form of events, achievements, individuals, institutions and communities so exceptional as to seem out of place in the region.

Such an exception—and the subject of this chapter—is Atlanta, Georgia, the Old South's biggest and richest city. Until very recently it was a complete anomaly in the region. It was a city of optimists in a region of prideful pessimists; a city marked with verve and zest at a time when these characteristics, while not altogether missing elsewhere in the region, were minimized and hidden behind a façade of genteel pokiness; a city striving to make its way from Southern backwaters into the mainstream of American life. The Atlanta of today is still dramatic in its vigor and growth, but in spirit, at least, it is no longer so atypical of the Old South as it once was. Profound changes are taking place throughout the region. With industrialization and the concomitant growth of towns and cities, the Old South is losing its once pervasive rural tone and character. Most of the burgeoning urban communities of the region look to Atlanta as their model.

In appearance and municipal accessories—if not in temperament and flavor—Atlanta could be a prototype for any large, progressive American city. Atlanta proper, the incorporated city, with a population of slightly more than a half million, has one of the most rapidly changing skylines in the United States. In an eight-year span in the 1960s, building

permits were issued for structures costing a total of more than a billion dollars. During this period, 95 new office buildings, well over 100 manufacturing plants, and numerous new apartment buildings, warehouses, motels, hotels, movie theaters and hospitals were erected. Yet despite this intense construction program, Atlanta has retained much of its old visual charm. The many parks, trees and unexpected patches of green scattered around the town are revered by the citizens and afford a pleasant relief from the massiveness of the tall buildings that are popping up all over town.

True, the city is also afflicted with the various blights common to almost all American cities. It has its festering slums and racial problems. Pollution afflicts its source of water, the lovely Chattahoochee River, and horrendous traffic jams morning and evening clog the peripheral highways as well as the downtown streets that follow the winding routes of former Indian trails and cowpaths.

Atlanta, however, enjoys at least one major advantage over many other sizable municipalities: it has space for growth in the surrounding countryside. Atlanta's metropolitan area, which includes the city proper, encompasses five counties, more than 1,000 square miles. Much of the land beyond the city boundaries is already occupied by small

towns—45 of them—industry and some of the nation's most beautiful suburbs, but there is ample acreage available for future development.

Some native Atlantans have mixed feelings about the changes taking place. As town boosters, they cheer growth, but as Southerners they find the faster pace and the new brand of commercialism that accompany growth less than congenial. "Although there is still the remnant of a gracious atmosphere in the dealings of the business world," one Atlanta reporter has said, "there is a new and unaccustomed sharpness and a certain abrasiveness that was not there until recent years."

Unencumbered by memories of an earlier Atlanta, newcomers to the city, especially executives sent in by Northern companies to man new offices and plants, often become the most enthusiastic residents of the city. On occasion this enthusiasm has posed problems for the parent companies. A number of transplanted executives who, in due course, have been assigned to other communities have offered their resignations rather than leave Atlanta.

Most Atlantans have no doubt that the city's growth will continue. City planners predict that the population of the metropolitan area—by the late 1960s it was nearing 1.3 million—will reach two million by the 1980s. Atlanta's assets, both man-made and natural, are indeed formidable. Ideally located to function as the transportation hub of the South, Atlanta is served by 13 railroad lines, an excellent highway system and a first-rate airport that is already the fourth busiest in the nation. In 1967 the airport achieved international status; passengers can now fly directly between Atlanta and Europe without changing planes. Such facilities have attracted an impressive number of diversified industries and businesses to the city.

The amenities of the city are also extraordinary. Atlanta, whose altitude of 1,050 feet is exceeded by only one other city of comparable size, Denver, is high enough to be spared the prolonged muggy summers of lowland Georgia but far enough south to enjoy generally mild winters. Thus year-round outdoor activities are usually possible in a handsome setting of gently rolling terrain, red soil, and an abundance of flowers and trees.

Atlantans exaggerate the resultant blessings of the city's altitude, but they were and are substantial. "There weren't no bugs," says Atlanta banker Mills B. Lane Jr., folksily overstating one of the attractions that existed for early migrants from lowland Savannah, his own hometown. Thanks to the scarcity of mosquitoes, Atlanta in the past had less yellow fever, the scourge of the Southern coasts

and lowlands in the 19th Century, as well as less malaria than they did.

To natural blessings modern Atlanta adds urban attractions. It provides major-league baseball and football—in a new $18 million sports stadium—a fairly solid theatrical season, a resident 89-piece symphony orchestra, museums, local ballet companies, an annual visit of the Metropolitan Opera Company, the intellectual stimulation of a gaggle of colleges and universities in the immediate area, and a generally cosmopolitan atmosphere.

From the beginning Atlanta's location was its greatest asset. The beginning, however, was fairly recent in the context of the Old South: as late as 1830 the site of the future city was forest. Nevertheless, the surrounding area had already begun to attract people. By the 1830s, numerous Georgians had moved from the humid coast and lowlands to the rolling uplands and less enervating climate of the Piedmont Plateau in the middle part of the state. This was hard on the resident Creek and Cherokee Indians, but they were soon evicted. Planters, farmers, and men of business and the professions had, for years, been trekking with their families and slaves from exhausted fields and towns in Virginia and the Carolinas to upland Georgia and beyond to upland Alabama and Mississippi.

Railroads, those new marvels of travel and trade, had already come to southern and eastern Georgia, and lines were projected into the developing uplands from south, east and north. The rail routes met on the surveyors' maps at a point in the forest about eight miles east of the Chattahoochee River and, with rather comic importance for the future Atlanta, seven miles from an Indian mound on which a lone peach tree was said to grow amid the pines. In 1837 an engineer drove a stake at the point where the projected rail lines intersected, and that area became in sequence the village of Terminus, the town of Marthasville (for a Georgia Governor's daughter), and finally, in 1845, Atlanta, in dual honor, apparently, of the Atlantic Ocean and one of the railroads, the Western & Atlantic. The solitary tree nearby fascinated the settlers, perhaps because it figured in pioneer and Indian lore as "The Standing Peachtree" and thereby provided the new community's one link with a local past. Later iconoclasts suggested that the tree, growing improbably far from the normal habitat of Georgia peaches, was really a pine "pitch tree," but Atlanta has never tolerated that notion. There was a Peachtree Road in the vicinity, connecting two wilderness forts, 33 years before there was an Atlanta. Today Peachtree Street,

Peachtree Road, Peachtree Industrial Boulevard and 25 other thoroughfares bear the name; so do a creek, a golf club, a commercial center, a subdivision, a hotel, a retirement home called Peachtree-on-Peachtree and a penthouse restaurant. A department store maintains three peach trees in pots on Peachtree Street, perhaps to help hold the city franchise on the name. A lively book about Atlanta is entitled, not unexpectedly, *Peachtree Street, U.S.A.*

Whether the first railroaders fully understood the potential of the site is uncertain, but Atlantans soon grasped the possibilities. Local boosters love to draw lines on maps—from New York to New Orleans, Chicago and Minneapolis to Miami, Kansas City to Savannah—and show (with a bit of distortion) how they intersect entrancingly near Five Points, the city's celebrated main intersection, where Peachtree Street joins four other avenues at the heart of the financial district. The city lies approximately midway between the Mississippi River on the west and the Atlantic Ocean on the east and also midway on the north-south axis from Chesapeake Bay to the Gulf of Mexico. The historic route of migration and trade down the eastern edge of the Appalachian range from the northeastern United States leads naturally to Atlanta, and a southerly break in the range near Chattanooga opens the way from Atlanta north to the Ohio and upper Mississippi Valleys. In consequence, Atlanta is the topographical and economic center of the American Southeast and of the five states of the Old South.

Of the nation's 500 largest corporations more than 400 are represented in Atlanta on a scale ranging from large manufacturing and assembly plants to warehouses and sales offices. Products made by the highly diversified industries include everything from automobiles and aircraft to textiles and chemicals, nearly 4,000 different commodities in all. The federal government has also been a factor in making Atlanta the economic center of the Southeast. The city has been the regional headquarters of the Federal Reserve Bank since 1914, and numerous other federal agencies and departments have regional offices there. So do scores of public and private organizations with regional interests, varying from churches to interstate educational services.

Atlantans suffer from no undue modesty in relating their city's accomplishments to anyone who will listen, a trait that sometimes annoys their neighbors in the Old South. In coastal Savannah, Georgia's oldest and once its biggest city, there is a saying that "if Atlanta could suck as hard as it

blows, it would be a seaport." Atlanta is sucking hard and anticipates the day when the Chattahoochee River, deepened, dammed and otherwise "improved" at federal expense, *will* make the city an inland port.

Much though topography has done for Atlanta, the place has ever affected Atlantans in ways that location, altitude and climate do not wholly explain. Before the Civil War, when it was a city only by legislative courtesy, the raw town was known for its "pushy people" (a phrase from *Gone With the Wind*, the novel that made Atlanta world-famous), its grabby ways, and its unabashed dedication to the pursuit and accumulation of wealth.

Getting and being rich was no sin in more sedate communities, including such repositories of the genteel tradition as Savannah and Charleston. But pillars of that tradition regarded the brash pushiness of Atlantans with a certain distaste, salted with envy. Atlanta was considered to be a kind of deviant upstart, accurately represented by the whores and vagabonds whom, on one occasion, it went through the motions of expelling. The city won a claim to Southern affections when General William T. Sherman and his army burned it in 1864. But its rapid recovery—Atlanta's official symbol is the phoenix, the mythical bird reborn of its own funeral-pyre ashes—and its postwar collaboration with the Yankee conquerors for mutual gain revived the impression that Atlanta was more in the South than of it.

To this day some Georgians have never quite forgiven Atlanta for inducing Reconstruction authorities to make it the state capital and bring the government there from Milledgeville, a serene and thoroughly Southern town in central Georgia. For their part, Atlantans are at once proud of the qualities that have distinguished their city and a little defensive about the feeling elsewhere in the region that they are somehow alien to it. In a 1954 guidebook Atlanta writer George Leckie took oblique note of the city's rather tenuous links with "the familial images of the Old South" and summarized the compensations in a revealing passage: "Gay, modern, colorful, energetic, and alert, Atlanta in its prime can well afford to substitute the cheerful realism of its present, and what this means for the future, for the traditional Southern uses of the past."

Atlanta has long been fortunate in having dynamic and dedicated leaders with copious quantities of that "cheerful realism." One of the earliest of the breed was Henry Woodfin Grady, managing editor of *The Atlanta Constitution* from 1880 to his

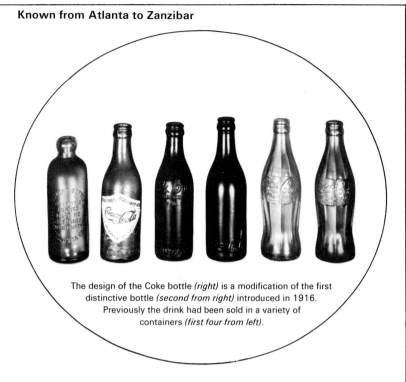

The worldwide fame of Coca-Cola is due in large measure to the guiding genius of the company's founder, Asa Griggs Candler. A firm believer in the power of advertising, Candler authorized a budget of more than $10,000 during the corporation's first year of operation, 1892. The resulting advertising campaign spread the name Coca-Cola across the country via soda-fountain clocks, calendars and posters. Annual sales increased more than 14,000 per cent within 20 years. One legacy of his management is the familiar Coke bottle *(far right)*, probably the best-known package on earth.

The design of the Coke bottle *(right)* is a modification of the first distinctive bottle *(second from right)* introduced in 1916. Previously the drink had been sold in a variety of containers *(first four from left).*

death in 1889. Soon after the Civil War he began urging the South to stop brooding over its ancient wounds and carve out a great and rewarding future through industrialization and the exploitation of its native resources and talents. To dramatize the South's neglect of industry, he told of attending the funeral of "a poor 'one-gallus' fellow" in Pickens County, Georgia: "They buried him in the midst of a marble quarry . . . and yet a little tombstone they put above him was from Vermont. They buried him in the heart of a pine forest, and yet the pine coffin was imported from Cincinnati. They buried him within touch of an iron mine, and yet the nails in his coffin and the iron in the shovel that dug his grave were imported from Pittsburgh. They buried him by the side of the best sheep-grazing country on the earth, and yet the wool in the coffin bands and the coffin bands themselves were brought from the North. The South didn't furnish a thing on earth for that funeral but the corpse and the hole in the ground. . . ."

When Grady died at the age of 38, Atlanta was despondent. A local jurist lamented, "Atlanta is so young and fiery, almost fierce in her civic energy, and pulls so hard on the reins." With Grady gone, "Who will drive us now?" But the mourner need not have worried; Atlanta has never lacked for drivers, and most of them have been and are wealthy businessmen. Their commanding role has been treated, at times with stupefying solemnity, as a phenomenon in itself by sociologists, political scientists and journalists who found in Atlanta a genuine leadership elite—a "power structure" readily definable.

Fortunately for Atlanta, its successful men of business, the professions and inherited wealth have traditionally identified their private interests with the general well-being (or the other way around) and, without entitling themselves to sainthood, have been conscious of their city's good and have tried to serve it. "These men love their city," a reporter familiar with Atlanta says, and there is ample reason to believe the statement. They have poured money as well as effort into projects for Atlanta's betterment. Their judgment has been disputed on a number of occasions, but rarely have their motives been questioned.

Most rich Atlanta families began accumulating their wealth in the 19th Century, and according to banker Mills Lane, the principal means were "patent medicine, real estate and Coca-Cola." Especially, he might have added, Coca-Cola.

If Atlantans revere the Coca-Cola bottle only slightly less than the Liberty Bell, and loyally drink far more of the stuff than other Americans do, the reason is understandable; Coke has created fortunes in Atlanta and the city has benefited handsomely from them.

The soft drink that brought and continues to bring great wealth was the invention of a pharmacist by the name of John Styth Pemberton, a native of Knoxville, Georgia, who came to Atlanta in 1869. A brewer and marketer of such patent medicines as Triplex Liver Pills, Globe of Flower Cough Syrup and French Wine of Coca—an "Ideal Nerve and Tonic Stimulant," Pemberton made his first batch of Coca-Cola syrup in 1886. He mixed it in a three-legged iron pot in his back yard, using an oar to stir the ingredients. Most of his customers in the beginning were men seeking a hang-over cure after drinking too much bourbon the previous night.

Apparently there were not enough heavy drinkers in Atlanta to encourage Pemberton because in the summer of 1887 he sold two thirds of his Coca-Cola interest to two druggists for $1,200 and the following spring let the remaining third go for $550 to a group of three purchasers, one of whom was a local pharmacist, Asa Griggs Candler. By 1891 Candler had bought out all the other owners and had exclusive rights to Coca-Cola at a total cost to him of $2,300.

The phenomenal success of Coke in the next quarter century was due almost entirely to Candler. He organized The Coca-Cola Company in 1892 and established a sales policy that ignored the drink's supposed therapeutic qualities and concentrated on its pleasurable ones. He also started to bottle the beverage; in the early days, Coke was mixed and sold only at soda fountains. The policy proved sound; he had amassed a fortune of some $50 million by 1916 when he resigned as president of the company to become mayor of Atlanta. He gave his stock to relatives, and they, much to Candler's annoyance, sold it for $25 million in 1919. It was quite a bargain for the new owners. A decade later the company's net profits were nearly $25 million a year.

Heading the syndicate that bought Coca-Cola was a Georgia financier named Ernest Woodruff. In 1923 his son Robert became president of the company and Coke was on its way to becoming an international as well as a national phenomenon. "Candler put us on our feet," one Coca-Cola executive said, "but Woodruff gave us wings." Robert Woodruff became the wealthiest man in Atlanta—his net worth in the late 1960s was estimated to be more than $100 million—and the city's most influential citizen, although he never held public office. The Woodruffs are not the only beneficiaries of Coca-Cola's prosperity, however. Much company stock is held by other Georgians.

A number of the wealthy families in Atlanta have contributed generously to the city, but the Candlers and the Woodruffs are outstanding in their philanthropy. Emory University has been the major beneficiary; this may explain why, at its athletic events, the chant often heard is: "We were raised on Coca-Cola/No wonder we raise hell." The Emily and Ernest Woodruff Foundation, a family enterprise, has also financed the establishment of a model community center in the Atlanta slums. With this center as a prototype the city was able to take early and maximum advantage of federal poverty programs and funds. The foundation's president, Boisfeuillet (maiden name of his mother, of French descent) Jones, who made a reputation for himself as an administrator at Emory University and in the federal government in Washington, is one of several Atlantans through whom Woodruff money and Woodruff influence are channeled.

An Atlanta institution only slightly less venerated than Coca-Cola is Rich's department store, which annually sells more merchandise than any other single establishment south of New York City. Started as a small retail dry-goods shop by Morris Rich in 1867, the store now has sales totaling about $150 million annually. It is one of the few remaining American department stores that is still family-run, and, says Celestine Sibley, author of *Peachtree Street, U.S.A.*, it is operated "with all the neighborliness and personal involvement in the community that the words 'family-run' imply." During December of 1930, for example, the Atlanta school system was without money and had to pay the teachers with scrip. The Rich management sent word to the authorities that the store had cash and that teachers could exchange their scrip for it without obligation. When the city finally got back on its financial feet, it redeemed $645,000 in paper held by the store. Friendly concern is such a tradition at Rich's that no one was especially astonished at the aggrieved complaint of an elderly woman who was picked up by the store police for shoplifting. "I've been getting things at Rich's for fifty years," she said, "and this is the first time they ever hurt my feelings."

Like many other wealthy Atlantans, the Rich family has shared its financial success with the city. Since the establishment of the Rich Foundation in 1943, the Georgia Baptist Hospital, Emory School of Business Administration, St. Joseph's Infirmary, Georgia Tech, and a radio station for the city and

county school systems have been among the beneficiaries. The Rich family takes an active part in city
affairs and urges its employees to do the same.
"We tell our people we want them to do *something*
for Atlanta," says Richard H. Rich, grandson of
the founder and chairman of the board of directors.
"We don't care what it is—church work, the Red
Cross, the PTA, anything they want—but service
beyond personal gain and one's workaday concerns
is, after all, the obligation of the citizen."

Among the younger generation of the wealthy
doing something for Atlanta is Ivan Allen Jr., who
was elected mayor of the city in 1961 and re-elected
for a second term in 1965. A second-generation
member of a family that operates a highly prosperous office-equipment company, Allen entered city
politics after a spectacular success in 1960 and
1961 as president of the Atlanta Chamber of Commerce. It was during his term as president of the
Chamber that the "Forward Atlanta" program
was launched with the major objective of creating
some 10,000 new jobs annually to take care of the
city's rapidly growing population. In 1961 the
Chamber, under Allen's leadership, raised $1.6
million in a month's time to entice new plants and
businesses to the city. The 10,000-job goal has
been comfortably exceeded each year since the program began.

The establishment of offices and plants in Atlanta by out-of-state firms has inevitably meant a
substantial influx of non-Southern executives. A
few of them have moved into Atlanta's power structure, but on the whole the established elite of the
city keeps a firm grasp on the reins. The newcomers, however, are not without effect. They give the
city a generally more cosmopolitan atmosphere,
and since they usually do not share the traditional
Southern attitude toward race relations they help
make the town more moderate in racial matters
than are other Old South communities.

Two additional moderating influences on the
city are its newspapers, the *Constitution* and the
Journal. The papers were merged in 1950, but each
continues to follow its own editorial policy. Of the
two, the *Constitution* has probably been the more
outspoken—and effective—thanks largely to the influence of a former sportswriter, now a columnist
and publisher of the paper, Pulitzer Prize-winner
Ralph McGill. Sometimes referred to as "the conscience of the South," McGill fought the Ku Klux
Klan at a time when many Southern leaders were,
if not members of the organization, so afraid of its
power that they dared not speak out against it. He
was a champion of Negro civil rights long before

Birmingham's move to diversify

Smoke billows from the stacks of the Old South's largest
steelmaking complex, the Fairfield Works of U.S. Steel in
Birmingham, Alabama. Birmingham, a rapidly growing center of
diversified manufacturing, has long been the heavy-industry
capital of the Old South. From its founding in 1871, it took
advantage of its proximity to plentiful lodes of coal, limestone and
iron ore—the three essential ingredients of steel—to dominate
the region in iron and steel production. Coal and limestone are
still mined locally, but not iron. Starting in the 1950s the
steelmakers found it less expensive to import rich iron ore from
Venezuela than to process the immediate area's low-grade ore.

Although the steel mills continue to prosper, Birmingham has
felt an increasing desire to lessen its dependence on a single
industry. Using its iron and steel production and other assets as
drawing cards, the city has attracted many lighter industries. It
has been successful in this endeavor despite the notoriety the city
received from the racial violence that erupted there in the early
1960s. By 1966 the number of factories had risen to almost 800
and the number of products manufactured to about 2,500.

integration of schools was even considered a possibility by the average Southerner. "McGill had guts when it wasn't easy to have guts," another Southern editor once said of him. Although both papers are usually enthusiastic supporters of the municipal programs of the power elite, they have no hesitancy about using the editorial lash when their editors feel it is needed.

How long Atlanta's white leaders will be able to exercise their present influence is another question. For a number of complex reasons, the growing racial imbalance between the central city and the outlying areas is hastening a radical shift in political power in the city itself. There is nothing especially "Southern" about this imbalance; in almost all American metropolitan areas Negroes are increasingly concentrated at the urban center while whites are a heavy majority in the suburbs. If Atlanta's problems with its Negroes, and the Negroes' problems with Atlanta, differ at all from the national urban norm, it is in the sense that at least through most of the 1960s these problems appeared to be less explosive than in such riven cities as New York, Newark, Detroit and Los Angeles.

In Atlanta the prospect is that Negroes, who constituted an estimated 45 per cent of the central city's population in the late 1960s, will be a ruling majority there by the 1970s. In the suburban towns and villages surrounding the city proper, on the other hand, they make up less than 10 per cent. Because of the overwhelmingly white suburbs, the racial composition of the metropolitan area as a whole—central city plus suburbs—is less than 25 per cent Negro.

A good deal of strain, civic and racial, results from these circumstances. Negro and white Atlantans alike are aware that the only way the whites can retain control of the city proper is by annexing the generally white outlying communities, and thus diluting the Negroes' political power. There are, of course, sound nonracial reasons for annexation— the desirability of reducing the profusion of local governments in the area is only one—and they are emphasized by the expansionists. But the racial factor permeates the arguments whenever the issue comes before the voters.

Annexation poses a difficult problem for most large American cities. Small communities, treasuring their political independence and a sense of entity, are usually reluctant to be annexed. In most cases a town or village votes for annexation only if its tax base is too limited to provide sufficient funds for adequate police and fire protection and similar services. Both elements—an unwillingness to be

annexed and an annexation through necessity—
were manifest in a 1966 Atlanta election. Because
of unusual circumstances, the combination proved
doubly frustrating to those who wanted to post-
pone Negro political ascendancy. The effort to
bring the predominantly white town of Sandy
Springs into the central city failed at the polls. On
the other hand, Adamsville, a smaller and poorer
suburb and one of the very few with a predominantly Negro population, voted to join Atlanta
proper. Thus annexation, instead of adding to the
whites' slender majority, actually increased the
proportion of black voters in the central city.

Whatever the pace of formal expansion may be,
the city appears to be entering a period described
in *Atlanta*, an excellent monthly magazine published by the Chamber of Commerce, as one in
which "it will be harder and harder for white politicians to stay in office in Atlanta." Negroes in high
city office will signify a "revolution," but "there is
no sign that it will be harmful to the interests of the
city's whites. It may, in fact, be what is needed to
get whites and Negroes working on Atlanta's problems as citizens of the same city, not as members of
different races." In other words, white economic
power will have to come to terms with black political power. In support of its calm appraisal, *Atlanta*

cited the belief of State Senator Leroy Johnson—an
Atlanta lawyer who in 1962 became the first Negro
elected to the Georgia Senate since the 1870s—that
"a coalition of Negro leadership and the best elements of the white leadership" will "keep this city
moving forward."

Such a coalition of racial equals is no more in the
tradition of Atlanta than of other American cities
and it will not be easily attained. At every level of
black Atlanta, from the slums to the lush residen-
tial sections that poor Negroes call "God's Country," there are militants and ambitious men who
reject any relationship dependent upon the good
will of even "the best elements" in the city's white
elite, and some who see more promise of power for
themselves in conflict than in peace. The established white leaders, including "the best," have
been accustomed to a working alliance, basically
patronizing, with Negro spokesmen whom they
chose to recognize. It is symptomatic that these
men, again including "the best," have to watch
their pronunciation of "Negro"—"nigra" comes
naturally and "nigger" more often than some may
realize. Yet there is a good chance that Atlanta will
fulfill the hopes of men like Leroy Johnson, white
and black. When they talk of achieving a valid coalition through "leadership" they are in the Atlanta
tradition, which among other things is a tradition
of success. Atlanta is used to following its leaders,
white and black, and to having—on balance and
over the years—leaders of high caliber to follow.

Negro Atlanta has its own elite, a more varied
and, in that respect, a more interesting lot than
white Atlanta's business-dominated leadership. No
authoritative list of the city's white dominance has
been known to include an educator, a minister, a
woman or anyone primarily concerned with human rights. But the Negro elite has these in even
greater number than men of business, and they are
at least equal to the businessmen in prestige.
Among the educators are the presidents and some
senior professors of Atlanta University and the four
colleges and a theological seminary that are associated with it, a group of schools making up what
has been termed "the world's largest center of Negro education." Outstanding among the women is
Mrs. Grace Towns Hamilton, a charming and cou-
rageous civil rights pioneer and state legislator
whose "Scotch-Irish and Negro" ancestry has been
reported by *The New York Times* to include "a pre-
Civil War governor of Georgia." The dean of
Atlanta's many active Negro ministers is the Reverend Dr. Martin Luther King Sr., pastor of the
3,100-member Ebenezer Baptist Church and father

of the Nobel Prize-winning civil rights leader. The Negro elite also includes almost a dozen millionaires—principally in real estate, banking, insurance, home mortgages and other personal finance.

But differences of opinion on tactics and objectives are numerous and sharp among Atlanta Negroes, and therefore the black elite does not have nearly as much influence with its people as the white elite does with white Atlantans. For want of generally recognized leaders in the Negro community, the white elite consults on occasion with a group of Negro businessmen, lawyers, politicians and others in what is called the Summit Leadership Conference. But no single group or class speaks with one voice for Atlanta Negroes nowadays, and such a qualified observer as Senator Leroy Johnson is by no means certain that the mass of Negroes recognize and follow any particular leadership.

This is quite a change from the period, dating from the 1940s, when the incumbent mayor had only to check with the late A. T. Walden, a wealthy lawyer and boss of the bipartisan Negro Voters League, to make sure that the Negro community would hold peacefully still for whatever the white leadership had in mind in the way of extending Negro rights. With Walden's help, William B. Hartsfield, who served as mayor from 1937 to 1961 with only a single 18-month interruption, molded Atlanta's national image as "the city too busy to hate." This biracial collaboration began to develop in 1944, after the U.S. Supreme Court required the Democratic Party in Atlanta, as elsewhere, to let Negroes vote in its hitherto all-white nominating primaries, which are the only elections of local importance. Mayor Hartsfield and his elite mentors had the practical sense, then extremely rare in Georgia and the South, to encourage rather than obstruct the increase in Negro registration and voting that resulted. A consequence was that Negroes soon were giving Hartsfield and eventually his successor, Mayor Allen, their winning margins over forthrightly racist opponents (including Governor-to-be Lester Maddox, who polled majorities among white working-class Atlanta voters in each of his two tries for the office of mayor).

Lawyer Walden's influence had faded before he died in 1965, but the white establishment continued the same style of chummy consultation on racial matters with other well-established Negroes, as in the Summit Leadership Conference. It was less than an ideal arrangement, for it was hardly a meeting of equals; a highly disproportionate share of the political and economic power was in the hands of the whites. But the unequal alliance worked well enough in a pragmatic sense through an exceptionally trying time.

All of the elements for a major racial explosion were present in Atlanta during the early 1960s when the city, yielding reluctantly to Negro demands, desegregated its trolleys and buses, municipal golf courses, lunch counters, restaurants, hotels and, at least on a token basis, its public schools. There was, however, a minimum of open conflict, thanks to hard and prolonged bargaining between Negro and white leaders. In every instance the white leadership granted only what federal law and local pressures compelled it to grant. Many of the white leaders were distressed by the concessions they had to make, but all of them were determined that "this city is not going to be torn to pieces." Although these concessions were probably the minimum that could be made to forestall violent protest, they amounted to much more than the majority of white Atlantans were prepared to welcome or might even have tolerated under less intelligent and respected leadership. The armistice that was achieved did demonstrate that Atlanta, if not exactly too busy to hate, was at least for the time being too prosperous and sensible to engage in self-destruction.

How long that armistice will last is a question that troubles all thoughtful Atlantans, black and white. One vital element in reaching the truce was Negro leadership that not only spoke for the black community but was willing to accept the slow pace of adjustment demanded by the whites. Now the Negro leadership is badly fragmented, and the Negro community, increasingly impatient with snail-like progress, is becoming more and more militant in its demands for decent housing, good schools, satisfactory employment and all the other advantages long denied most black citizens. This militancy is evident not only among Negro slum dwellers but in the race's middle class and upper-middle class as well. On the other side of the racial fence is a large concentration of "nigger-hating" whites, "red-necks" from the rural areas of the South who have moved to Atlanta in recent years. They are equally militant in their determination to block Negro gains whenever and however possible. Thus violence is a real and constant threat in the city.

Whether Atlanta can continue to contain these potentially explosive elements and make the inevitable accommodations without falling victim to bloodshed and destruction remains to be seen. Atlanta's past success in meeting its problems offers its best hope today.

Astride small, power-driven craft called Sea Jeeps,
vacationers skitter over the waves off Miami Beach.
Tourism, Florida's largest industry, is now a year-round
business, bringing in some four billion dollars annually.

The fabled land called Florida

Despite historical ties with the Old South and a sharing of many attitudes, Florida is a startling anomaly in the region. But then Florida would be unique in any grouping of states. Its 58,560 square miles encompass primordial swamps and space-rocket bases, small fishing villages and great cattle ranches, bustling industry and some of the nation's most popular vacationland—all, so it often seems, awash in a sea of orange juice. The youngest of the Old South states—it came into the Union as a slave state in 1845—Florida had the smallest population in the region as late as 1940. Then within two decades its inhabitants increased from less than two million to nearly five million, and it became the most populous state in the Old South. Filled with unquenchable verve and an anything-is-possible spirit, Florida reflects the era in which it came to maturity.

A wicked archipelago reformed

The Florida Keys, a string of some 25 major islands extending in a 150-mile arc southwest from the tip of Florida, were a haven for pirates, smugglers and adventurers when the archipelago was a Spanish possession. Soon after the islands became part of the United States in 1819, the federal government largely ended these activities. Salvaging kept the islanders prosperous for some time, however. Because there were no lighthouses on the Keys, ships frequently ran aground on reefs, and the natives would claim the cargoes. But a warning system, built by the government in the 1830s, drastically cut the number of wrecks. In the decades that followed, such enterprises as fishing *(below)* and cigarmaking provided a modest living for the islanders. Prosperity returned to the Keys in the late 1940s when tourism became Florida's golden flood.

The Spanish coins above—gold doubloons, a silver "pillar dollar" *(top center)* and a silver "piece of eight"—were salvaged by treasure-hunter Art McKee from a wreck off the Keys. The sunken ships, part of the Spanish "Plate Fleet" of 1733, carried $68 million in jewelry, gold and silver.

By day, the shrimp fleet that sails out of Key West anchors in port with nets wrapped in colorful chafing mats. These boats sail to islands some 65 miles west, where the shallow waters teem with valuable night-feeding shrimp.

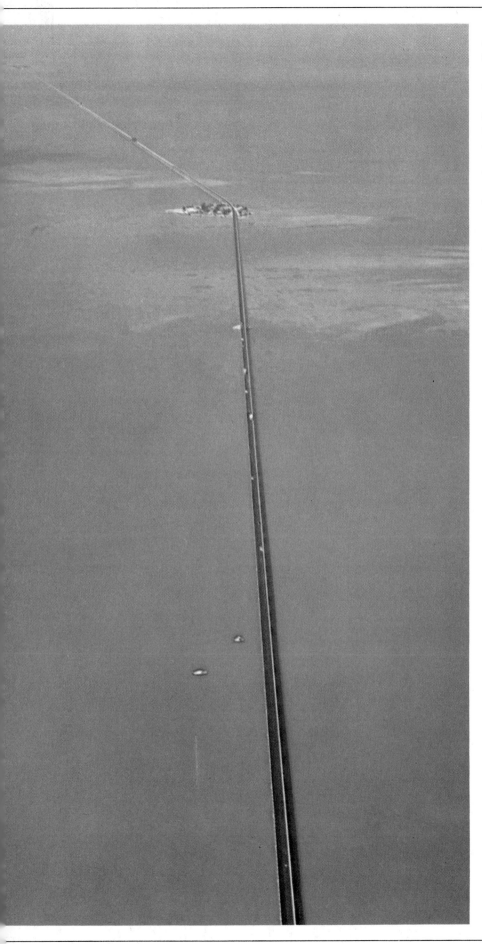

Binding the islands to the mainland and to each other, the Overseas Highway *(left)* spans the clear waters that separate the Florida Keys. This 122-mile road was built over the battered roadbed of the ill-fated Florida East Coast Railway. An ambitious $50 million project, the Florida East Coast, which ran to Key West, was wrecked by a hurricane in 1935. Completion of the highway in 1938 brought Key West within four hours of Miami by car, and the resulting increase in tourism has sparked this area's economic resurgence.

The Florida Keys are former coral reefs that have been thrust above the surface, usually by underwater upheavals. Reefs are created by the accumulation of common types of coral such as the massive star coral—a single boulder may weigh several tons—and the tall, angular staghorn coral *(below)*. Such coral is made by tiny sea animals that cluster in colonies. When the animals die, their skeletons remain, gradually building up on the sea floor to form reefs. The delicately patterned sea fan, another type of coral commonly found among the Keys, is nonrooting and therefore will not form reefs.

STAR CORAL

STAGHORN CORAL

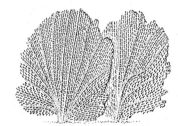

SEA FAN

The place of winter dreams

The Gold Coast along the eastern tip of Florida adds to the winter of discontent of snowbound citizens in the Northern states. But Florida's appeal is no longer limited to the cold months. Because of low "off-season" rates, the Gold Coast now has more tourists in the summer than in the winter. Until the 1890s this region was a dreary stretch of sand and marshes. Then oil magnate Henry Flagler saw the area had a future as a resort center and extended a rail line south to Miami. Other entrepreneurs followed; soon hotels were sprouting all along the coast. Tempting ads of a land of perpetual summer were used to lure Northerners to the Gold Coast. Few campaigns have ever been more successful.

A sunset to delight the Chamber of Commerce gilds Miami Beach *(right)*. Here, on about seven square miles of land, are jammed approximately 400 hotels—some ornate, some beautiful, some an architect's nightmare, and all expensive at the height of the winter season. Separated from Miami proper *(visible in the background)* by Biscayne Bay, Miami Beach is a man-made playground; it was created out of a jungle-matted sand bar in 1913 by automobile tycoon Carl Fisher, who financed the dredging that created 1,200 acres of filled land and went on to build the first big hotel.

Basted with lotion and turning every hour, vacationers brown slowly at Miami Beach *(below)*. Gold Coast resorts such as Miami Beach, Fort Lauderdale (which gained notoriety as a sandbox for the college set) and Palm Beach (a favorite winter retreat for wealthy socialites) are synonymous with vacation glamor. Of the 20 million tourists who come to Florida annually, more than half come to the Gold Coast.

A damp, uncharted wilderness

The Everglades—a giant tray of water filled with fields of saw grass, irregular clumps of mangrove trees and islands lush with tropical vegetation—remains one of the few sections in the United States that has not yet been fully explored. The part set aside as a national park in 1947 now encompasses 1.4 million acres and is one of the nation's great wildlife preserves. It is monotonously flat; the highest land is only 10 feet above sea level. Its water level is maintained partly by heavy rainfall—50 inches annually—and partly by the fact that the Everglades acts as a giant, slow-moving river that begins 120 miles north at Lake Okeechobee and flows into the Gulf of Mexico. Perhaps the area's Seminole Indians had the most descriptive name for the Everglades. They called it Pa-hay-okee, or "Grassy Water."

Strewn like pieces of a jigsaw puzzle, mangrove clumps *(right)* jut from the water along the western edge of the Everglades. Of all the Everglades' flourishing vegetation—more than 1,000 known seed-bearing plants and countless varieties of ferns, moss and lichens—the mangrove trees are the most distinctive. Able to survive in both fresh and salt water, they are known as "walking forests"; the seedlings of these hardy trees drift on water until they reach low ground, where they root. The western sector of the Everglades has some of the best-developed mangrove forests in the world.

Birds fly in the twilight sky *(below)* near a mangrove island in the park, which is one of the nation's most populous rookeries. The Everglades is a bird watcher's paradise; one writer, John O'Reilly, described a trip along a quiet stream: "A little blue heron flapped across the river. A kingfisher clattered shrilly as it flew along the bank; cormorants became airborne and mullets shone silvery in the afternoon sunlight as they leaped from the water. On a tall, dead tree to the right sat a bald eagle. . . . [The river] was so narrow that the mangroves, festooned with air plants and wild orchids, met in a green tangle overhead."

The Everglades National Park has within its borders some 600 species of vertebrate animals. They range from rare birds such as the roseate spoonbill *(top)* to reptiles like the alligator *(center)* and such common mammals as the raccoon *(bottom)*. With enforced protection of wildlife in the park, many species threatened with extinction by hunters—among them the beautiful roseate spoonbill, great white heron and snowy egret —have recently increased their numbers. The greatest threat to the animals now is the Everglades' changing ecology. Water diversion and flood-control projects to the north have diminished the flow of water through the area. Many conservationists have warned that a prolonged drought, coupled with the restricted inflow of water from Lake Okeechobee, could dry up the park in a few years. In the mid-1960s the first of a series of canals designed to maintain the park's water level was started.

Southcentral cowboy country

Southcentral Florida—dominated by giant Lake Okeechobee—has long been a major food-producing area. Covering more than 700 square miles, Okeechobee is the second-largest (after Great Salt Lake in Utah) body of water wholly within the United States. Around it and on the grassy prairies to the north are concentrated the state's beef-cattle ranches. Florida is not yet up to the leading cattle states in terms of production and efficiency—but the state has made amazing strides. Because of improved breeding practices and better management, the number of beef cattle rose more than fourfold in the four decades following the late 1920s, and the amount of marketable meat has increased more than 1,000 per cent. Drainage projects around the lake—first begun in 1905—have reclaimed large areas of rich black soil, and on this fertile land farmers grow sugar cane and truck crops to add substantially to the state's agricultural income.

Florida's growing importance as a beef-producing state can be traced in large part to accomplishments in crossbreeding. Mixing desirable traits of different breeds has led to the development of animals able to withstand the hot, humid climate and provide the maximum amount of meat when slaughtered. One of the most successful hybrids being raised by Florida ranchers is a Brahman-Angus crossbred *(right)*, which combines the best qualities of its parents —the beefiness of the Angus and the Brahman's resistance to the diseases common in a semitropical climate. This combination of characteristics has made the Brahman-Angus crossbred highly popular not only in Florida but in other Gulf Coast cattle states as well.

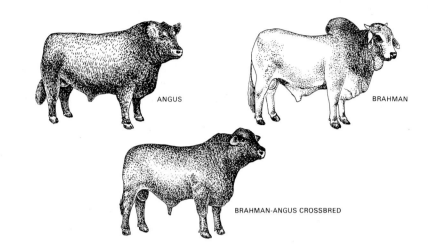

ANGUS

BRAHMAN

BRAHMAN-ANGUS CROSSBRED

Straddling the top rail of a corral, a Seminole keeps an eye on his herd. In Florida many of the "cowboys" are Indians; for example, the Muskhogeans, who live on a reservation on the northwest shore of Lake Okeechobee, depend on cattle raising for their living.

A bull leads a herd of cattle *(left)* in an afternoon romp across a pasture at the J Box Ranch in Okeechobee. One of Florida's larger spreads, the 12,000-acre J Box boasts a herd of 6,000, almost all crossbred for the subtropical climate from Brahman stock.

Benches for the old, business for the young

The Sun Coast on the Gulf of Mexico, along which lie such cities as St. Petersburg and Tampa, is often characterized as an area devoted exclusively to elderly residents who congregate on ubiquitous green benches, play shuffleboard and collect Social Security checks. This impression comes largely from St. Petersburg, which does have one of the world's largest shuffleboard clubs, and also has a large proportion of residents over sixty-five—28 per cent, compared to the U.S. average of 9 per cent. But this is only one aspect of the area. Since 1950 the population of the Sun Coast's six counties along the gulf has more than doubled, and a good deal of this increase is attributable to new or expanding business. St. Petersburg now boasts thriving electronics and research firms, which, along with the other Sun Coast industries, are attracting younger people. Tampa is a shipping center for phosphate and the home of the state's largest shrimp fleet. Land development *(right)* is another bustling enterprise, especially in the Fort Myers area. Some developers now furnish free airline tickets to prospective customers to get them to visit the sites. Perhaps the coast's future was foreshadowed in 1966 when a St. Petersburg newspaper sent one of the city's famous green benches to Miami Beach, which by then had a higher median age than the Sun Coast city.

Elderly people sun themselves and chat on the benches *(left)* that have long been identified with St. Petersburg, the city known as "the retirement capital of the United States." In 1907 a real-estate salesman set the first benches outside his office. The idea caught on throughout the community, and in 1914 the size, shape and color (green) were regulated by city ordinance. The law was later altered, and since 1961 most of the benches have been painted in pastel colors.

Cape Coral *(above)* is one of the largest planned communities in Florida. This area near Fort Myers was once covered with pine and scrub palmetto trees. By the mid-1960s, developers had cleared the area and had cut canals *(top)* along the Caloosahatchee River to provide waterfront homesites. By April 1968, a decade after land development and marketing began, 101,000 homesites had been sold, and Cape Coral could boast a population of nearly 10,000.

The billion-dollar trees

The central lake and the Indian River sectors are the center of Florida's most famous industry: citrus growing and processing. The first citrus trees are thought to have been planted in Florida by Ponce de León, who came to the area in 1513 in search of the legendary "Fountain of Youth"; according to the story, he brought seeds with him from Spain. For a number of decades, citrus fruits have been Florida's leading crop, the foundation of a billion-dollar industry that today produces three fourths of the nation's citrus products and one quarter of the world's. Oranges are the most important crop, but Florida also grows tangerines, limes, grapefruit (the pink and seedless varieties were developed here) and such hybrids as the limequat, a cross between the lime and the kumquat.

The Valencia oranges shown above are destined for one of Florida's 33 plants that produce frozen orange-juice concentrate. This industry, pioneered in Florida, makes some 70 million gallons of concentrate annually, or enough to make almost six billion glasses of juice. About 60 per cent of the entire Florida orange crop is now concentrated and frozen.

TEMPLE ORANGE   VALENCIA ORANGE

Two of the best-known varieties of Florida oranges are the easily peeled and readily sectioned Temple, primarily a "hand," or eating, orange, and the thin-skinned, juicier Valencia, used mainly for juice. Today, some 80 per cent of the state's orange crop is processed in various forms, compared to only 1 per cent in the mid-1930s. Canned and frozen orange juice is now so readily accepted by the public that even in Florida restaurants freshly squeezed juice is a rarity. A writer with an aversion to frozen products once reported with irony that, while in Florida studying the citrus industry, he had to buy his own squeezer to get fresh juice.

Vital to citrus growers in the area, the lakes near Orlando sparkle in the morning sun. Groves are often planted near water, for lakes retain part of their daytime warmth and help prevent nighttime chills that harm fruit.

Citrus trees rise symmetrically from the sandy soil of Florida's Ridge *(right)*, an area between Leesburg and Sebring that contains the world's greatest concentration of citrus trees.

The languid north

It is the northern sector of Florida that most noticeably marches to the cadence of the Old South. Here picturesque rivers flow lazily through pine and oak forests; here the towns are mostly small and steeped with the flavor of the Old South. And here, too, was the area in Florida where slavery flourished on large cotton and sugar plantations. By 1845, when Florida entered the Union, the plantation owners were sufficiently powerful to bring it in as a slave state. But Florida never developed a plantation economy on the scale of the rest of the Old South. Partially, this was the result of a late start; the Spanish, who ruled Florida until 1819, were primarily missionaries, explorers and traders rather than farmers. Although there were some plantations in Florida while the Spanish were in control, the major movement toward large holdings and slavery did not come until Florida became an American possession. Today northern Florida probably most closely resembles Mississippi in its slow adjustment to the economic revolution taking place in the Old South. Those advances that have been made are most apparent in the cosmopolitan bustle that pervades Jacksonville.

St. Augustine's ivy-covered chapel *(above)* of the Nombre de Dios Mission stands on the site where Mass was said on September 8, 1565, the day that the Spanish explorers landed. It was modeled after the original chapel and, like many Spanish missions, is built of coquina—crushed sea shells and coral.

Huge live oak trees *(right)*, heavily laden with the Spanish moss that is ubiquitous in the area, are abundant on the Live Oak Plantation near Tallahassee. Called live oaks because their foliage remains green the year round, the trees were prized for shipbuilding in the days of wooden vessels.

The Suwannee River *(left)*—with a slightly different spelling it is one of the world's best-known rivers—flows between banks lined with moss-draped trees. Composer Stephen Foster made the northern Florida stream famous with his song "Old Folks at Home":

> *Way down upon de Swanee ribber,*
> *Far, far away. . . .*

Foster, a Pennsylvanian who never saw the river, got his spelling of the name from an atlas that was in error. Despite his unfamiliarity with the region and the stream, he captured the tranquil mood in both music and words:

> *When will I see de bees a humming*
> *All round de comb?*
> *When will I hear de banjo strumming*
> *Down in my good old home?*

The Suwannee retains its old, slow-moving charm. There are only seven towns along its 250-mile length, and none of them has as many as 1,000 inhabitants.

The state's stepchild

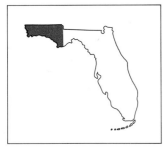

In some ways, Florida's panhandle, a fairly narrow strip of land between Alabama and the Gulf of Mexico, is a microcosm of the entire state. Like Florida as a whole, it has farms and industry, sizable government installations and numerous tourist attractions. But the panhandle is growing at a far slower pace than the rest of the state. Most of the area's farms are small, devoted to such crops as tobacco and peanuts. Lumbering is well established, and some heavy industry and a number of chemical and synthetic-fiber plants are sprinkled along the coast, but wide diversification is yet to come. The Navy has a large airbase at Pensacola, and the Air Force has one at Fort Walton Beach. Tourism currently provides one of the brightest economic lights in the area, thanks to the beautiful beaches *(right)* and fine resorts along the gulf. The panhandle has long been something of a stepchild in Florida, but it may soon be sharing the state's rich heritage.

Like an enormous desert of glistening sugar, broken only here and there by vegetation-coated dunes *(right),* the white beaches of Florida's panhandle stretch for 100 miles, curving with the crescent coastline of the Gulf of Mexico. The pure silica composition of the sand and the absence of organic matter give these beaches their dazzling whiteness, and on the dunes cling stunted live oak, golden aster *(above)* and wax myrtle. This area is especially popular with vacationers from other Old South states.

6

The Drive for Growth and Change

In 1938 President Franklin D. Roosevelt took a long, appraising look at the U.S. South and, in a famous pronouncement, declared the whole region to be "the Nation's Number One economic problem," adding, for emphasis, "the Nation's problem, not merely the South's." The South was, indeed, in desperate straits. Although the President's various New Deal agencies had pumped large amounts of cash into the area during the 1930s, the South, and especially some of the poorer states in the Old South, seemed mired in poverty. The average annual income there was only about half that of other regions. The rest of the country was also suffering the effects of the Great Depression, but the South was so much worse off that, said Roosevelt, its poverty produced an "economic unbalance in the Nation as a whole."

Today the situation has changed remarkably for the better. Compared with the mid-1930s, the states of the South, including the five of the Old South, are rolling in wealth. Admittedly, they still lag behind "the Nation as a whole" and thus an

Rising from the sandy lowlands of Florida's coast, huge gantries at Cape Kennedy stand ready to launch rockets into space. Although the cape's rapid development is unusual, it symbolizes the remarkable economic comeback of the Old South region.

"economic unbalance" continues to exist. Individual incomes there still average less than those of the other states, but the gap is not nearly as significant as it once was, and certainly the region could no longer be termed "the Nation's Number One economic problem."

One result of President Roosevelt's concern over the South's economy was a 1938 federal report which said in effect that the Number One problem area could become the nation's Number One economic opportunity if the South's chronic wastage of human and material resources were halted and its immense potential for development were realized. This is happening, and has been happening throughout the intervening decades. No one factor has been responsible for this revolutionary change. In fact, there have been dozens of impulses propelling the South forward economically.

Among the first and most important has been the high level of federal expenditure in the area for defense during World War II and for the space program and military purposes in the postwar years. Another has been the nationwide boom of the past decades, which has penetrated to all but the most backward areas of the Old South. A third factor, and perhaps the most decisive, has been the South's new ability to attract industry; and not just marginal, low-paying cotton-processing mills, but solid, efficient industrial plants producing high revenues and paying substantial wages. Plenty of open land, a large and available work force, and, often, important tax concessions are among the lures used to bring in new industries.

Measured by total wealth, the states of the old Cotton South were among the nation's richest just before the Civil War. Their recent climb back from the economic depths toward national levels of affluence would inspire the hoisting and downing of many a julep if the grandees of that vanished time were present to applaud.

No more impressive example of growth in the Old South can be found than the case of Huntsville and its neighboring cities in northern Alabama. A once-somnolent town of 15,000 that called itself "The Watercress Capital of the World," Huntsville was violently propelled into the space age when, in 1950, its Redstone Arsenal, moth-balled after World War II, was reactivated as the U.S. Army's missile research complex. Later Huntsville became the home of the George C. Marshall Space Flight Center, where the giant Saturn rockets have been developed and tested. These two installations alone employed some 30,000 workers by the late 1960s. So pervasive is Huntsville's enthusiasm over its role in space that the breakfast menus in local restaurants have featured such energizing morning specials as "The Lift-off" (eggs) and "The Blast-off Special" (sweet rolls with coffee).

The economic thrust generated by Huntsville and its rockets has given a lift to other towns up and down the Tennessee River, which reaches into the northern edge of the Old South. (All of them, with Huntsville, benefit from that mighty federal effort of the 1930s, the Tennessee Valley Authority, which provides the area with massive amounts of cheap electric power.) Decatur, just up the river, has plants producing goods for a startling number of large, well-known national companies, among them Goodyear, Chemstrand, Amoco, 3M (formerly Minnesota Mining and Manufacturing), Fruehauf and Prestolite. Reynolds Metals, Ford and Union Carbide operate large plants near the TVA's Wilson Dam on the outskirts of the town of Florence. Smaller companies abound, including several that make elasticized polyester fibers for clothing, automobile seat covers and other purposes. Even chicken feed has become big business in northern Alabama; Decatur's Nebraska Consolidated Mills turns out food for poultry by the trainload. Nearby Albertville claims to have the largest chicken-slaughtering plant in the United States, producing some 750,000 broilers a week.

This, of course, is northern Alabama, which all Alabamians, and all Southerners for that matter, will tell you is a world apart—an area so untypical of the Old South, so "Northern" in its bustle and its concentration on science-oriented industry, that some Southern traditionalists would almost like to disown it. Alabama, everyone agrees, is really two places, divided by a line that runs across the state from east to west somewhere south of the steelmaking city of Birmingham. The southern half of the state, with its rich Black Belt farming area, so called because of its dark soil, is still largely rural and comparatively backward. But even here, as in other long-remote and agriculturally oriented parts of the Old South, some remarkable changes have taken place since the mid-1930s.

The town of Dothan, which lies in the southernmost sector of Alabama, is an excellent example of the effects that postwar industrialization has had on numerous communities all across the state and across the entire Old South. The change is not as dramatic as around Huntsville, but it is nonetheless notable. Dothan, located just north of the Florida border in an area that had long been looked down upon by other Alabamians as the state's ragged stepchild, was selected during World War II as the site for an Army airfield. During the early 1940s, there was plenty of near-empty farmland around for student pilots to fly over, and the land needed for runways and barracks was cheap. The military pumped some money into Dothan's economy, but the fighter pilots who trained at Napier Field, and the ground crewmen who kept the Curtiss P-40s airworthy, noticed little prosperity. What they saw was a typical dusty, sleepy Old South town. Dothan's main street boasted a rather new (and rather graceless) brick hotel, but the rest of the two-block-long business district was largely made up of elderly, unprepossessing one- and two-story structures. The principal streets were paved, but in the Negro district south of the center of town, and even in the white neighborhoods to the north, the pavement quickly petered out and gave way to dirt roads. The bus station, where the soldiers had to wait for transport back to the airfield after an evening in town, was little more than a rickety shack.

Why the GIs bothered to come into town at all was something of a mystery. The local movie houses usually presented films of the sort that *Variety*, the show-business trade journal, once characterized as "stix pix," movies so trite and simpleminded that they were rarely shown in big-city theaters. Virtually the only other amusement was buying a bottle of whiskey to take to one of the town's roadhouses, where "setups" were available —state law forbade liquor sales by the glass—and a roaring jukebox battled the inevitable tedium of Army life.

In 1945 Dothan was what Southerners sometimes call a "Saturday town"; it bustled only on the one day in the week when farmers came in from the surrounding rural areas to sell produce, buy supplies or just gossip. Dothan had a stockyard— whose odor engulfed the town when the wind was right—half a dozen cotton-ginning plants, several peanut-oil mills and one small hosiery manufacturing firm.

The change that has taken place in Dothan since the war ended and the airmen left is nothing less than astonishing. Although it is still the market town for its area's farmers, it has also become a busy and prosperous industrial and commercial center. Since 1946 it has acquired an average of two new industries a year—a fantastic growth rate for any small town, north or south—and these industries had a combined annual payroll of some $20 million by the late 1960s. The old stockyard has been enlarged and improved, packing plants have been built, and Dothan has become the largest pork-producing and -processing center in the state. With all this industrial growth, the population more than doubled between 1940 and the late 1960s, from about 17,000 people to 39,500. Some of the newcomers are plant managers and such from elsewhere, including the North, but others are farmers who have now come to town for good, taking jobs in the new factories.

All this growth has had a profound effect on the quality of life in Dothan. Families there spend more money on consumer goods than their counterparts anywhere else in Alabama; the new industries have given the people the power to buy all manner of merchandise that was beyond their reach in the mid-1940s. The old icebox has been replaced by a refrigerator, the furniture is newer, and the food is better and more plentiful. This buying boom, of course, has benefited the local merchants and created more wealth. And the new wealth is going into things once unheard of in Dothan. The town not only has a little-theater group but also a civic ballet and a concert association affluent enough to engage touring artists. It also has an art league that sponsors regular art exhibitions.

Perhaps most important of all for the future, the town's schools have been improved until they are among the best in the state. Between 1946 and 1968, Dothan spent more than four million dollars on its school facilities, and today it pays its teachers so generously that their income stands well above the state average. When it comes to schools, says Chamber of Commerce official Larry Register, "we never have to pinch pennies." An astonishing 75 per cent of the white high-school graduates go on to some form of higher education. Unfortunately, the percentage of Negro graduates going on with their schooling is smaller, but it is not negligible. Some of these students, black and white, stay right in Dothan, for the town now possesses a junior college plus a technical and trade school; both are integrated. Their combined enrollments total about 1,000 students.

These developments would certainly astonish the crewmen and pilots who knew the town in the mid-1940s. What would astonish them even more is the fact that their modest airfield has become a busy municipal airport serviced daily by big commercial jets, with regular jet flights from Dothan to Washington, D.C., and New York City. To the town's residents, the busy airport is a clear sign that Dothan has "arrived."

The most encouraging thing about such economic gains is that they tend to be self-reproducing. When an industry comes to a Southern town like Dothan, the wages it pays enable the people to buy more and better goods. This new market encourages manufacturers to build new plants to make the desired products and to set up these plants in the South, near the market. Thus new industries beget more new industries.

The effects of this upward spiral are clearly visible in Alabama's largest city, Birmingham. Long the leading steel-producing city in the Old South, it was for decades dominated by this heaviest of heavy industries. When times were good and the demand for steel was high, Birmingham prospered, but when depressions or recessions struck, it suffered. Now the city has diversified considerably— new plants have attracted still more new plants— and there are now almost 1,000 factories turning out some 3,500 different products ranging from truck bodies to wrist watches.

It may be a little too much to say, as one informed local observer has, that Alabama is "rapidly becoming a Northern industrial suburb," but he is surely right when he says that there is "not a region of the state that hasn't been influenced by industrial expansion." Not everyone is enthusiastic about the change. "If you ask me, this whole state's going to hell in a hurry," says a diehard descendant of the old agricultural aristocracy. "All they think about is industry and money." But most Alabamians, while they remember with nostalgia more leisurely times, heartily approve the new prosperity. Back in 1937, according to John Samuel Ezell, a distinguished historian of the South, industrial wages in the region averaged $865 a year, while tenant farm families, of which Alabama and the other states of the Old South had a distressing number, had to get along on an average of $73 per person for a year's work. By contrast, factory workers in Alabama in the mid-1960s averaged about $96 a week compared with a national average of approximately $112.

The story is much the same throughout the Old South, although less so, as we shall see, in Mississippi, which has always been the poorest of the states and has clung to old ways with greater tenacity than have the others. The economy of Georgia, for example, has wholly changed complexion since 1950. At that time, according to the U.S. Census, about half the people made their living from the land. Just a single decade later there were almost 10 times as many nonfarm jobs as there were jobs in farming. In a mere two and a half years in the mid-1960s the state counted 872 new industrial plants or significant plant expansions that created 36,300 new industrial jobs. Some were in traditional low-wage industries—textiles and lumber, for example—but many were in the high-pay category—chemicals, transportation equipment and machinery.

Progress is being made in South Carolina, too, with far-ranging results not only for prosperity in the state but for education. No state of the Old South is prouder of its Southern character, and none has suffered more grievously from the less kindly consequences of that character. The 1960 census classified 230,789 (20.3 per cent) of South Carolinians aged 25 and over as functional illiterates, i.e., they had less than a fifth-grade education. Some 51,000 of them—34,000 Negroes and 17,000 whites—had never attended school at all. Of those who started school, appalling proportions (nearly 90 per cent of the Negroes, 60 per cent of the whites) dropped out before reaching the 12th grade. The prevailing indifference to these facts was underscored in 1955 when South Carolina repealed its compulsory school attendance law in order to impede racial integration.

Now South Carolina cares—not because segregation is a lost cause, or because of social and humanitarian considerations, but because the state began to run out of workers qualified for jobs in the industries it was vigorously seeking. "We found ourselves scraping the bottom of the barrel and mighty sick about what we found there," a leading industrial spokesman said in 1966. The result is perhaps the best adult-education program in the Old South. By the late 1960s nearly 85,000 uneducated or woefully undereducated men and women, black and white, of all ages, in racially integrated classes, had enrolled in courses from elementary through high-school levels. In addition, the state has given thousands vocational training, fitting them for jobs in industry.

A large proportion of these newly skilled workers has been absorbed by the state's enormous and swiftly modernizing textile industry—South Carolina manufactures more than half of all the textiles made in the U.S. Others have been hired by some relatively higher-paying industries. Utica Drop Forge, Westinghouse Airbrake, Lockheed Aircraft —these and many more are giving the state a much-needed boost. A measure of this boost can be seen in the old port of Charleston. As recently as 1947 it ranked 65th in the U.S. in terms of volume of foreign trade handled; less than a decade later it had climbed to 15th place.

Florida, for its part, has undergone an almost incredible boom in the last decades. And it has done so not, as many people suppose, solely because of increased tourism and the nation's apparently unslakable thirst for the state's orange juice. Manufacturing expansion has accelerated to such an extent that Florida has taken the lead among all the southeastern states in the rate of industrial growth. Much of this has been spurred, of course, by Cape Kennedy and the space program. But many other industries, having nothing to do with space, have also built plants in the state.

There is obviously—at last!—a "New South," the goal that the region has been proclaiming and pursuing for more than a century. Economic conditions in the Old South are still worse than those of most of the rest of the country, but at last the region is laying a tax base on which it can furnish better education—which it has so desperately needed—better services, better health and a better way of life. Its period as "the Nation's Number One economic problem" lies behind it.

The reasons the Old South had fallen so low economically are as numerous as the reasons behind its post-World War II renaissance. But perhaps the key to them all, as the report of 1938 to President Roosevelt said, was waste—waste of both natural and human resources.

For many decades, one of the major causes of this waste—and the stock villain in many books on

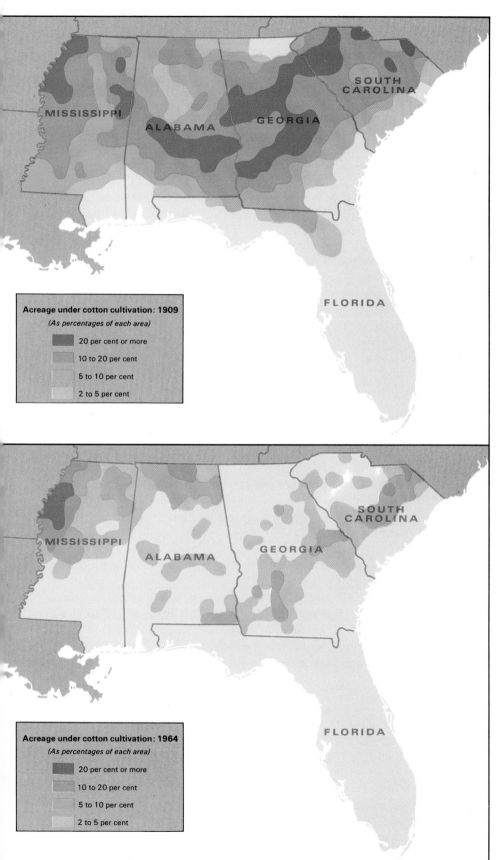

Acreage under cotton cultivation: 1909

(As percentages of each area)

- 20 per cent or more
- 10 to 20 per cent
- 5 to 10 per cent
- 2 to 5 per cent

Acreage under cotton cultivation: 1964

(As percentages of each area)

- 20 per cent or more
- 10 to 20 per cent
- 5 to 10 per cent
- 2 to 5 per cent

The decline of King Cotton

The concentration on cotton farming that once dominated the economy of the Old South has disappeared in the past half century, as indicated on the acreage maps at left. In 1909 *(top)*, when cotton acreage reached its maximum in this region, this crop was grown in almost every part of four of the five states; by 1964 *(bottom)* only one fifth as many acres were devoted to cotton. King Cotton's decline was due to several factors. First, early cotton farmers exhausted the soil in many areas. Second, the onslaught of the cotton-eating boll weevil, an insect that caused widespread damage to cotton plants in the 1920s, forced many farmers to raise other crops. Third, Negro field hands began leaving the South in increasing numbers after World War I, depleting the planters' labor force. Finally, price supports in the 1930s fostered a restriction of cotton acreage. As cotton lost its hold over the Old South, the Old South also lost its dominance over the cotton market; today the leading cotton-producing state is Texas; Mississippi and California vie for second place.

Fully as dramatic as the decline in cotton acreage in the Old South, however, is the huge increase in yield per acre. Thanks to such improvements as modern farm machinery and chemical fertilizers, the output of a single acre of cotton today is three times what it was in 1909, and total cotton production in the region has dropped only 15 per cent.

the South—was cotton. Far too large a proportion of the Old South's good agricultural land was planted in that one crop decade after decade. Even in good years the returns on cotton were not high; in bad years, when the price dropped, the returns were appallingly low. In one post-Civil War decade, the price plummeted from 23 cents a pound to 15 cents and then to seven cents. The same thing happened later as the Great Depression began to deepen. In 1929, as textile mills cut back production, the price of cotton dropped from 20 to 12 cents a pound. In 1930 it fell to eight cents and later to less than five cents.

The result, of course, was disaster for everybody dependent on cotton—the banker, the landlord and especially the small farmer. In Mississippi one farm in every 10 went bankrupt and had to be sold. Tenants and sharecroppers became even more hopelessly mired in grinding debt. All were suffering from the fact that the Old South was locked in a system of one-crop farming marked by high risks and low returns.

Some attempts had been made even before the Civil War to escape from such dependence on cotton farming. One, logically enough, was to establish mills in the South to weave the region's own cotton into cloth, which would, it was hoped, bring in more money than the sale of the raw material. By the 1880s an almost religious mania for industrialization swept the South, and locally financed cotton mills went up in hundreds of little towns. A revivalist preacher in Salisbury, North Carolina, spoke for the whole South when he exclaimed that "next to the grace of God, what Salisbury needs is a cotton mill!" The trouble was that many of these mills were too small for efficient operation. Further, their semiskilled mill hands, working with sometimes outdated machinery, were incapable of producing anything but the cheaper grades of cloth. Wages were low—incredibly so by modern standards. Thus, although these mills did represent some progress, it was not enough.

The later influx of Northern cotton-goods manufacturers did little to improve the situation. They came south partly because they wanted to be near the cotton supply and closer to certain markets, and partly because there was abundant water power and cheap land. But the major attraction was the low wage levels that prevailed in the South. An experienced New England weaver in 1906 could command daily wages of about $1.70; in the Old South adequate textile weavers could be had for $1.20 a day, a saving of nearly 30 per cent. The result was that although the mills might hum, and

produce high profits for their proprietors, only a small proportion of the wealth they generated went into the pockets of the workers and thus into the Old South's economy. Therefore the towns of the Old South had little if any money to build better schools, upgrade public services or care for public health. The South was paying an enormous social price for its low-wage type of industrialization.

Many other industries besides cotton milling came to the Old South throughout the period from the end of the Civil War to the beginning of World War II, but the benefit to the region was in most cases marginal. For example, logging became a major enterprise. Thousands of back-country sawmills sprang up—along with some big lumbering operations. Large sums of money were made by the owners, but precious little fell into the hands of the workers. The long-run result was that one of the world's finest timber stands was gutted and millions of acres turned into eroded wasteland. It was, according to one expert, "the most ruthless destruction of forests known in history." To this wholesale destruction was added another form of waste: too much of the lumber was sold to consumers outside the South as just that, plain lumber. The South largely failed to benefit from the extra jobs and extra profits that would have come from turning its lumber into furniture and other finished products.

But the picture was not altogether bleak in the Old South. In Birmingham the region had its own "Pittsburgh of the South"; by 1900 the city ranked fifth in the nation in the production of iron and steel. Birmingham also manufactured rails and rolling stock for the region's burgeoning railroads. The Gulf Coast area became a major source of sulfur after 1903 when a new process for extracting the mineral from deposits deep underground was developed. Georgia granite came to compete with stone from Vermont and New Hampshire. Local sources of cement and gravel were exploited, spurring the ambitious highway programs undertaken in several Old South states in the 1920s.

Diversification and mechanization were also attempted in agriculture. Up to the 1930s Depression and even beyond, however, both had lagged sadly. With its diversity of climate and soil, the Old South could have grown a wide variety of crops. There was plenty of excellent grassland, yet livestock production was scant. In addition, farms tended to be too small for modern agricultural methods and the average farmer too poor to afford modern equipment. The South as a whole had more than half of the farmers in the U.S. during the 1930s and yet possessed less than one fifth of the nation's farm equipment; the five states of the Old South were particularly badly off in this regard. Again, as in other realms, the story of agriculture in the Old South was one of waste—and not just of natural resources but of human resources as well. Because of the Depression and lack of modern tools, excellent farmers, men devoted to the soil from birth, were increasingly being forced off the land or reduced to the peonage of sharecropping and tenant farming.

All of this tragic wastage of men and land, while somewhat ameliorated by New Deal programs and money in the 1930s, did not really begin to right itself in the Old South until World War II. Generally speaking, Southern agriculture, like Southern industry, began to change radically in the 1940s. There was, first of all, a sudden and dramatic increase in farm mechanization. The number of larger farms, on which machines could be used efficiently, showed a steady increase. This meant, of course, that the total number of farms shrank, the smaller and less efficient places being absorbed or forced to close down. Combined with increased mechanization, this threw a large number of farmers and field hands off the land. But it was not wholly a misfortune. Many of the displaced men were able to find jobs in the growing towns.

Another important element in the revitalization of the Old South's agriculture was a new determination among the region's farmers to diversify their crops. By 1950 the major proportion of the U.S. cotton crop was being grown, not in the Old South, but west of the Mississippi River, in Texas and in irrigated parts of the Southwest. In its place, Old South farmers were producing a healthy variety of other crops such as corn, hay, wheat, soybeans and peanuts. The most startling growth, however, occurred in the raising of livestock. Today broad sweeps of grassland dotted with herds of cattle are to be found in many parts of Mississippi, Alabama and Georgia, and most especially in northern Florida, where some ranches boast more than 200,000 acres, challenging the giant "spreads" of Texas. (Much of this land had been depleted by poor farming practices. Restoring it for crops would have been prohibitively expensive but it serves well for grazing.) Nor have Southern farmers neglected such profitable stock as hogs and chickens. Northern Georgia leaped into the forefront of chicken raising during the post-World War II decade, and dozens of new meat-packing plants across the region converted fat swine into bacon and pork chops.

All of this dramatic progress, in agriculture as in industry, has changed the Old South from a region largely sunk in poverty, lethargy and even despair to one of the most economically vigorous in the nation. It must be added, however, that large and serious defects remain. Too many farmers, especially in the hill country, are still trying to scratch a living from hard, grudging and exhausted soil. Too many Negro farm workers who lost their jobs to machines remain without steady employment. Behind such problems lies a basic fact: the Old South states were so depressed for so long that, with all their recent strides forward; they have simply been unable to close the gap between their standards of living and the steadily rising average standard of living of the rest of the nation.

The difficulties still facing the Old South are revealed most sharply in Mississippi. It is, and has long been, the most backward and problem-plagued of the five. It serves, in effect, as a magnifying mirror of the region.

An illustration of the problem can be found in the state's frustrating experience with its per capita income. Between 1950 and 1965 the Mississippi average income more than doubled, going from $775 to $1,608. In the same years the national average increased from $1,496 to $2,746—considerably less than double. But, as an official Mississippi publication sadly notes, the gap in numbers of dollars between the Mississippi and national averages actually *increased*.

The reasons? The same ones that we have already considered, although in more virulent forms. For years Mississippi had lured industry by unsubtle allusions to "willing and able labor," with the result that most industries that came to the state were low-wage, low-skill enterprises in flight from Northern costs and unions.

Despite the flaws, however, the shape of the economy and with it the way of life in Mississippi are changing very much as they are in the rest of the Old South. In the mid-1960s, for the first time, the number of people employed in manufacturing (some 152,000) about equaled the number employed on farms. Manufacturing had become the primary source of income for the state of Mississippi, with farm income well behind. Especially for anyone familiar with Mississippi as it used to be, there was a look and feel of real affluence.

Even in the Mississippi Delta country some industrialization—and with it more jobs and better pay—has been achieved. Not, however, without tribulation, anxiety and tension. The D. H. Baldwin piano and organ manufacturing concern has had its share of all three since it established a large plant in the old cotton town of Greenwood in 1960.

Greenwood is not, even by Mississippi standards, either a prosperous or a progressive town. Its streets are narrow, laid out in a confusing tangle of unplanned triangles, and lined with a motley collection of red brick stores and corrugated-tin warehouses. In the words of a local observer, "The buildings of Greenwood press upon one another like a disheveled group of small, untidy boys jammed into the insufficient confines of a makeshift clubhouse." The town, long committed to cotton, tends to be ingrown and conservative, resisting change both in its commercial life and in its attitudes toward the race problem. The birthplace of the Citizens' Councils, it is a seat of Ku Klux Klan activity. There has long been wealth in the town, but it has belonged to very few—the cotton barons and the bankers. Most of the rest of the people have been poor, especially the field hands of the cotton plantations, both white and Negro.

Baldwin chose to establish a plant in Greenwood for a number of reasons. One was that its sales of pianos had been steadily increasing in the South and Southwest, and Greenwood was handy to this expanding market. Another was that lumber for piano making would be readily available nearby. And, of course, Baldwin knew that there was plenty of labor to be had.

All these advantages have proved to be real, but Baldwin was not quite prepared for some of the problems it would face operating in such a long-backward area. Among the first of these was the low educational level of some of the workers it hired. Downright illiteracy proved distressingly common. In its other U.S. plants Baldwin had long hired only high-school graduates. In Greenwood it had to lower its standard to an eighth-grade education, and even then found that some of the workers simply could not comprehend specifications and work orders. Baldwin also encountered an extraordinarily high degree of absenteeism. Most of the workers had never been in an industrial plant and did not fully understand the idea of coming to work every day, and on time. Many of them had never had jobs that lasted year round; their work on fields and farms had been seasonal. After working six months or a year, some of these employees just up and quit, apparently responding to a compulsion to move on. To counter these problems Baldwin early set up an intensive counseling program to help workers settle into the world of time clocks and to explain the benefits—health insurance and the like—that accrued to workers able to adjust to the daily routine.

Almost as bothersome, and much more fraught with tension, was the matter of race. Entering such a bastion of white supremacy, Baldwin moved cautiously. At first it played the game by the local rules: no Negroes were taken on the payroll. Then, slowly, it began to hire Negroes until the plant was fully integrated by 1967. At that time Baldwin's Greenwood plant had 800 employees, and some 60 per cent were Negro. "This is about the same as the percentage of Negroes in the community," a Baldwin spokesman argued, plainly trying to mollify segregationists and disclaim any crusading on the company's part.

The argument has not always worked. There have been only isolated instances of violence, but members of the Klan and the Citizens' Council have periodically campaigned against Baldwin with acrimonious hate literature, distributed clandestinely in the night. Sometimes the leaflets have been scattered about town; sometimes workers have found them in the plant when they reported for work in the morning.

For the most part, however, Greenwood has accepted even the integrated Baldwin plant. It has done so for the very good reason that Baldwin has done much for the town. The plant's yearly payroll of $4.5 million is a powerful stimulant to the town's economy. Since Baldwin moved in, Greenwood has expanded its airport and acquired a new shopping center and several new motels. Business in the downtown stores has increased. And since Baldwin hires only local workers, it has put at least $4,000 a year in the pockets of at least 800 Greenwood citizens. The company also contributes to fund-raising drives such as the Community Chest.

What Baldwin means for Greenwood's future is probably more important than anything it has done to date. It has exposed many hundreds of workers to industrial equipment, to time clocks, to regular workdays and to a taste of affluence. This, along with Greenwood's other advantages, will, sooner or later, attract another industry to the town, and then another. When they come they will promote job competition and higher wages and these will further raise Greenwood's living standards. In time, it seems reasonable to predict, some of this increased affluence will be put into improving the town's schools, beautifying its buildings and generally upgrading the whole tenor of life in this part of the Delta. Even the town's bristling animosity on the race question might be modified. All this has already happened in Huntsville, Dothan and many other Old South towns. There is no reason why it should not happen elsewhere.

As a workman checks the tension of the strands, gleaming synthetic fibers are fed into a chemical treating unit that increases their pliancy and strength. The mill, owned by J. P. Stevens & Company, is in Greenville, South Carolina.

An industrial giant rejuvenated

The Old South's textile industry, once characterized by poor management and lack of imagination, is now one of the most vigorous enterprises in the region. Most of its mills were first established there in the early 20th Century, drawn by low wage scales. This competitive advantage, though less marked than it once was, has enabled the area to achieve its position as the U.S. textile center. The dramatic rejuvenation of textiles began in the late 1940s when well-financed research-and-development programs became an integral part of the business. From these programs have come improvements in production techniques and a host of new and better products. The new products have, in turn, helped bring about the establishment of an enormous chemical industry in the Old South to make the raw materials for the mills.

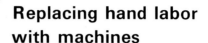

In one of the few sheet-making operations still performed by hand, women fold sheets for packing at the J. P. Stevens mill in Clemson, South Carolina.

Replacing hand labor with machines

The old-fashioned textile mill, characterized by rows of sweating, lint-covered workers attending clanking machinery, is a thing of the past today, and nowhere more noticeably than in the Old South. In its place is likely to be a clean, air-conditioned plant of modern design, housing automatic, high-speed equipment that requires only periodic checks by trained technicians. In the decade or so following the mid-1950s, the U.S. textile industry spent nearly seven billion dollars for new factories and machinery, much of it in the South. The results were a marked increase in productivity and simultaneously a reduction in the number of workers needed for each operation. In one South Carolina plant, the entire process of making bed sheets, from unbaling the raw cotton to packing the finished product, requires only 14 minutes of hand labor per sheet.

Because of the opening of new plants and the expansion of existing facilities, the effects of automation on employment have been slight thus far. But the trend toward fewer, more highly skilled workers could have many repercussions in such states as South Carolina, where the textile industry employs nearly half of all manufacturing workers, and in Georgia, where the figure is about 25 per cent. To meet the new requirements of the mills, the state and the industry are combining forces to train people for the new jobs in textiles. The task is huge, for until recent decades there has been slight demand for men and women with skills.

High-speed looms run with a minimum of attention in the J. P. Stevens Dunean plant. Only 80 to 90 operators are needed to tend 2,000 looms.

The spreading empires
of fabrics and chemicals

As indicated on this map, which for clarity shows only key plants or groups of plants, the textile industry now has plants in all five Old South states, with the heaviest concentration in South Carolina, the lightest in Florida. The cities shown are the centers of five leading textile production areas.

The colored pins represent different kinds of plants, following a classification system often used in the industry. Cotton mills produce either fabrics by the yard or finished goods (like shirts and sheets) in which the basic ingredient is cotton, though it is frequently blended with synthetics. Woolen mills perform comparable operations using wool, often combined with synthetics. Synthetic-fiber plants principally convert raw chemicals into fibers for use in other mills producing fabrics and finished goods. Tufted carpet and fabric mills produce rugs, carpets and other tufted goods from wool, cotton and synthetics. Hosiery mills take synthetic fibers and make stockings.

Until recently, most cotton mills produced only fabrics rather than the completed goods that consumers buy. Today the trend is toward plants that perform complete, integrated operations, taking in raw material at one end and putting out finished goods at the other. Another trend is toward cotton mills making only cotton-and-synthetic blends; today the mill producing goods solely of cotton is becoming rare.

 COTTON

WOOL

SYNTHETIC FIBERS

TUFTED CARPETS AND FABRICS

HOSIERY

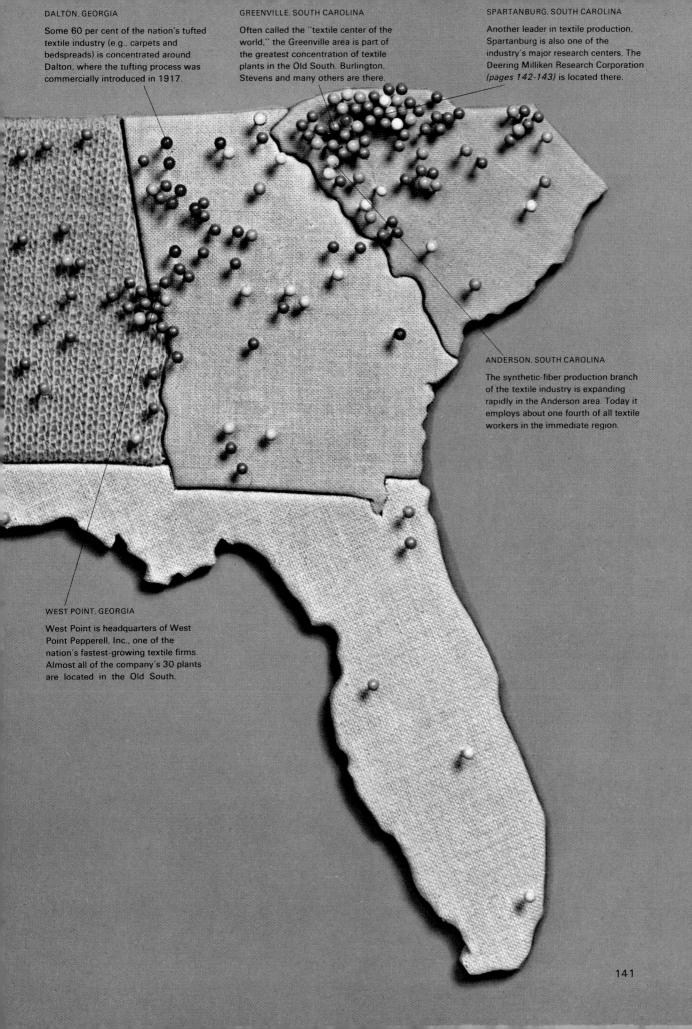

DALTON, GEORGIA

Some 60 per cent of the nation's tufted textile industry (e.g., carpets and bedspreads) is concentrated around Dalton, where the tufting process was commercially introduced in 1917.

GREENVILLE, SOUTH CAROLINA

Often called the "textile center of the world," the Greenville area is part of the greatest concentration of textile plants in the Old South. Burlington, Stevens and many others are there.

SPARTANBURG, SOUTH CAROLINA

Another leader in textile production, Spartanburg is also one of the industry's major research centers. The Deering Milliken Research Corporation *(pages 142-143)* is located there.

ANDERSON, SOUTH CAROLINA

The synthetic-fiber production branch of the textile industry is expanding rapidly in the Anderson area. Today it employs about one fourth of all textile workers in the immediate region.

WEST POINT, GEORGIA

West Point is headquarters of West Point Pepperell, Inc., one of the nation's fastest-growing textile firms. Almost all of the company's 30 plants are located in the Old South.

141

A computer-operated color analyzer tests fabrics for color accuracy as well as uniformity of hue by comparing pieces of the finished materials to standard samples.

Survival through innovations

Hard pressed by both domestic and foreign competition and by consumer demand for greater convenience and lower prices, the once hidebound textile industry has found that innovations in materials and production techniques are prime requisites for survival. Today almost all the large companies maintain research-and-development units concerned with creating new materials, improving established goods and finding ways to reduce manufacturing costs.

The largest textile research center in the Old South is operated by the Deering Milliken company in Spartanburg, South Carolina. Among its other activities, the center creates and tests new textiles. As shown here, samples are twisted, pulled and pounded by special devices to determine their durability. The center also tests new machinery and production methods. Since its founding in 1945, the Deering Milliken Research Corporation has received more than 300 patents, including one for the first advance in one stage of yarn spinning since the early 19th Century.

A technician testing resiliency uses a stop watch to find how long creased samples take to recover their shape.

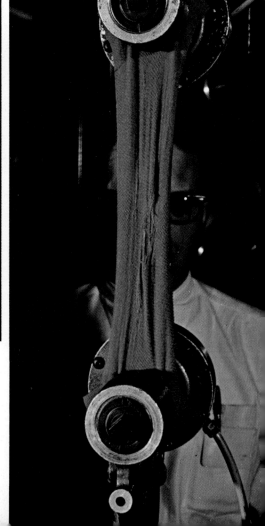

A strength-testing machine shows how much stretching a fabric sample will stand before tearing.

Stretching and rubbing fabric *(left)* determines how the finished product will withstand normal wear and tear.

A machine twists fabric *(below)* to find if the sample measures up to specifications.

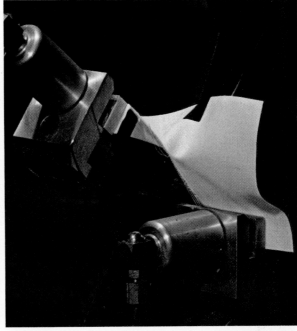

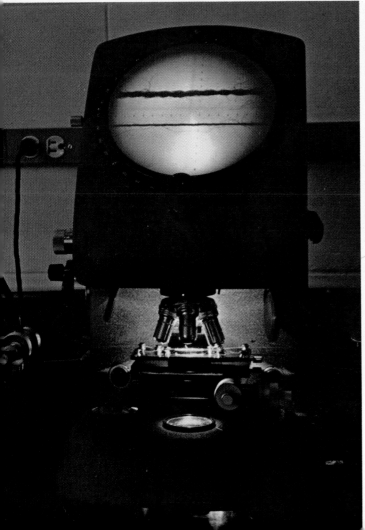

Abrasion wheels grind a carpet sample *(above)* to test its ability to withstand heavy wear.

A magnified view of individual strands of yarn is projected onto a screen to permit accurate comparison of fibers.

143

A multicolored, patterned carpet, usually made only by costly weaving techniques, is created by an inexpensive screen printing process at the plant of E. T. Barwick Mills in LaFayette, Georgia. To penetrate the deep pile, metal-impregnated dyes are used. During the printing operation, a magnet pulls the dye-covered particles into the carpet.

The high-flying carpetmakers

Carpetmaking, a craft that dates back thousands of years, is today a branch of the textile industry that is receiving particular benefits from research-and-development programs. By adapting man-made fibers to their purposes, for example, manufacturers can now weave carpets to be used outdoors and withstand not only the pedestrian traffic of a busy New York sidewalk but the most severe year-round weather. The researchers have also developed production innovations such as the electromagnetic dyeing process *(above),* the automatic design reader *(top right)* and the electronically controlled tufting machines *(right).* These new processes and machines drastically cut costs, producing inexpensive carpets with qualities once found only in the high-priced types. Even more immediately obvious advantages may come from studies now underway. The familiar static-electricity shock—the kind experienced after walking across a thick carpet on a cold, dry day and then touching a metal doorknob—may soon become a thing of the past.

How a rug is tufted under electronic control in West Point Pepperell's Cabin Crafts plant at Dalton, Georgia, is shown at right. In the control center *(top right),* an automatic pattern reader scans a picture of the design to be created in the rug. Some 600 electric eyes detect which parts of the pattern, painted on a clear plastic sheet, are black and which are clear. The eyes in turn control the tufting machine *(right),* turning the black parts of the pattern into a raised design on the finished rug. This electronic control, introduced in 1968, works more precisely than any previous device, creating rugs with such sharp patterns that they appear hand-crafted. Perhaps the biggest advantage of the device is that little time is required to create entirely new rugs. A new design can simply be painted on a plastic sheet, then exchanged for the old pattern in a matter of minutes.

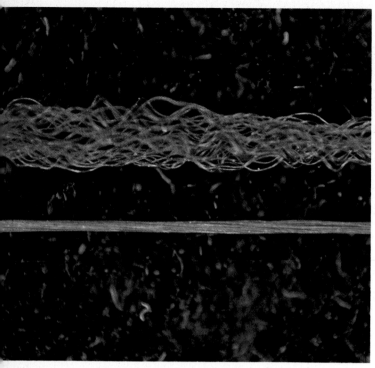

Acetate filaments, weak and loose when first extruded
(top), are twisted into tight fibers, doubling their strength.

Growth of an ally
in chemicals

Because of the constantly increasing use of synthetic fibers in the textile business, a giant multimillion-
dollar chemical industry is being established in the
Old South to meet the demands of the region's mills
for raw materials. The first man-made fiber, rayon,
was introduced in the late 19th Century, but synthetics were of relatively little importance until the
invention of nylon in the late 1930s. In the decades
since then, synthetics have skyrocketed in popularity. In the 1920s, man-made fibers accounted for
less than 1 per cent of the textile market; four decades later the figure was nearly 45 per cent.

The chemical industry produces two basic kinds
of fiber for the Old South's textile plants: rayon and
acetate, which are made from the natural material cellulose; and those others, like nylon and
Orlon, that are created wholly from chemicals. The
latter group is, by far, the dominant one today.

Lights burn far into the night at Hercules Incorporated in
Spartanburg, South Carolina. The plant produces a
chemical called DMT, used to make polyester fibers.

146

7

Great Writers in an Unlikely Setting

The Southern Literary Renaissance . . . ," says critic John M. Bradbury, "is a phenomenon unparalleled in American history. The country has experienced significant creative revivals in the past, principally in New England and the Midwest, but never before has a region so suddenly, so widely, and so effectively burst into literary activity as has the South since 1920."

No student of American letters—nor any statistician, for that matter—would challenge this statement. Both at home and abroad, Southern writers have received a cornucopia of honors. In the years between 1929 and 1967, for example, authors in the region were awarded one Nobel Prize for literature and 21 Pulitzer Prizes: 14 for fiction—more than a third of those given during the period— three for drama and four for poetry. The New York Drama Critics' Circle began making awards for the best American play of the year in 1936; of the 24 prizes handed out between then and 1967, eight went to playwrights from the South. From 1950, when the first National Book Awards were made,

until 1967, nine Southern writers—four novelists and five poets—were among the recipients. "In sum," Bradbury says, "the South which was offering almost nothing to American letters before World War I has since been earning a considerably larger share than its population warrants of the literary kudos."

One of the most astonishing aspects of this literary renaissance is the major contribution made by the five states of the Old South, generally regarded as the nation's cultural backwater. By 1950, for example, Mississippi was producing, on a per capita basis, more creative literature than any other state in the Union. Along with the late William Faulkner, winner of the Nobel Prize, Mississippi includes among its native sons and daughters such outstanding writers as Tennessee Williams, Eudora Welty, Negro novelist Richard Wright, Ben Ames Williams, David Cohn, Stark Young and Hodding Carter. The other states in the Old South could put forth lists almost equally impressive.

Probably this flood of contemporary literature from the Old South tells us more about the changing attitudes and intellectual ferment of the region than any other single indicator. A host of excellent poets, novelists, playwrights and short-story writers have given the world penetrating insights into

Cabbage Row, a quaint Charleston court made famous as Catfish Row in George Gershwin's folk opera *Porgy and Bess*, appears quiet in the soft light filtering through the trees. Gershwin's work was based on the DuBose Heyward novel *Porgy*, set in this street.

the dark and tragic spirit of the contemporary South and, by extension, into modern man himself. And in so doing they not only reflect their own time but often anticipate the future. Their concern is not solely with the effect of history upon one generation but with the probable influence of that generation upon the next.

Exactly why this tremendous upsurge of literary productivity began in the 1920s is a question that baffles most observers. Certainly there was nothing in Southern history that foreshadowed the renaissance. In fact, the very word "renaissance"—from the French *renaître*, "to be born again"—is a dubious choice. This era of creativity in the South, and especially in the Old South, is less a rebirth than a literary Athena born fully armed from the head of a Dixie Zeus.

For generations the South had produced little of literary importance. As late as 1917 editor and essayist H. L. Mencken was sufficiently appalled by the creative sterility of the region to describe it as "The Sahara of the Bozarts." This appraisal was painfully accurate at the time it was made. But if Mencken meant his observation as prophecy, implying that the South was destined to remain a literary desert, he was as far off the mark as the French art critic who opined that the young Paul Cézanne lacked any potential as a painter.

Strangely enough, the renaissance was neither preceded nor followed by any dramatic improvement in the general intellectual health of the Old South. The illiteracy rate is still the highest in the nation. Public education on the grade- and high-school levels continues to be poor in many areas; when states are ranked according to the amount of money spent per pupil, South Carolina and Mississippi occupy the last two places on the list, and Alabama, Florida and Georgia are well below the national average. On a per capita basis the Old South buys fewer books than any other part of the country, and the writers who have dealt realistically with the region are often treated as pariahs. When the news that Faulkner had won the Nobel Prize was released, the *Daily News* in Jackson, Mississippi, editorialized: "He is a propagandist of degradation and properly belongs to the privy school of literature." Such facts only add to the mystery surrounding Southern literary aptitude. "I can't explain the phenomenon," a Midwestern author said recently. "For the Old South suddenly to begin producing quantities of outstanding writers seems as unlikely as New England's suddenly producing bevies of great bullfighters."

Undoubtedly World War I was an important factor in starting the renaissance. Many Southerners, including potential writers, left the Old South for the first time as members of the armed forces. Faulkner, for example, had never been out of Mississippi until he went to Toronto to join the Royal Flying Corps. (Earlier he had been turned down as a pilot by the U.S. Army because he had not completed two years of college.) For these future writers the war meant exposure to men from other cultures, and travel, in many instances to Europe. Quite a few remained in England and France after the armistice to study. Inevitably these experiences breached the wall of provincialism.

Also the postwar years were a period of intellectual revolution. Creative men, disillusioned by a war that had been labeled a great crusade but that now seemed to have been little more than a sordid bloodletting for markets, were out to topple the traditional gods. Old values, old concepts, old faiths were falling before the onslaught. It was the era of the "new freedom" in literature, and the young writers, returning to their homes in the Old South, were eager to become a part of the movement.

The South, they found, was also going through a transformation. Industrialization, stimulated by war-begot factories, was continuing to spread and to change the region. Two kinds of cultures were in uneasy coexistence. "Both the old and the new culture abounded in sharp contrasts and logical paradoxes," wrote sociologist Howard W. Odum. "There were many Souths yet *the* South. It was preëminently national in backgrounds, yet provincial in its processes. . . . There were romance, beauty, glamor, gayety, comedy, gentleness, and there were sordidness, ugliness, dullness, sorrow, tragedy, cruelty. There were wealth, culture, education, generosity, chivalry, manners, courage, nobility, and there were poverty, crudeness, ignorance, narrowness, brutality, cowardice. . . . It was a South getting better, a South getting worse."

To many writers in the Old South these paradoxes proved a powerful stimulus. Here was an enigma to be studied, understood and interpreted. "I discovered that my own little postage stamp of native soil was worth writing about," Faulkner once said and added that he would "never live long enough to exhaust it." There were enough novelists, poets, playwrights and short-story writers who felt, and continue to feel, as Faulkner did to create one of the greatest schools of regional writing in all literary history.

The aftermath of World War I evoked a similar blossoming of regional writing in the Midwest. But whereas the Midwestern movement did not survive

Eudora Welty of Mississippi writes of her native state and its people with great skill and profound feeling. Critics usually rate her as one of the best of contemporary women writers.

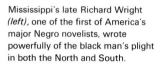

Mississippi's late Richard Wright *(left)*, one of the first of America's major Negro novelists, wrote powerfully of the black man's plight in both the North and South.

Erskine Caldwell of Georgia, one of the best-selling authors of all time, has written numerous novels depicting life in rural Georgia, among them *God's Little Acre* and *Tobacco Road*.

the 1930s, that of the South has been going on for decades and still shows no signs of withering. How do we account for its longevity and continued vigor in this unlikely setting? Certainly the only comparable period of prolonged regional creativity in the United States, the one that occurred in New England during the 19th Century, is far more easily explained. There the cultural roots were deep and strong—broad-scale education, respect for learning and the tradition of writing could be traced back to the Massachusetts Bay Colony—and the intellectual atmosphere of the region during the 1800s continued to encourage creative work. But the reverse is true in the Old South: except in such cities as Charleston, Savannah and Atlanta, the roots are few and shallow, and the general atmosphere remains hostile.

Perhaps some clues to the mystery may be found in a similar phenomenon that has been taking place in Ireland since the beginning of the 20th Century. Like the Old South, Ireland is poor, culturally backward and often repressive to new concepts; until about 1900 it was without a substantial literary tradition. But since that time Ireland has produced a wealth of playwrights, poets and novelists whose works are among the greatest of contemporary literature. James Joyce,

George Bernard Shaw, Sean O'Casey and William Butler Yeats are just a few of the Irish giants of their era.

"There are some interesting parallels between the southern and Irish writers," a literary historian said recently. "A period of unrest—mounting Irish nationalism in the early part of this century—was a powerful spur to Ireland's writers just as the changing South in the post-World War I years was to southern authors. Also the hostility that both the Irish and southern writers often find in their surroundings may be the irritant sand that creates the pearl in an oyster. In a tribute to Yeats, [poet W. H.] Auden wrote, 'Mad Ireland hurt you into poetry.' By changing 'Ireland' to 'Dixie,' this observation would probably apply to many creative men and women in the South."

The Irish also share two human qualities with Southerners: both are great storytellers and both have a deep love of the spoken language. The Southerner, the late Georgia novelist Flannery O'Connor said, "possesses a story-telling tradition. When a southerner wants to make a point, he tells a story; it's actually his way of reasoning and dealing with experience." The Southerner's feel for language may be attributed to the fact that most Southerners are steeped in the Bible and that this has had a large influence on their use of words and on the color and rhythm of their speech.

Almost total immersion in the language and ideas of the King James Bible—a legacy not shared in most of Ireland—is only one aspect of the South that makes its intellectual history distinctive. In the backwoods communities of the Old South during colonial times, the Bible was often the only book with which the people were thoroughly familiar. Usually this familiarity was acquired by listening to preachers, for a high proportion of the people were illiterate. Poor education for most of the people, and none at all for many, has burdened the Old South throughout its history.

As late as 1770 Governor William Bull of South Carolina wrote from Charleston: "We have not one good grammar school, though foundations for several in our neighboring parishes. All gentlemen who have anything of a learned education, have acquired it in England. . . . We have a provincial free school, the master and usher whereof are paid by the public, but their salaries being established at the early age of the province, are insufficient to engage and retain fit men. The masters when tolerably well qualified have frequently quitted the laborious task of teaching boys, for the more easy office of preaching in some country parish."

The rich and powerful planters, who might have done something about the situation, adopted the English attitude that education was primarily a private matter and not a concern of the state. Throughout the colonial period, formal education was almost exclusively a privilege of the wealthy landowners who hired tutors to teach their children. The purpose of this training, says historian Francis Butler Simkins, was theoretically to endow "the children of the leisure class with the adornments of mind and the habits of application and restraint which set them apart from the poor and the less fortunate. The aristocratic child was taught the proper accent, the correct style of writing, the use of Greek and Latin phrases, and studies such as law that fitted him for exercise of political power."

During this pre-Revolution era, many of the plantation owners, especially those in South Carolina, sent their older sons to Eton, Oxford and the Middle Temple in England for their advanced education. The English influence, in fact, was the mainstay of the culture of upper-class Southerners. Says historian Clement Eaton, "They refined and embellished their lives by the importation of books from England in the returning tobacco ships . . . ; they themselves aspired to live like English country gentlemen—a formative ideal; they built beautiful homes, furnished with engraved silver, candelabra, and elegant mahogany furniture; they had their portraits painted; they sought through the church, especially the Church of England, to improve their spiritual life; and they developed a peculiarly Southern emphasis on the art of conversation, hospitality, and polished manners." The gentry aspired to a versatile, Renaissance type of education for their children, but the realization "was often defeated by the laziness of Southern youth . . . by their passionate love of horses and out-of-doors life and by their delight in dancing, fine clothes, and gay parties."

Actually the cultural interests of the older generation were on the whole no more profound than those of the young people. The majority of planters were men of action, not students. "They are more inclinable to read men by business and conversation, than to dive into books," said Hugh Jones, an 18th Century historian, "and are for the most part only desirous of learning what is absolutely necessary, in the shortest and best method."

Of the communities in the Old South, Charleston showed the liveliest interest in the arts. During the first half of the 18th Century, the Charleston Library Society was founded and soon had a quite respectable collection of books for circulation. Also a Charleston theater was opened and soon Shakespeare's plays and the latest British successes were being performed by traveling companies of English actors. In 1762 the St. Cecilia Society was organized to provide concerts for the town's music lovers.

The first successful newspaper in the Old South was another of Charleston's innovations; another had been established somewhat earlier in South Carolina but survived only about six months. In 1731 Thomas Whitmarsh, one of Benjamin Franklin's printers, came to town supplied with Franklin presses and Franklin financial backing. The following January Whitmarsh established the *South-Carolina Gazette*, a publication that was to play an important part in arousing support for the Revolution in the colony.

In modern terms the *Gazette* was less a newspaper than a magazine; the columns were filled with political articles, social satire, poetry and similar material. Much of the writing was done by the subscribers. The paper actively encouraged this participation with such announcements as "All Articles of Intelligence, Essays, Poems, &c. from the Ingenious, will be thankfully received, and inserted gratis. . . ." There was no mention of payment. To editors of colonial newspapers and magazines,

Tennessee Williams *(below)*, a native Mississippian, is one of the most widely acclaimed of modern playwrights. He has won two Pulitzer Prizes.

The late Carson McCullers *(above)* of Georgia became an outstanding writer after abandoning her ambition for a career as a concert pianist.

Alabama's Harper Lee *(right)* won prominence in 1960 with her first novel, *To Kill a Mockingbird*, a poignant story about racial injustice.

Samuel Johnson's dictum, "No man but a blockhead ever wrote except for money," was wild-eyed radicalism. Despite the *Gazette*'s open-door policy toward writers, none of lasting importance developed in Charleston.

Savannah, Georgia, also became a cultural center but never as active a one as Charleston. Savannah did not even have a newspaper until 1763, when James Johnson established the *Georgia Gazette*, one of the last to be founded during the colonial era. Education in Georgia was even more deplorable than in South Carolina. But Georgia was fortunate in one group of immigrants who helped to brighten the intellectual scene considerably and to provide much-needed leadership. In the 1750s a group of New England Puritans who had left Massachusetts and had settled in South Carolina about the turn of the 18th Century decided to move on to southeastern Georgia. The Puritans brought their love of learning with them. From their small group came ministers, political leaders and teachers so far out of proportion to the community's population that historian William Bacon Stevens referred to the Puritans as "the moral and intellectual nobility of the province." In the 1770s these former New Englanders played a major role in bringing a reluctant Georgia into the

Revolutionary movement. The colony had boycotted the First Continental Congress, but thanks largely to the efforts of the Puritans, Georgia finally joined forces with the other 12 colonies.

For some years after the successful Revolution, strong democratic currents were felt in the Old South. Now, for example, an increasing number of prominent Southerners were questioning the moral basis of slavery. "The most elevated and liberal Carolinians abhor slavery," wrote Rhode Islander Dr. Joseph Brown Ladd in 1785; "they will not debase themselves by attempting to vindicate it." And there was the growing feeling that ownership of property should not be considered a requisite for voting; suffrage should be extended to all white adult males.

The old concept of education as a private responsibility—and therefore a privilege restricted to the rich—also faced renewed questioning at the beginning of the 19th Century. There was considerable agitation for a broad-scale public-school system such as the North was establishing, but in the Old South this aspiration was largely undermined by population distribution, by reluctance of the rich to pay the necessary taxes, and by the apathy and resentment of the poor.

In the backwoods areas there were only a few

people per square mile, and the mountainous terrain and inadequate roads cut children off from community schools. Such obstacles proved more difficult to overcome in the Old South than elsewhere in the young nation, perhaps because a far more important handicap to all public education in the region was the refusal of the rich planters to spend money for the purpose. Taxes were very low, and plantation owners wanted to maintain that comfortable situation. A number of public schools were opened, but the ruling class made attending them as humiliating as possible for the children of the poor. These schools were unmistakably labeled pauper institutions; parents had to sign a statement of poverty before a child could be admitted. It is questionable, one historian says, "whether the training children received in these schools counterbalanced the stigma of their attendance." Finally, because of the general apathy of the agrarian poor toward education, there was no strong counterforce, such as the early organizations of laboring men in the North, striving to correct the situation. Many of the poor expressed contempt for "book larnin'." Besides, they said, the children were needed as field hands except, perhaps, during the three winter months.

The pattern of illiteracy inherited from colonial times continued to handicap the entire South. As late as 1850 the federal census, which may have erred on the side of leniency, found that more than 20 per cent of the native white population in the South was illiterate compared with less than half of 1 per cent in New England. In some parts of the South at least a third of the whites could not read and had to sign their names with an "X."

Meanwhile, the intellectual climate of the South was being chilled still further by two important changes in the education of the gentry. The tutorial system, prevalent during colonial times, was rapidly losing favor; in the post-Revolutionary years it was no longer considered fashionable to send sons to English universities. Largely taking the place of the private tutors and British training were privately supported "old field schools" (so called because they were built in unused fields) and academies, which offered little more than a good high school does now. To many contemporary observers these academies were a poor substitute for sound college training. In a letter to John Adams in 1814 Jefferson referred to "these petty academies . . . which are starting up in every neighborhood, and where one or two men, possessing Latin and sometimes Greek, a knowledge of globes, and the first six books of Euclid, imagine and communicate this as

the sum of science. They commit their pupils to the theatre of the world, with just taste enough of learning to be alienated from industrial pursuits, and not enough to do service in the ranks of science." Southern families who wanted their sons to have an advanced education usually sent them to Harvard or Yale.

However, some actual colleges and universities were established in the Old South in the years between the late 18th Century and the beginning of the Civil War. The College of Charleston, for example, was founded in 1785 and was officially taken over by the city in 1837; it is the oldest municipal college in the United States. The University of Georgia came into existence in 1801, and South Carolina College (now the University of South Carolina) four years later. The University of Alabama opened its doors in 1831, and the first class entered the University of Mississippi in 1848. Florida, which came into the Union in 1845, did not have a college or university until after 1852.

The second change in Southern education came in the 1830s: a pernicious intellectual blight that inevitably afflicted almost all institutions of learning in the region. That was the decade in which Southern leaders, reacting to abolitionist sentiment in the North, began to defend slavery, not on an economic basis but on a moral one. Slavery became "a positive good," and soon anyone who questioned this belief was hounded unmercifully. The rigid orthodoxy of thought applied to this subject quickly spread to other fields; the status quo became sacred and dissidents and doubters of any stripe were not tolerated. Financially, at least, Southern academies and colleges benefited. Also their number increased. Many wealthy Southern families, who had once sent their sons to Harvard and Yale, were no longer willing to expose them to the dangerous atmosphere of the North. The obvious solution was to expand educational opportunities at home, where unacceptable concepts would receive no hearing. Thus the region's schools became "an intellectual protective tariff" to keep out inimical ideas. "We must have certain security . . ?"—editorialized one Southern newspaper—"that at State Universities at least we will have no canker worm preying at the vitals of Southern institutions." Questioning the essential rightness of slavery was only one of the thorny issues that a prudent academician avoided. For example, Thomas Cooper, President of the University of South Carolina, was a strong supporter of slavery, but he was tried and dismissed from his post in 1832 because of his unorthodox religious and political beliefs.

There was a concerted effort, political scientist Ronald Howell has said, "to seal off the South as a vacuum package, to reject all that seemed 'alien' or 'subversive,' to despise and fear 'efficiency' and 'newness' and 'industrialism' and 'progress' as diseased imports from the North—these were the sentiments that then permeated the Southern campus, no less than the Southern home, church, courthouse, and marketplace."

Partly because of this atmosphere, creative writing in the five states of the Old South was meager during the antebellum years. One of the region's few authors of note was William Gilmore Simms, the Charleston-born son of an Irish immigrant. Simms was an ardent admirer of the Southern gentry, and he wrote glowingly of them in such romantic novels as *Mellichampe* and *The Scout*. He also valiantly defended Southern institutions in his other writings. But Simms's love for the upper class of South Carolina was unrequited. His lowly birth and lack of fortune prevented him from entering the charmed social circle, and the members of it took no notice of him even after he had become well known as a writer in New York and London. "All that I have [done] has been poured to waste in Charleston . . ." he wrote in 1858.

Georgia's Augustus Baldwin Longstreet, one of the most popular of the Old South's antebellum writers, explored the other side of the social tracks. As a young lawyer, Longstreet had traveled extensively in rural Georgia, and when he began to write he used his experiences as the raw material for his highly entertaining *Georgia Scenes*. He had an excellent ear for the speech of the backwoodsmen, a good eye for revealing detail and an uncommon talent for writing humor. One of his most ardent admirers was young Edgar Allan Poe, who found in *Georgia Scenes* "a sure omen of better days for the literature of the South."

Writing was an avocation for Longstreet. In addition to practicing law, he served at various times as a judge of his state's superior court, as editor of the *Augusta State Rights Sentinel*, as a Methodist minister and as a college president. Because of the popularity of *Georgia Scenes*, editors were constantly urging him to write more sketches. He finally complied. Some of them were collected under the title *Master William Mitten: A Youth of Brilliant Talents Who Was Ruined by Bad Luck* and were published in 1864, six years before his death. Early in the 20th Century other pieces by him were reprinted in book form under the title *Stories with a Moral Humorous and Descriptive of Southern Life a Century Ago*. Neither measured up to his earlier work. However,

Longstreet did have an important influence on later Southern humorists by showing them the rich vein of material to be found in their own environs.

But if little fiction and poetry were written in the Old South during the antebellum years, there was an outpouring of books and essays defending states' rights and the institution of slavery. John C. Calhoun, the most distinguished Southern political figure of the era, wrote *A Disquisition on Government* and *A Discourse on the Constitution and Government of the United States*, in which he argued that the states have the power to nullify federal action. Calhoun also advanced the thesis that the Union, as formed, was a compact between sovereign powers, so that a state could reserve the right to secede whenever the arrangement proved unsatisfactory.

While Calhoun discussed the fundamental relationship between state and federal governments, other Old South writers were specifically defending the institution of slavery. Everything from the Bible to the works of Aristotle was used to justify the enslavement of the black man. "Scientific" argument to prove the natural inferiority of the Negro race was also advanced by such men as Dr. Josiah C. Nott, a Mobile, Alabama, physician, and George R. Gliddon, an archeologist, in their collaborative effort, *Types of Mankind*. Senator James H. Hammond of South Carolina went so far as to denounce the Declaration of Independence and its doctrine of the equality of men. Negro slavery, he argued, was "a mudsill" in the structure of a white democracy.

One of the most important media for disseminating racist prose at this time, and later, was the region's newspapers, which flourished in the Old South and gave popular currency to the ideas of the pundits. Despite the high ratio of illiteracy in the region, the papers delivered their message. On town squares groups of citizens who could not read gathered to listen to literate members of the communities read the papers aloud. Like the contemporary politicians, the papers made bald appeals to the emotions and prejudices of the populace. Strident in tone, flamboyant in style, the publications sacrificed reasoned discussion for grossly oversimplified arguments defending the Southern cause.

By the eve of the Civil War the Old South was nearing intellectual bankruptcy. Illiteracy was terrifyingly high; orthodoxy was sternly enforced; schools and colleges were not stimulating rational examination of ideas but, instead, were spoon-feeding accepted beliefs and brooking no questions; writers, often the bold nonconformists of a society, were meekly supporting the status quo; newspapers and politicians were concerned with stirring passions, not with provoking thoughtful debate.

The tragic result of this intellectual climate was perhaps best summed up by the historian and philosopher Henry Adams when he wrote of Rooney Lee, a son of Robert E. Lee's, and other young Southerners he knew at Harvard in the 1850s. For a year or so, Adams wrote, Lee was the most popular and prominent member of his class, "but then seemed slowly to drop into the background . . . He was simple beyond analysis; . . . No one knew enough to know how ignorant he was; how childlike; how helpless before the relative complexity of a school. . . strictly, the Southerner had no mind; he had temperament. He was not a scholar; he had no intellectual training; he could not analyze an idea, and he could not even conceive of admitting two."

Those pre-Civil War years became a favorite subject of Southern literature in the following decades, the time between Reconstruction and World War I. But the harsh realities of the antebellum era were almost wholly ignored by these later writers. In a flood of romantic, cloyingly sentimental novels, stories and poems, the Southern myths were given permanent cast, and the North as well as the South quickly came to accept this folklore as fact. It was regional writing, but regional writing of a never-never land. The antebellum South was portrayed as a land of warm, happy folk with a cultured gentry whose males were all handsome, gallant cavaliers and whose women were all beautiful, gentle and of such virtue that, by comparison, the vestal virgins seemed a sorority of wantons. (This kind of writing came readily to Southerners; Sir Walter Scott had been the South's favorite author for generations.) Slavery was pictured as a thoroughly benevolent institution and the slaves as among its most ardent admirers. Thus the Confederacy became the noble "Lost Cause," the defense of a great civilization against a power unaware of what it was destroying.

Northern book and magazine publishers eagerly sought out the work of Southern writers to supply an apparently insatiable national appetite for the antebellum fables. Many readers in the North may have had a strong sense of guilt about the havoc visited upon the South, and reading the books about the region may have served as a gentle kind of penance. Through this penance, says one historian, the North was "honoring in death a culture that had proved an anathema in life." It was a victory of sorts for the South but a costly one. The literature that provided solace for Northerners blinded most Southerners to their own history.

Slavery was always benign in this fictional world. Faithful old "uncles" and "mammies" were forever holding forth on that happy time when they had been chattels of the white man. Here is a fairly typical bit of dialogue spoken by Sam, an emancipated slave, in a post-Reconstruction story of 1887: "Dem wuz good ole times, marster—de bes' Sam ever see! Niggers didn' hed nothin' 'tall to do—jes' hed to 'ten' to de feedin' an' cleanin' de hosses, an' doin' what de marster tell 'em to do: an' when dey wuz sick, dey had things sent 'em out de house, an' de same doctor come to see 'em whar 'ten' to de white folks when dey wuz po'ly. Dyar warn' no trouble nor nothin'."

The Negro, almost neglected in Southern writing before the Civil War, became a favorite character —and a monumentally false stereotype—during the postwar decades. When he was not being portrayed as a mourner over the lost institution of slavery, he was usually shown as the lovable, carefree, happy-go-lucky fellow who spent much of his time raiding watermelon patches. He was also on occasion the dispenser of folk wisdom, always delivered with comic language difficulties.

Among the writers of the Old South, Irwin Russell, a Mississippi poet, was one of the most popular portrayers of the Negro. Russell's dialect poetry in "Uncle Cap Interviewed" and in "Christmas Night in the Quarters" appeared in *Scribner's Monthly* and won national acclaim. Joel Chandler Harris of Georgia, however, established a far more durable reputation with his 10 volumes of Uncle Remus stories. Although many modern readers find Harris basically patronizing to Negroes, the stories continue to have a quaint, nostalgic charm for a considerable audience.

One of the most important and least typical of the Old South's writers during the post-Civil War period was a poet, novelist and critic, who was also a professional musician, Sidney Lanier of Georgia. Although he was a Confederate veteran whose health had been permanently impaired in a Union prisoner-of-war camp—he was to die at age 39— Lanier was devoid of the bitterness and hatred that consumed many of his fellow Southerners. In one of his early poems, "Nirvâna," he wrote:

> *I slew gross bodies of old ethnic Hates*
> *The stirred long race-wars betwixt states and states; I*
> *stood and scorned these foolish dead debates,*
> *Calmly, calmly, Nirvâna.*

Lanier was contemptuous of the sentimentality of many of the Southern novels of his time, and he tried, not always successfully, to avoid the fault in his own work. He wrote one novel, several volumes of criticism, many essays, and a study on the interrelationship of poetry and music, but he gained his greatest fame as a poet. Such poems as "Corn," "The Symphony," "The Marshes of Glynn" and "Song of the Chattahoochee" received critical praise and won him a national audience.

On the whole, however, the writing done in the Old South during the 1865-1919 span included little of lasting interest. More important, the romantic version of history that many of the writers presented had an unfortunate effect on the South. For Southerners this simplistic concept served as a kind of narcotic; dwelling on the supposed glories of the past dulled the pain of the present and thereby made the need for effective therapy seem less urgent.

In this half century or so after the Civil War, the colleges and universities of the Old South did almost nothing to restore a sense of reality to the region. In fact, say John C. McKinney and Edgar T. Thompson in their *The South in Continuity and Change*, "they mirrored society's (a narrow, regionally defined society) concern with its past rather than helped it to face its future." Despite the region's obvious economic needs, the authors say, there was "little emphasis upon training in the utilitarian arts, and almost no concern with the creation of the future." The South lagged behind the rest of the nation in the teaching of science, engineering and agriculture; these disciplines, say McKinney and Thompson, remained "the weakest areas of education in all but a few institutions. . . ."

There was one highly important development in higher education in the Old South during this post-Civil War period: a number of Negro colleges and universities were founded. Half a dozen, including Atlanta University, were established in Georgia. Tuskegee Normal and Industrial Institute, with Booker T. Washington as its first president, and Selma University opened their doors in Alabama. Four colleges, Tougaloo and Jackson among them, were started in Mississippi. Allen University and Claflin College were two of seven set up in South Carolina, and in Florida the Florida Agricultural and Mechanical College was founded. Usually financed by Northern church groups, almost all of these institutions had serious money problems—Atlanta University's first classroom was an abandoned freight car—but they at least began to fulfill a desperate need of the black people of the Old South.

Certainly little in this generally dismal background foreshadowed the great Southern literary renaissance that followed World War I. For nearly a century—from 1830 to 1920—the South, and especially the Old South, had been a self-made cultural invalid. It was trapped in a stifling atmosphere of anti-intellectualism and afflicted with poor education from grade school through college, appallingly high illiteracy, rigidly enforced conformity and intense provincialism. The literary heritage of the region was meager.

And yet this most unlikely of times and places did produce the great era of creativity. The first intimation that something was afoot came in the early 1920s with the appearance of three Southern literary magazines, *The Double Dealer*, *The Reviewer* and *The Fugitive*. Within a decade or so there were similar publications in almost all of the Southern states. The Old South had its full quota: *The Nomad* and *The Gammadion* in Alabama, *Verse Craft*, *Shards* and *Bozart* in Georgia, *Blues* in Mississippi, and *The Cycle* and *The Dragon Fly* in Florida. Many of these magazines were devoted largely to poetry, and there was no trouble filling the columns. "Poets," says John Bradbury, "came out of the towns, the hills, and the bayous."

The general purpose of all of these publications was perhaps best expressed by the editors of *The Double Dealer:* they wanted their magazine "to be known as the rebuilder, the driver of the first pile into the mud of this artistic stagnation which has been our portion since the Civil War." This theme was developed by Basil Thompson in an early issue. There is a need for a new Southern literature, he claimed, to replace "the treacly sentimentalities" of "lady fictioneers" and "the storied realm of dreams, lassitude, pleasure, chivalry and the Nigger." Writers should be concerned with "the physical, mental and spiritual outlook of an emerging people—the soul-awakening of a hardy, torpid race, just becoming reaware of itself."

That precisely was the concern of most of the Southern writers who returned from World War I to take a hard, new look at their nation and their region. Much of their inspiration came from a book that captured the mood of the times: Sinclair Lewis' *Main Street*, published in 1920. *Main Street* was a harsh, satirical, cynical presentation of the foibles and hypocrisies of small-town life in the Midwest, but Southern writers found numerous parallels in their own area.

But these authors of the 1920s did not restrict their interests to the mores of the small-town middle class. They also wrote of the city worker, the Negro field hand and the sharecropper. There was little sentimentality in the new approach. If Job

were alive today, says a character in Dorothy Scarborough's *In the Land of Cotton*, "he'd be a cotton farmer, a share-cropper, I reckon." Of particular importance was the abandonment of the Negro stereotype that earlier writers had created. For the first time in Southern literature the Negro was recognizable as a man. Before the end of the 1920s decade such white writers as Roark Bradford, DuBose Heyward and Julia Peterkin were presenting attitudes and conditions in Southern communities from the black man's viewpoint.

The new school of writing understandably provoked considerable popular outrage, and partly because of this, writers tended to huddle together in literary centers—Faulkner, Roark Bradford and Hamilton Basso, for examples, gathered in New Orleans, while Robert Penn Warren, John Crowe Ransom, Allen Tate and Randall Jarrell were part of the Nashville coterie known as the "Fugitive Group" because they published *The Fugitive.* These centers were important not only because the authors who came found stimulation and encouragement in a region that offered little of either, but because the communities attracted still more writers who might otherwise have gone into such fields as journalism and advertising.

As the Southern literary movement gathered force, a number of colleges and universities in the Old South were rapidly gaining in intellectual vigor and setting higher academic standards, especially in the humanities, than before. Some of these institutions soon established courses in creative writing. The program at the University of Alabama was especially effective; among the many writers who received their early training there are William Bradford Huie, Frances Tillotson, Carlyle Tillery, Alice Fellows and Robert Gibbons. One of the most influential academic voices heard by writers all over the South was that of Professor Frederick Henry Koch at Chapel Hill, North Carolina. "Write what you know," he told his students. "If you observe the locality with which you are most familiar, and interpret it faithfully, it will show you the way to the universal."

Perhaps Allen Tate has best described the unique position of the Southern writers during the 1920s. After World War I, he wrote, "the South again knew the world, but it had a memory of another war; with us, entering the world once more meant not the obliteration of the past but a heightened consciousness of it; so that we had . . . a double focus, a looking two ways, which gave a special dimension to the writings of our school."

That "heightened consciousness" of the past

manifested itself dramatically—and foolishly in the opinion of many critics—with the publication in 1930 of *I'll Take My Stand*. A collection of essays by writers who came to be known as the "Agrarians" —Tate, Ransom and Warren of the old Fugitive group were among their number—*I'll Take My Stand* lashed out at industrialized society and America's "Cult of Science." Its authors proposed a society "in which agriculture is the leading vocation, whether for wealth, for pleasure, or for prestige."

In much of their criticism of the evils of industrialization, the Agrarians were on solid ground, but in their glorification of agrarian life in the South, they came dangerously close to espousing the romantic myths perpetrated by earlier Southern writers. Critics had a field day. "Young Confederates," "typewriter agrarians," "a socially reactionary band," were among the epithets hurled at the Agrarians. One reviewer asked, "Are they unaware of pellagra and hookworm, two flowers of Southern agrarianism?" In retrospect the socially conscious critics of the early 1930s seem overly severe with the Agrarians. In 1941 W. J. Cash, hardly an admirer of the group, admitted that there was "a good deal more realism in them than in any of the earlier apologists and idealizers" of Southern life.

But as the literary renaissance in the South progressed, not all of the region's writers were casting nostalgic looks at the past. Hugh Holman was actually describing many of them when he wrote of Thomas Wolfe as "torn by the tensions and issues that thoughtful Southerners feel, oppressed . . . with the tragic nature of life, and feeling . . . a sense of guilt that demands some kind of expiating action." Certainly these words applied to the giant of the movement, Mississippi's William Faulkner.

This aspect of Faulkner dominated *Sartoris*, the first of his novels about his fictional Yoknapatawpha County. Published in 1929, it was his fourth book. Earlier in the decade he had published *The Marble Faun*, a book of verse, and two novels, *Soldiers' Pay* and *Mosquitoes*, none of which received much critical acclaim. In *Sartoris* the author dealt with what was to become a recurring theme: the tragic end of a guilt-ridden, worn-out aristocracy. Even in the sound of the name Sartoris, Faulkner wrote, there was "death . . . a glamorous fatality, like silver pennons downrushing at sunset, or a dying fall of horns along the road to Roncevaux."

In such following books as *Light in August*, *The Sound and the Fury*, *As I Lay Dying*, *Absalom! Absalom!*, *The Unvanquished*, *The Hamlet* and *Intruder in the Dust* and in his numerous short stories, Faulkner continued to turn the harshly brilliant light of his genius upon the "doomed and cursed" land and people of Mississippi. The decadence of the poor whites trying to scratch a living from soil impoverished by greed, the Negro as the victim and the ever-present reminder of the white man's sins, the despair and madness visited upon the sons and daughters of the exploiters and wreckers of a great natural heritage—such were the materials he used to build a giant literary monument, at once regional and universal.

Other Mississippi writers were also making their marks in the 1930s and 1940s. The Negro novelist Richard Wright, who had been born of desperately poor parents on a plantation near Natchez, wrote searingly of the black man's plight in such novels as *Uncle Tom's Children* and *Native Son*. He was one of the first Negroes in the Southern renaissance to enjoy critical and popular success, and his books stirred national controversy. Eudora Welty of Jackson, one of the most important women authors of modern times, published her first short story in 1936, and in the decade that followed wrote three books, *The Robber Bridegroom*, *The Wide Net* and *Delta Wedding*. Columbus-born Tennessee (christened Thomas Lanier) Williams made his debut as a playwright in 1940 with the Theatre Guild's production of *Battle of Angels* and followed it with such acclaimed plays as *The Glass Menagerie* and *A Streetcar Named Desire*.

The other states of the Old South were also making their contribution to the Southern literary renaissance. In 1929 Erskine Caldwell of Georgia published two short novels, *The Bastard* and *Poor Fool*, but he was little noticed until 1932 when *Tobacco Road* appeared. A year later it was adapted to the stage and became one of the most successful plays in the history of the American theater. *God's Little Acre*, *Trouble in July* and *Georgia Boy* were among the many novels that followed. Although Caldwell and Faulkner wrote generally of the same kinds of people, Caldwell's work lacks Faulkner's great tragic vision. However, it is laced with wild, unpredictable humor, a highly developed sense of the ridiculous and the absurd. He has "one of the most fertile humorous imaginations in American literature," said one critic.

Another of Georgia's early entries in the Southern literary movement was Laurence Stallings, who, in collaboration with Maxwell Anderson, wrote the jolting war play *What Price Glory?*, first produced in 1924. Stallings' only novel, *Plumes*, was published in the same year. Later Stallings returned to the theater and again collaborated with

Anderson to write *First Flight* and *The Buccaneer*.

In the 1930s Georgia's late Margaret Mitchell, probably the most famous one-book novelist in history, won national attention with *Gone With the Wind*. It became an immediate bestseller all over the globe, won a Pulitzer Prize for its author, and was soon made into a motion picture that is still revived every few years and never fails to find a huge and appreciative audience. But Miss Mitchell did not live to enjoy her continuing success; in 1949 she was hit and killed by an automobile while crossing a street with her husband.

Carson McCullers was one of a number of Georgia writers whose work first appeared in the 1940s. At age 22 she wrote the beautiful and surprisingly mature *The Heart Is a Lonely Hunter* and followed it with such first-rate novels as *Reflections in a Golden Eye* and *The Member of the Wedding*.

Julia Peterkin and DuBose Heyward were two of South Carolina's writers first published in the 1920s, and both turned to the Negro for inspiration. At the urging of poet Carl Sandburg, Miss Peterkin began writing sketches about the Negroes on her plantation, Lang Syne, and in 1924 these works appeared as a collection entitled *Green Thursday*. Three years later her first novel, *Black April*, appeared and in 1928 she published another, *Scarlet Sister Mary*, that was awarded the Pulitzer Prize. She portrayed her characters sympathetically and with respect, but also with a frankness that shocked many of her readers, including those neighbors who bought the book. "I said things that no nice South Carolina lady ever says," she admitted with no hint of remorse.

Meanwhile Heyward, a poet and refugee from the insurance business, published his first novel, *Porgy*, in 1925. Although his characters were romanticized, they were believable. *Porgy* became a play in 1927, and in 1935 George Gershwin set the story to music in *Porgy and Bess*, a folk opera that has scored a huge success in almost every nation on the globe. Heyward's later works include *Angel*, *Mamba's Daughters* and *Star Spangled Virgin*.

Among the many writers whom Florida contributed to the Southern renaissance, two of the most outstanding are women, Marjorie Kinnan Rawlings and Lillian Smith. Miss Rawlings, a Floridian by adoption—she was born in Washington, D.C.—made little splash with her novelette, *Jacob's Ladder*, published in 1931, but two years later *South Moon Under*, a story of the Florida scrub country, brought her both critical and popular success. *The Yearling*, which appeared in 1938, is a minor classic that tells about a boy and his pet deer. The book had huge

sales and won a Pulitzer Prize for the author.

Lillian Smith, a native of Jasper, Florida, won immediate acclaim in 1944 with her first published novel, *Strange Fruit*. A tragic love story about a Negro girl and a white man, *Strange Fruit* was bitterly attacked; attempts were made to ban the book, but the American public responded by buying some three million copies, and later it was published abroad in 15 languages. Among her other books are *Killers of the Dream*, an exploration of the psychological bases of racial prejudice, and *The Journey*, an account of her personal experiences.

Poet and novelist Clement Wood was one of the Alabama writers who caused a stir in the literary world during the early days of the Southern renaissance. A graduate of the University of Alabama and then of the Yale Law School, Wood soon became chief presiding magistrate of Alabama's Central Recorder's Court. He did not last long in this position, however, being removed for "lack of the judicial temperament," a mild enough rebuke in view of the fact that he had jailed the lieutenant governor of the state for contempt of court. It was then that Wood decided to become a writer.

After several books of his poetry had appeared, he published *Nigger* in 1922. In this novel, Wood explored an area almost wholly ignored by other Southern writers up to that time; he traced a Negro family from the days of slavery in the Black Belt to modern bondage in the slums of Birmingham. A prolific writer, Wood published about 50 books of poetry and prose during his lifetime.

The era of creativity in the Old South did not end with the writers who began their careers during the first three decades of the Southern literary movement. Among the authors who made their professional appearances in the 1950s and 1960s were Georgia's Flannery O'Connor, who wrote such novels as *Wise Blood* and *The Violent Bear It Away;* Mississippi's Charles East, the author of *Where the Music Was;* and Florida's George Garrett, with *The Sleeping Gypsy* and *Do, Lord, Remember Me*.

The poets, novelists and playwrights of the Old South—only a comparatively few of whom have been mentioned in this account—encompass the literary spectrum. Their number has included tough realists and romanticists, experimentalists and traditionalists, despairing conservatives and hopeful liberals, religious-minded individuals and existentialists. Together they have explored almost every facet of Southern life and history, but their collective work achieves more than a great canvas of a region; it is a miniature of the victories and defeats of Western man.

Faulkner shortly before his death.

A land honored by genius

One of America's great writers, winner of the Nobel Prize, William Faulkner devoted some of his most famous novels to picturing the land and people of a not-quite imaginary region he called Yoknapatawpha County—in reality Lafayette County, Mississippi, and its principal town, Oxford, his "own little postage stamp of native soil." His evocations of his "native soil," excerpted from his writings and from an interview he gave, are used on these pages to accompany photographs of Oxford and its environs taken by Martin J. Dain for his book *Faulkner's County: Yoknapatawpha.* They and Faulkner's words re-create the Old South as the author saw it, "opaque, slow, violent, shaping and creating the life of man in its implacable and brooding image."

A great writer's friends and neighbors in his hometown

I write about the people around Oxford. I know them, and they know me. They don't much care what I write. "Why, look here," they'll say. "Bill Faulkner's gone and got his picture in the New York paper. It says here he's written a book." So they come around and try to borrow money, figuring I've made a million dollars. Or else they look twice and figure I couldn't make a thousand.

THE NEW YORK TIMES, NOVEMBER 7, 1948

William's uncle J.W.T. Falkner II. (The author added a "u" to his name.)

Phil Stone, a lawyer and young Faulkner's literary mentor.

Mrs. Calvin Brown, a longtime acquaintance.

Eph and Ed Lowe, friends of the author's.

Red Brite, Faulkner's hunting companion.

The busy yet placid center of Oxford life

Courthouse square.

Through the long afternoon they clotted about the square and before the jail—the clerks, the idle, the countrymen in overalls; the talk.

But above all, the courthouse: the center, the focus, the hub; sitting looming in the center of the county's circumference like a single cloud . . . musing, brooding, symbolic and ponderable, tall as cloud, solid as rock, dominating all: . . .

REQUIEM FOR A NUN

Elderly resident at midday.

A farmer homeward bound.

**Along a sun-baked road
seemingly endless**

The sharp and brittle crack and clatter of its weathered and ungreased wood and metal is slow and terrific: a series of dry sluggish reports carrying for a half mile across the hot still pinewiney silence of the August afternoon. Though the mules plod in a steady and unflagging hypnosis, the vehicle does not seem to progress. It seems to hang suspended in the middle distance forever and forever, so infinitesimal is its progress, like a shabby bead upon the mild red string of road.

LIGHT IN AUGUST

Fishing in a flooded woodland.

A welcome solitude where a man can breathe

Deer hunter.

It is just dawn, daylight: that gray and lonely suspension filled with the peaceful and tentative waking of birds. The air, inbreathed, is like spring water. He breathes deep and slow, feeling with each breath himself diffuse in the neutral grayness, becoming one with loneliness and quiet that has never known fury or despair.

LIGHT IN AUGUST

Lives beyond
desperation and hope

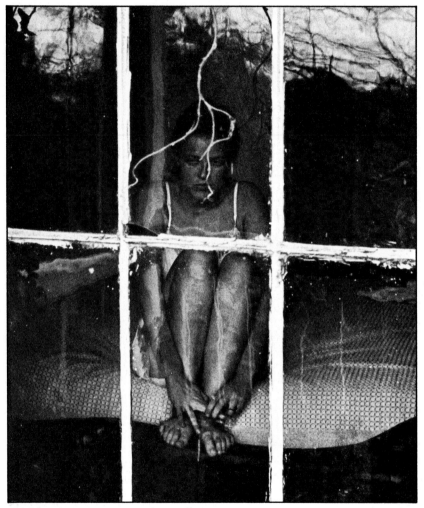

Summer rain.

In the old Oxford jail.

How do our lives ravel out into the no-wind, no-sound, the weary gestures wearily recapitulant: echoes of old compulsions with no-hand on no-strings: in sunset we fall into furious attitudes, dead gestures of dolls.

AS I LAY DYING

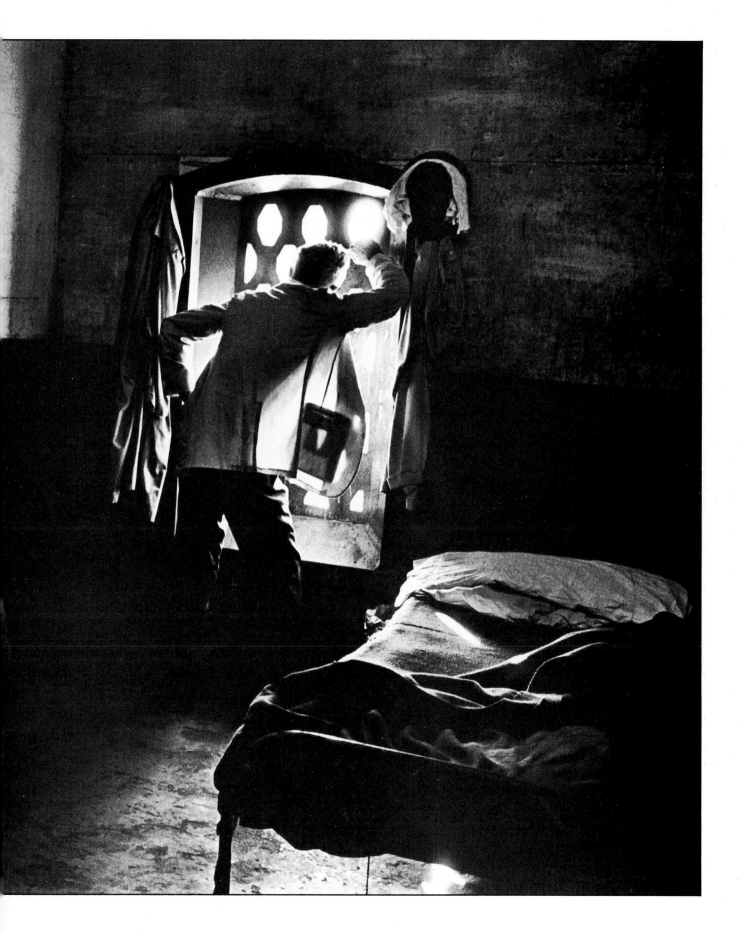

Thoughts of past glory, of
dead men and fallen mansions

The grave of a man killed by Faulkner's great-grandfather during a quarrel.

The Shipp place outside Oxford.

Think of all that has happened here, on this earth. All the blood hot and strong for living, pleasuring, that has soaked back into it. For grieving and suffering too, of course, but still getting something out of it for all that, getting a lot out of it, . . . But you can't be alive forever, and you always wear out life long before you have exhausted the possibilities of living. And all that must be somewhere; all that could not have been invented and created just to be thrown away. . . .

BIG WOODS

Suggested tours

On the following pages six maps show sections of the Old South that are of unusual interest. No attempt has been made to show every road or town. Instead, scenic routes, parks and other special features have been emphasized. The text accompanying each map gives a brief description of the area. Opening dates and hours, especially of the business tours, should be confirmed locally, since they may vary during the year. The six areas covered are shown in the small map below, with a key to the symbols used.

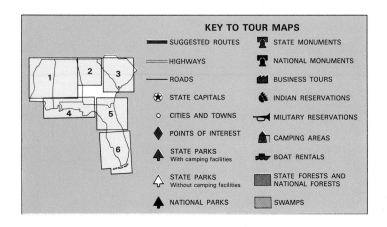

KEY TO TOUR MAPS

▬▬ SUGGESTED ROUTES	🔔 STATE MONUMENTS
═══ HIGHWAYS	🔔 NATIONAL MONUMENTS
─── ROADS	🏭 BUSINESS TOURS
★ STATE CAPITALS	🪶 INDIAN RESERVATIONS
○ CITIES AND TOWNS	🎺 MILITARY RESERVATIONS
◆ POINTS OF INTEREST	⛺ CAMPING AREAS
▲ STATE PARKS With camping facilities	🚤 BOAT RENTALS
△ STATE PARKS Without camping facilities	STATE FORESTS AND NATIONAL FORESTS
▲ NATIONAL PARKS	SWAMPS

1. Mississippi and Alabama

This section of the Old South, dotted with many of the nation's finest antebellum homes, also offers visitors a close look at sites of early Indian settlements, several Civil War battlefields, natural caves filled with colorful rock formations, and even a space-age installation. A good starting point for a tour of the region is Natchez, Mississippi (*bottom left*). Every spring this show place offers tours of many of its antique-filled mansions (*pages 15-31*). At nearby Vicksburg a national military park commemorates the 47-day siege of the city by Union forces in 1863. Northeast of Jackson, the state capital, off Route 397, is Nanih Waiya, the site of a 1,500-year-old Indian ceremonial mound and legendary birthplace of the Choctaw tribe. In the north-central part of the state, at Oxford, the Mary Buie Museum displays prizes awarded the town's famous author, William Faulkner. Ivy Green, birthplace and childhood home of Helen Keller, the remarkable woman who rose to greatness despite being blind and deaf, is on view near Florence, Alabama, northeast of Oxford on Route 72. At nearby Huntsville, NASA's Space Orientation Center offers exhibits of modern rocket engines and man-made satellites. At Russell Cave, in the northeast corner of Alabama, there is a display of relics of Indians who lived in the cave from about 7000 B.C. to 1650 A.D. The tour continues south through Birmingham to Montgomery, capital of Alabama and site of the 1840 house that once served as the home of Jefferson Davis, President of the Confederacy.

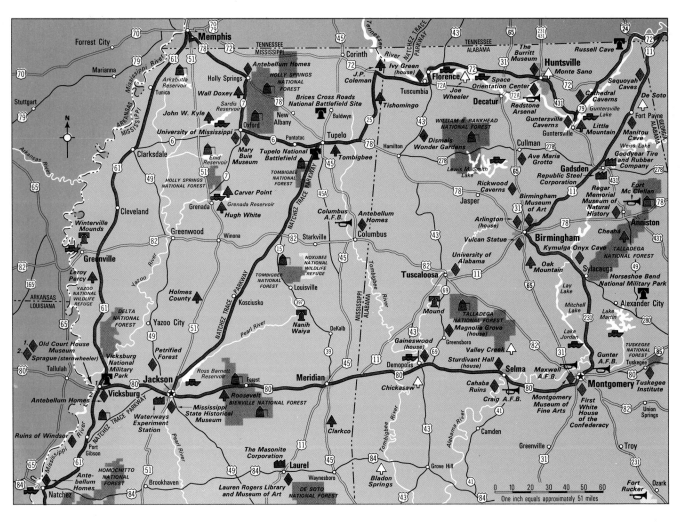

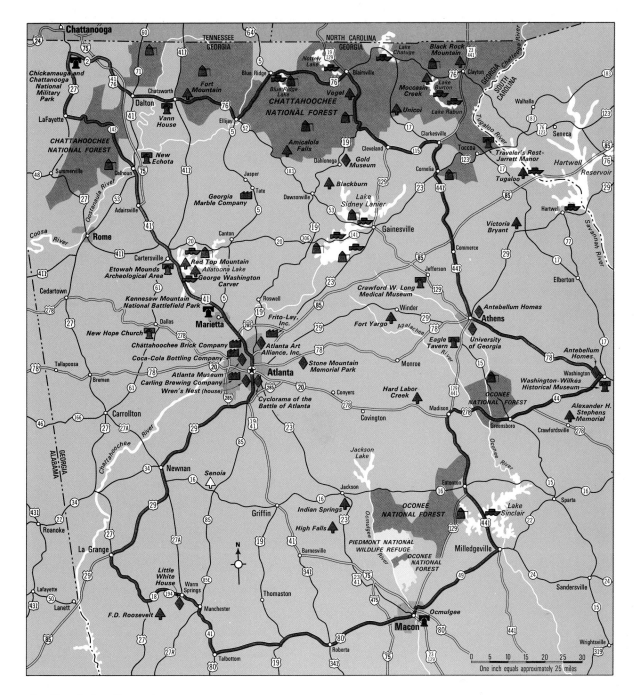

2. Northern Georgia

The scenic mountains and foothills surrounding Atlanta, Georgia's capital, are rich in reminders of the diverse cultures that flourished in the region, from early Indian tribes to the antebellum plantation society. Atlanta itself abounds in urban attractions, among which are numerous museums and galleries. At Grant Park, the Cyclorama depicts the Battle of Atlanta in a three-dimensional combination of a circular painting 50 feet high and 400 feet around and a realistically arranged tableau of scaled, seemingly life-sized figures of Confederate and Union soldiers locked in combat. South of Atlanta the route leads through rolling farm country, past peach orchards and pecan groves to Warm Springs and the Little White House, vacation home of President Franklin Roosevelt. The house is preserved as it was when he died there in 1945, and a nearby museum displays many of his personal effects. East of Warm Springs, near Macon, is Ocmulgee National Monument, where numerous mounds have been excavated to study the Indian mound-building civilization that thrived in the region from about 8000 B.C. to the 1700s A.D. To the northeast lies Washington, one of Georgia's most attractive towns, with some 30 well-preserved antebellum homes. The tour now leads northwest, past Athens, site of the University of Georgia, and through some of the South's most mountainous terrains. A short detour south on Route 19 takes the traveler to Dahlonega, site of a gold rush in the early 19th Century. To the northwest, beyond the Chattahoochee National Forest (ideal for camping), the town of Chatsworth contains the restored 19th Century home of James Vann, sponsor of a mission school for Cherokee Indians. Nearby, the Chickamauga and Chattanooga National Military Park commemorates bloody Civil War battles fought in the area.

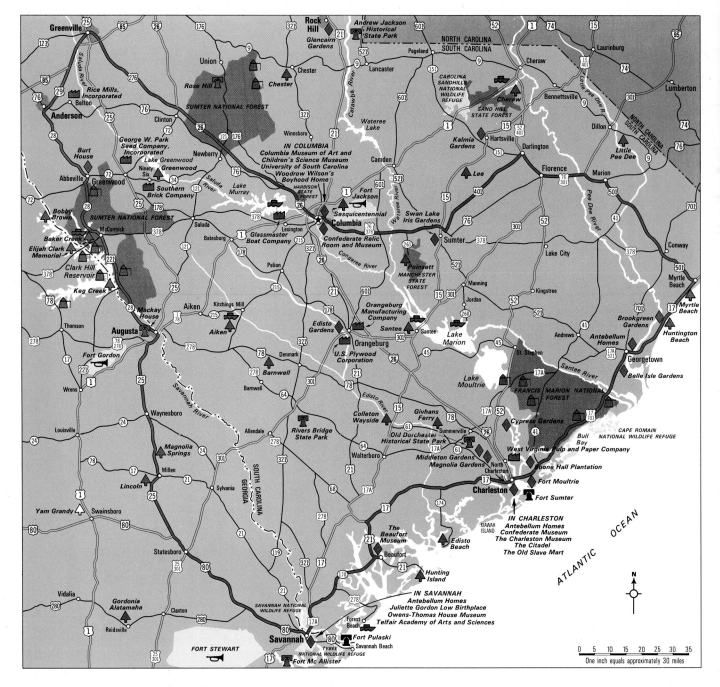

3. South Carolina and eastern Georgia

South Carolina and eastern Georgia, among the first areas to be settled in the Old South, are popular both for their rich historical atmosphere and for their mild climate, which make this region a nearly year-round vacationland. A circular tour will cover major points of interest along the island-dotted coast as well as the pine-forested interior.

Savannah (*bottom center on map*), an ideal starting point for such a tour, was Georgia's first city and its first capital. As a defense against Indian raids, British General James Oglethorpe, who planned most of the town, set up a system of 52 squares that served as rallying points for armed men; these squares are now small but attractive parks that enhance the city's charm. Route 170, northeast out of Savannah, leads to Beaufort, South Carolina, site of The Beaufort Museum, with relics of the region's settlements dating back to the 1560s. Charleston, often

called the coast's most attractive city, is northeast via Routes 21 and 17. It was founded by Englishmen in the 17th Century and is still filled with homes dating from the late 1700s and early 1800s. In Charleston Harbor, motor launches take visitors to Fort Sumter, where the first shots of the Civil War were fired. Farther north on Route 17 is Myrtle Beach, in the heart of the Grand Strand, South Carolina's seashore resort area. Along with broad, white beaches, this section offers some of the East Coast's finest golfing, with five championship courses open year-round. Now turning inland, the road passes through low marshland and past fields of cotton and tobacco to Darlington. There stock-car racing fans gather every May for the Rebel 300 race, and in September for the Southern 500. Southwest on Route 401 near Sumter are the Swan Lake Iris Gardens, displays of jasmine, wisteria, Japanese iris and Cherokee roses that

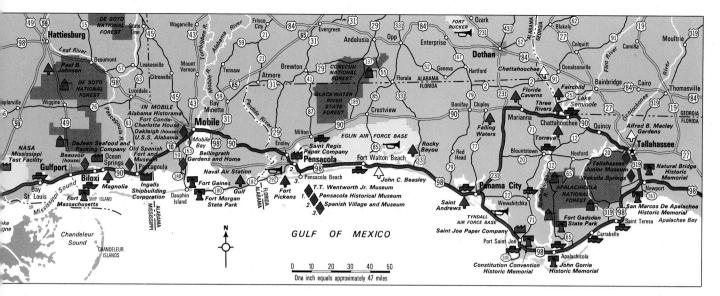

One inch equals approximately 47 miles

4. The Gulf Coast

The north coast of the Gulf of Mexico, which includes parts of Mississippi, Alabama and Florida, is an area of lush semitropical beauty that is also rich in history, from the era of Spanish colonization through today's ventures into outer space. Entering this region from the west, a traveler on Route 90 passes NASA's Mississippi Test Facility, on the Louisiana-Mississippi border near Bay St. Louis. There visitors may tour the installation where rockets destined for use in moon flights are tested. In Biloxi the retirement home of Confederacy President Jefferson Davis, Beauvoir, is now a museum. At Pascagoula is the Old Spanish Fort and Museum, built in 1718 of wood, mud, moss and shells; it houses relics from the time of the Indians and Spanish colonies to the Civil War era. Across the border, Mobile, Alabama, is set on the shores of beautiful Mobile Bay. Some 35 miles of the streets in and around the city have been marked off as the Azalea Trail, a route best followed in February and March when the flowers are in bloom. A highlight in any season is Oakleigh, an antebellum house completed in 1838 and furnished today in early Victorian, Empire and Regency styles. Bellingrath Gardens and Home, south of

Mobile, is an 800-acre estate of formal gardens, azalea-lined trails and forests. In the center of the estate, the Bellingrath home contains a fine collection of china and rare porcelains. Farther east is Pensacola, known as the "City of Five Flags" because it has been governed by Spain, France, England, the Confederacy and the United States. At Pensacola's well-known Naval Air Station, exhibits show the growth of flight and include models of the Navy's first airplanes and an original training biplane from World War I. Now and then visitors may see the Navy's precision jet flying team, the Blue Angels, which is stationed at Pensacola. East of Pensacola, at Panama City, travelers may either continue along the coast highway (Route 98) or turn inland, first along Routes 231 and 90 to Marianna and Florida Caverns State Park. There a cavern hollowed from limestone reveals unusual underground rock formations. Route 90 continues east to Tallahassee, the state capital, where the Tallahassee Junior Museum displays a 40-acre restoration of an 1880 Florida farm. Nearby Wakulla Springs, one of Florida's biggest springs, offers trips in glass-bottomed boats across waters nearly 200 feet deep yet clear as crystal.

surround a small lake populated by black and white mute swans. Among the sights of Columbia, the state capital, are the University of South Carolina and Woodrow Wilson's Boyhood Home. Northwest, beyond Sumter National Forest (with its excellent camping facilities), is Greenville, the center of South Carolina's textile manufacturing district. At Abbeville, to the south via Routes 29 and 28, the pre-Civil War Burt House has been preserved as it was when the Confederate Cabinet held its last meeting there in May of 1865. Nearby, forming part of the border between South Carolina and Georgia, the Clark Hill Reservoir offers excellent boating and fresh-water fishing. The adjacent Elijah Clark Memorial State Park, in Georgia, honors the Revolutionary War hero and American leader during the Battle of Augusta. Augusta, Georgia, is famed as the site of the Masters Golf Tournament, played there every April.

5. Northern Florida and southern Georgia

This region, with its wildlife preserves, historical sites, beautiful lakes and dazzling beaches, is perfectly geared to the vacationer. In its upper part lies Waycross, Georgia, gateway to the Okefenokee Swamp. Now largely a national wildlife refuge covering more than 300,000 acres, the swamp was called the "land of the trembling earth" by the Seminole Indians. Board walks extend into the swamp and guided boat tours can be arranged.

Southwest of the swamp, on the Suwannee River at White Springs, Florida, is a memorial to composer Stephen Foster. In this 243-acre park, animated dioramas illustrate some of Foster's most famous folk songs, and there is a collection of antique musical instruments and Foster memorabilia. Gainesville, to the south, is the home of the University of Florida.

South of Gainesville is Silver Springs, largest of Florida's celebrated springs. At the entrance to Silver Springs is a museum that features antique automobiles,

and glass-bottomed boat trips are offered through the springs' underground caverns.

Southeast of Silver Springs lies Orlando, one of Florida's most beautiful cities. Near Orlando hundreds of small lakes offer excellent bass fishing. East of Orlando, near Titusville, is the spectacular John F. Kennedy Space Center. Here the visitor can tour the nation's space port, view an exhibit of spacecraft and see the world's largest building, the 52-story Vertical Assembly Building.

North of the space center the route passes Daytona Beach, famous for its speedway, and the delightful Marineland of Florida with its noted porpoise acts. Farther north lies Saint Augustine, the oldest city in the nation. Founded in 1565, Saint Augustine offers numerous monuments, among them the Castillo de San Marcos National Monument, the oldest masonry fort in the U.S. Begun in about 1672—it was never completed—the fort withstood the assaults of pirates, Indians and the English.

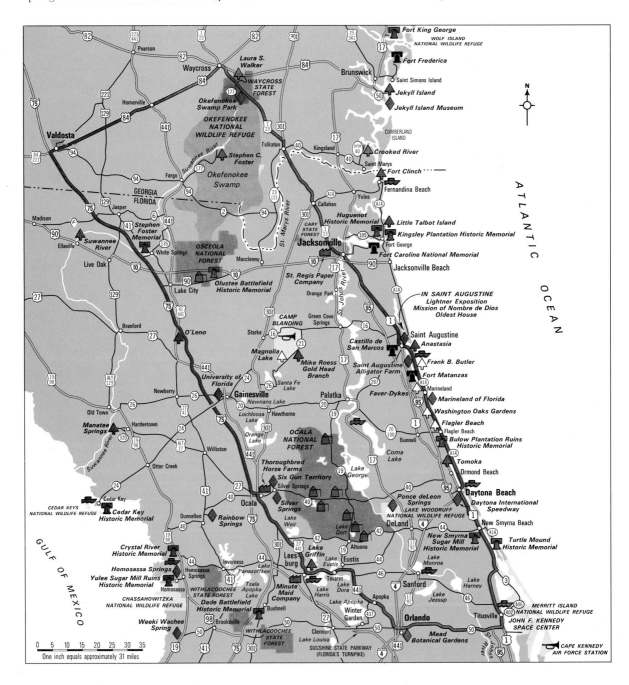

6. Southern Florida

Southern Florida is a something-for-everybody place: a year-round playground and a quiet area for those who want to relax; a historical site and a circus midway; an exotic wildlife refuge and a busy center for sports-car racing; a plush haven for the champagne set and a budget vacationland for the coffee-and-doughnut crowd.

Most of the region's major attractions can be seen on a circle tour starting in Saint Petersburg (*upper left of map*). In that city, the local Historical Society Museum displays Florida flora and fauna as well as relics and memorabilia from early Indian times, the era of Spanish colonization and the Civil War years. Across the bay in Tampa, the Anheuser-Busch brewery offers tours of its elaborate Busch Gardens, which includes a reproduction of the African veldt stocked with lions, zebras and other wild animals. East, on Route 17, outside of Winter Haven, is Cypress Gardens, with its lush flowers and popular water-skiing show. Continuing eastward, Route

60 leads to the Atlantic Coast and Vero Beach, where the Piper Aircraft Corporation conducts visitors through its aircraft assembly lines. From here, Route 1, the coast drive, leads south past impressive white beaches and nearby the elegant resort town of Palm Beach. Some 60 miles farther south is the southern goal of thousands of vacationers, winter and summer, Miami Beach, with accommodations and activities for every taste and pocketbook. South of Miami Route 1 continues to the sea and across open water and low coral keys to Key West. The highway from Miami back toward Saint Petersburg (Route 41) goes across the Everglades, through Naples, with its spectacular Caribbean Gardens, to Sarasota, one of the state's most popular retirement communities. There the 37-acre estate of circus entrepreneur John Ringling has been turned into a public museum containing a collection of baroque art and such memorabilia of circus life as wagons, costumes and early circus posters.

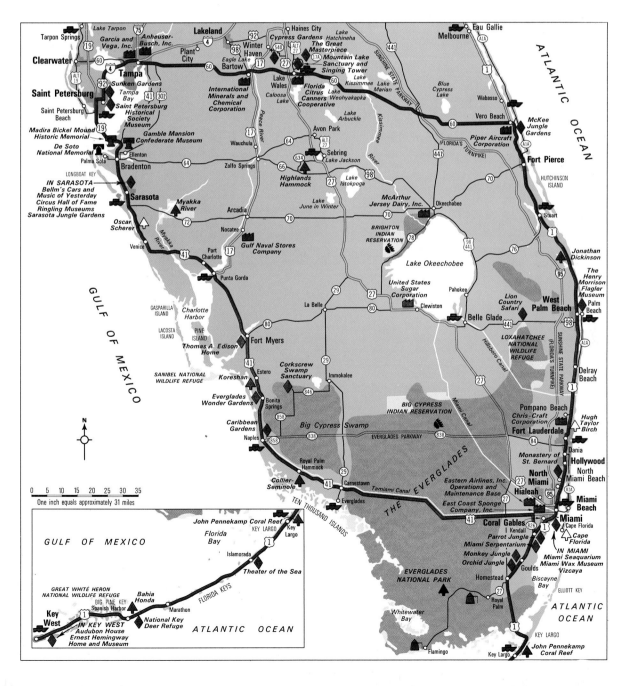

Museums and galleries

Alabama

Anniston
Regar Memorial Museum of Natural History, 1411 Gurnee Ave. Zoology; Indian artifacts. Tues-Fri 10-5:30; Sat 10-5; Sun 2-5.

Birmingham
Arlington Historical Society, 331 Cotton Ave., S.W. Civil War weapons; doll display; antebellum furnishings. Mon-Sat 9-5; Sun 1-6.

Birmingham Museum of Art, Oscar Wells Memorial Bldg., 200 8th Ave. Paintings; American Indian and pre-Columbian artifacts. Mon-Sat 10-5; Sun 2-6.

Huntsville
NASA Marshall Space Flight Center, Space Orientation Center. Exhibits of rockets and spacecraft. Tours Mon-Sat 8-4:30; Sun 1-5.

Montgomery
First White House of the Confederacy, Washington and Union Sts. Home of Jefferson Davis and family; personal property; war relics. Daily 9-4:30.

Montgomery Museum of Fine Arts, 440 S. McDonough St. Paintings; Civil War items. Tues-Sat 10-5; Sun 2:30-5.

Moundville
University of Alabama Museum of Natural History, Mound State Monument. Artifacts from the area illustrating traits and characteristics of prehistoric people. Daily 9-5.

Tuscumbia
Birthplace of Helen Keller, 300 W. North Commons. Historic 1820 main house and small cottage used as school; original furniture. Mon-Sat 8-5; Sun 1-5.

Tuskegee
Tuskegee Institute, George Washington Carver Museum. Dioramas of Negro contributions to civilization; sculpture and paintings by American Negroes. Mon-Sat 10-4; Sun 12-4.

Florida

Bushnell
Dade Battlefield Historic Memorial Museum, 3180 Dade Battlefield Memorial. Artifacts of Seminole Indians; site of Dade Massacre. Daily 9-5.

Cape Kennedy
Air Force Space Museum, Complex 26. Site of first U.S. satellite launching; complete space museum; German V-1s; Titan, Minuteman and Polaris weapons systems. Sun 9-4:30.

Jacksonville
Fort Caroline National Memorial, 12713 Fort Caroline Rd. French colonial memorabilia. Mon-Fri 8:30-5; Sat, Sun, hols 9-5:30.

Key West
Audubon House, Whitehead and Green Sts. John James Audubon prints. Tues-Sun 9-12, 1-5.

Ernest Hemingway Home and Museum, 907 Whitehead St. Built of native limestone, home of author from 1931-1961; mementos and furnishings. Daily 9-5.

Marineland
Marine Studios, State Rte. A1A. Deep-sea life; tropical fish. Daily 8-6.

Miami
Historical Museum of Southern Florida and the Caribbean, 2010 N. Bayshore Dr. Indian artifacts; area history; aviation exhibits. Tues-Sun 1-5.

Miami Seaquarium, Virginia Key. Sharks, rays, turtles; species of reef and game fish. Porpoise and seal shows. Daily 9-5:30.

Museum of Science and Natural History, Inc., 3280 S. Miami Ave. Birds, reptiles, amphibians; planetarium. Mon-Sat 9-5; Mon eves 8-10; Sun 2-5.

Miami Beach
Bass Museum, 2100 Collins Ave. Renaissance painting; sculpture; French drawings. Tues-Fri 10-11:30, 1-9; Sat 10-11:30, 1-5.

Palm Beach
The Henry Morrison Flagler Museum, Whitewall Way. Seventeenth Century fans; antique china; railroad room. Tues-Sun 10-5.

Pensacola
Naval Aviation Museum, U.S. Naval Air Station. Naval aviation and warfare relics; models. Tours daily at 1:30.

St. Augustine
Castillo de San Marcos and Fort Matanzas National Monuments. Historic documents; Indian archeology. Daily 8:30-5:30.

The Oldest House, 14 St. Francis St. 1702-1727 house; Spanish glass and furniture. June 15-Sept 1: daily 8-8; Sept 2-June 14: daily 9-6.

Sarasota
The John and Mable Ringling Museum of Art, 5401 Bay Shore Rd. European paintings; decorative arts; theater history. Mon-Sat 9-5; Sun 1-5.

Ringling Museum of the Circus, 5401 Bay Shore Rd. Illustrated history of the circus; circus equipment; model circus. Mon-Sat 9-5; Sun 1-5.

Georgia

Athens
University of Georgia, Georgia Museum of Art, Jackson St. Collection of American artists. Mon-Fri 9-5:30; Sat 9-12.

Atlanta
Atlanta Art Alliance, Inc., 1280 Peachtree St., N.E. Kress collection of Italian Renaissance art; European, American and Oriental art. Mon 5-10; Tues-Sat 10-5; Sun 12-5.

Atlanta Museum, 537-539 Peachtree St. Items from Georgia, Confederate and world history; paintings, sculpture, prints. Mon-Sat 10-5.

Atlanta University Center Gallery, 233 Chestnut St., S.W. Contemporary and Negro American art. Tues, Thurs, Sat, Sun 2-5.

Augusta
Augusta Museum, 540 Telfair St. Archeology; ethnology; Civil War and local history. Tues-Sat 2-6; Sun 2-5.

Calhoun
New Echota, State Rte. 225. Restoration of 1825 Cherokee Nation capital. Winter: Mon-Sat 9-5; Sun 2-5; summer: Mon-Sat 9-6; Sun 2-6.

Columbus
Columbus Museum of Arts and Crafts, Inc., 1251 Wynton Rd. Contemporary art; French and Italian prints; china; ivories; Persian rugs. Tues-Sat 10-5; Sun 3-6. Closed last two weeks of Aug.

Fort Benning
The Infantry Museum, Ingersol St. Weapons, equipment and documents of the U.S. Army from French and Indian Wars to present. Tues, Thurs 10-2; Wed, Fri-Sat 12:30-4:30.

Fort Oglethorpe
Chickamauga and Chattanooga Military Park, Chickamauga Battlefield Visitor Center. Civil War relics; collection of arms. Daily 8-5.

Macon
Macon Youth Museums, Inc., 4182 Forsyth Rd. Archeological, anthropological and historical items; native wildlife; planetarium. Tues-Sat 9-5:30; Sun, Mon, hols 2-5:30. Closed Sept.

Savannah
Juliette Gordon Low Birthplace, 10 E. Oglethorpe Ave. Possessions of Juliette Gordon Low, founder of the Girl Scouts of the United States of America; Girl Scout memorabilia. Mon-Sat 9-4:30; Sun 2-4:30.

Telfair Academy of Arts and Sciences, Inc., 121 Barnard St. American paintings of 18th-20th Centuries; graphic and decorative arts. Mon 12-5; Tues-Sat 10-5; Sun 3-5. Closed Aug.

Savannah Beach
Fort Pulaski National Monument. Civil War artillery and ammunition. Daily 8:30-5:30.

Warm Springs
Franklin D. Roosevelt Warm Springs Memorial Commission. Little White House. Sept-June: daily 9-5; July-Aug: 9-6.

Mississippi

Biloxi
Jefferson Davis Shrine and Memorial Gardens. Last home of Jefferson Davis; antique furniture; apparel; firearms. Daily 9-5.

Jackson
Old Capitol State Historical Museum, Capitol and N. State Sts. Chronological exhibits of Mississippi history. Tues-Sat 9:30-4:30; Sun 12:30-4:30.

Ridgeland Visitor Center, Natchez Trace Pkwy. History of the Natchez Trace. Daily 9-4:45.

Laurel
Lauren Rodgers Library and Museum of Art, 5th Ave. at 7th St. Furniture of 18th and 19th Centuries; paintings; sculpture; prints. Oriental and Indian artifacts. Tues-Fri 10-12, 2-5; Sat 10-12; Sun 2-5

Pascagoula
Old Spanish Fort and Museum, 200 Fort St. Built of pine, oyster shells, mud and moss; Indian

artifacts; Revolutionary and Civil War weapons. Daily 9-5.

Vicksburg
Mississippi River Museum and Hall of Fame, Vicksburg City Waterfront. *Sprague,* 1901 stern-wheeler; paintings, photographs, models. Daily 8-dusk.

Vicksburg National Military Park, Confederate Ave. Civil War relics and displays. Daily 8:30-5.

South Carolina

Charleston
The Charleston Museum, Rutledge Ave. and Calhoun St. Founded in 1773; rice culture; pottery, ironwork, silver; small arms; natural and cultural history. Mon-Sat 10-5; Sun 2-5.

The Citadel Memorial Military Museum, Moultrie St. and Hagood Ave. Citadel history; military art; military equipment. Mon-Fri 2-5; Sat 8-5; Sun 2-5.

Confederate Museum, Market and Meeting Sts. First Confederate flag raised over Fort Sumter; items related to Robert E. Lee and Jefferson Davis. Mar-May, July, Aug: Mon-Fri 9-1.

Old Powder Magazine, 79 Cumberland St. Memorabilia of colonial South Carolina. Sept-July: Tues-Sat 9-4.

The Old Slave Mart, 6 Chalmers St. Documents; maps; slave-made handicrafts. Mon-Sat 10-5; Sun 2-5.

Columbia
Columbia Museum of Art and Children's Science Museum, 1112 Bull St. Science displays; natural history; planetarium; Indian relics; period furniture; costumed dolls. Tues-Sat 10-5; Sun 2-6.

Kings Mountain
Kings Mountain National Military Park. Revolutionary War items. Mon-Sat 8:30-5; Sun 9:30-5:30.

Lancaster
Andrew Jackson Historical State Park, State Rte. 1. Indian relics; household objects; tools; firearms; textiles; art collection. Tues-Sat 9-5:30; Sun 1-6.

Santee
South Carolina Indian Museum, State Rte. 95. Artifacts of Indians who lived nearby. Mon-Fri 8-6; Sat, Sun 9-6.

Spartanburg
Regional Museum of Spartanburg County, 501 Otis Blvd. Regional furniture; early American lighting devices; dolls. Tues-Sat 10-1, 3-5; Sun 2-5.

Walnut Grove Plantation, near intersection of Rtes. 26 and 221. Furnishings; wrought iron; earthenware. Mar-Nov: Tues-Sat 10-5; Sun 2-5; Dec-Feb: Mon-Fri 11-4.

Sullivan's Island
Fort Sumter National Monument. Fascinating items from Revolutionary and Civil War periods. Daily 8-4:30.

Local festivals and events

Alabama
Azalea Trail Festival, Mobile. Dazzling azalea displays; Mardi Gras parades and balls; jazz festival; tours of Mobile's antebellum houses; selection of America's Junior Miss. Feb—Mar.

South Alabama Annual Rattlesnake Rodeo, Opp. For months preceding the event, local people scour the hills for rattlesnakes and display them at the rodeo; also exhibitions of snake handling, venom milking; rattlesnake barbecue. Late Feb.

National Shooting Dog Championship, Sedgefield Plantation, Union Springs. Bird-dog field trials in which hunters on horseback use blank shells. Mar.

Southern Skirmish Association, Fort Gaines, Dauphin Island. "Black powder" target competition for Civil War cannon, muskets and pistols. Twice a year: Apr and Aug.

Guntersville Boat Races, Lake Guntersville. Annual event features races for all classes of power- and sailboats; beauty contest. Last week in July.

Florida
Greyhound Dog Racing, Miami. West Flagler Kennel Club. Year-round.

Stephen Foster Week, White Springs. Daily bell concerts of composer's works from 200-foot, 97-bell Carillon Tower. Mid-Jan.

Silver Spurs Mid-Winter Rodeo, Kissimmee. Top U.S. cowboys compete with local talent; livestock show; rodeo-queen crowning. Feb.

Edison Pageant of Light, Fort Myers. Thomas A. Edison's winter home, with a laboratory attached, was in this city for half a century; eight-day celebration includes Grand Parade, fireworks, coronation of Queen. Second week in Feb.

Gasparilla Pirate Invasion, Tampa. Full-rigged pirate ship sails into the harbor and buccaneers take the city; parade of floats and bands. Second week in Feb.

Gator Bowl Festival, Jacksonville. Various sporting events, including a basketball tournament and a football game pairing two of the nation's top college teams. Last two weeks in Dec.

Orange Bowl Festival, Miami. Eighteen days of festivities, including regattas, tennis tournaments and parades, topped off by North-South football game in Orange Bowl Stadium. Dec 14—Jan 1.

Georgia
Continental Field Trials, Quitman. Nationally recognized trials to pick top bird dogs. Mid-Jan.

Masters Golf Tournament, Augusta National Golf Course, Augusta. One of the most prestigious professional golf tournaments in the world. Four days, early Apr.

Atlanta Arts Festival, Piedmont Park. Outdoor exhibitions of pottery making, hand carving, painting; also concerts ranging from folk to classical. One week, late May.

Atlanta Classic, Atlanta. Championship PGA golf at the Atlanta Country Club. Late May—early June.

Coaches All-America Football Game, Atlanta Stadium. Sixty former All-America football players take part in the season's first football game. Late June.

Rattlesnake Roundup, Whigham. Natives and visitors join for a weekend of snake hunting. Late Sept.

Mississippi
Dixie National Livestock Show and Rodeo, Jackson. One of the largest in the South; features nightly championship rodeo at coliseum; judging of every kind of stock from cows to quarter horses. Early Feb.

Pilgrimages, state-wide. Guided tours of antebellum houses and gardens in most of the big cities. Mar—May.

Dixie Showboat Players, Vicksburg. Melodramas in old riverboat style. Fri-Sat eves, Mar—Aug.

Mississippi Arts Festival, Jackson. Art exhibits, concerts, dramatic and musical productions. Late Apr.

Shrimp Festival, Biloxi. Ushering in the shrimp season, this festival includes blessing of the fleet, crowning of King and Queen. Early June.

Neshoba County Fair, Philadelphia. Major state political campaigns are traditionally opened here; daylong speeches; agricultural exhibit. Early Aug.

South Carolina
Polo Matches, Aiken. Both professional and amateur players take part. Suns, Feb—Apr.

Carolina Cup Races, Camden. Steeplechase and flat racing; main event is a three-mile race over obstacles in open country. Late Mar.

Sun Fun Festival, Myrtle Beach. Largest state festival; sand-castle-building contests; stock-car races; crowning of Miss Sun Fun U.S.A. Early June.

Carolina Summer Jazz Festival, Columbia. Nation's leading Dixieland and progressive jazz exponents play all day and half the night. July 4.

Southern 500 Festival, Darlington. Parades, street dances, beauty contests and barbecues culminate in annual stock-car races. Labor Day.

Bulls Island Annual Bow and Arrow Hunt, McClellanville. Hunters are welcome to hunt for deer, wild turkey, raccoons and squirrels. Dec.

Wildlife of the Old South

A sampling of the natural life frequently found in the Old South is given on this and the following pages. In each case both the common name and scientific name of the plant or animal are given. The information supplied is not intended to be comprehensive; for additional material on the fauna and flora of the region the reader should refer to specialized books on wildlife. A number of useful reference works that contain such information are listed on page 188.

Mammals

Virginia opossum

When threatened, this omnivorous, cat-sized marsupial, *Didelphis virginiana*, "plays possum," i.e., feigns death so it will be passed up by predators.

Seminole bat

The tree-dwelling, mahogany-brown *Lasiurus seminola*, three to four inches long with a wingspread of about a foot, is rarely found outside the South.

Eastern fox squirrel

Sciurus niger, a slow walker and clumsy climber, is the largest Eastern tree squirrel, up to 28 inches long. In search of food, it will forage over nearly 10 acres.

Southeastern pocket gopher

Geomys pinetis, named for its pocketlike cheek pouches, spends most of its time in underground tunnels, which it can dig at the rate of up to 300 feet a night.

Rice rat

Oryzomy palustris ranges from forest clearings in the Piedmont to coastal salt marshes, where in colonial times it was a threat to the plantations' rice crops.

Florida water rat

Also called a round-tailed muskrat, *Neofiber alleni* lives in marshes and on boggy ground, where it digs tunnels leading to its basketball-sized grassy nest.

Marsh rabbit

An oddity among rabbits, the *Sylvilagus palustris*, found among the marshes of the coast, can walk as well as hop and is an excellent swimmer.

Key deer

Smallest of the Eastern deer, *Odocoileus virginianus clavium* lives on Florida's southernmost Keys. Once nearly extinct, the deer are increasing in numbers.

Fish and reptiles

Black crappie

Sometimes called a calico bass, *Pomoxis nigro-maculatus* stays in large schools in ponds and sluggish streams. Though tasty, it is not caught commercially.

Large-mouth black bass

Micropterus salmoides is the largest of the black bass; some that live in the mud-bottomed ponds and swamps of Florida may weigh up to 25 pounds.

Tarpon

Tarpon atlanticus, the "silver king," is one of the most prized of game fishes. Easily hooked, it puts up a lengthy and spectacular fight, making it hard to land.

Great barracuda

A fast-moving predator, *Sphyraena barracuda* has been known to attack man. Usually it follows schools of fish, darting in swiftly to make its catch.

182

Spanish mackerel

Scomberomorus maculatus, the familiar Spanish mackerel, is one of the South's most important commercial fish, with an annual catch of some 10 million pounds.

Atlantic sailfish

Istiophorus americanus, mounted with its sail-like dorsal fin extended, is a favorite trophy of fishermen. Landing it may take an hour or more of hard work.

Pompano

Trachinotus carolinus is found along the west coast of Florida from midwinter to early spring. A favorite with gourmets, it brings a high price on the market.

Dolphin

Coryphaena hippurus, sometimes reaching a length of six feet, is among the fastest-swimming fish, partly because of its tapered, streamlined shape.

Pensacola red snapper

The red snapper *(Lutianus blackfordi)*, an important food fish, stays almost exclusively in deep water from Brazil to Florida, feeding on other fish.

Sheepshead

Another popular game fish, *Archosargus probatocephalus* ranges from the North Atlantic to the Gulf of Mexico, occasionally swimming up fresh-water rivers.

American alligator

Distinguished from the sharp-nosed crocodile by a broadly rounded snout, *Alligator mississippiensis* inhabits swamps in all the states of the Old South.

Yellow-bellied turtle

Due probably to its ability tc scavenge, *Pseudemys scripta scripta* is managing to survive in many of the South's polluted lakes and streams.

Atlantic loggerhead turtle

A marine giant weighing up to 900 pounds, *Caretta caretta caretta* has some commercial value as food; its meat looks much like beefsteak.

Southern fence lizard

When chased from its perch on a log or fence, the four-to-seven-inch *Sceloporus undulatus undulatus* easily scampers to safety up a nearby tree.

Eastern coral snake

Micrurus fulvius fulvius can be distinguished from harmless banded snakes by noting that its yellow band ("caution") touches the red ("stop").

Eastern cottonmouth

When aroused, the poisonous *Agkistrodon piscivorus piscivorus* vibrates its tail and opens its mouth, revealing the white interior that gives it its name.

Birds

Water turkey

Anhinga anhinga leucogaster, named for its long, turkeylike tail, lives in rice fields and swamps, where it swims with only its head and neck above water.

American egret

Snowy-white, yellow-billed *Casmerodius albus egretta* is extremely shy in the wild, but loses its fear and suspicion of man when raised in captivity.

Wood ibis

Properly called a stork, *Mycteria americana* nests in trees in swamps from South Carolina to Texas, wandering as far north as New England in the summer.

Marsh hawk

In search of its prey of mice, frogs and snakes, *Circus cyaneus hudsonius* gracefully glides just above the tops of the bushes on its flexible, four-foot wings.

Wild turkey

Once abundant as far north as Nova Scotia, *Meleagris gallopavo* still lives in Southern fields and meadows, and in deep woods where it roosts in trees.

Purple gallinule

Porphyrula martinica is one of the most colorful of water birds, with a deep-purple head and under parts, green back, yellow-tipped red bill and yellow legs.

Eastern willet

Also called a stone curlew, *Catoptrophorus semipalmatus* is named for its constant high and clear musical call, which sounds something like *pilly-willy-willet*.

Laughing gull

The song of *Larus atricilla* sounds like a harsh, high-pitched laugh. The gull is often seen far out at sea, circling around or following vessels in search of castoff food.

Carolina wren

Thryothorus ludovicianus is the largest of the wrens. Singing the year around, regardless of the weather, it nests in both tree branches and hollow stumps.

Mockingbird

A common bird of the Old South, *Mimus polyglottos polyglottos* can mimic the songs of a dozen other birds in addition to singing its own wide variety of songs.

Pine warbler

The green-and-yellow *Dendroica pinus* nearly always nests in pine trees, and feeds on pine seeds and berries when its normal diet of insects is not available.

Painted bunting

With its indigo head, green back and red breast, the male *Passerina ciris* is one of America's most colorful birds. But it usually perches too high to be spotted.

Flowers and trees

Pine lily

Lilium catesbaei, also called a leopard lily, is a common flower in moist pine woods and swamps. The petals are mostly red and are long and sharp-pointed.

Southern blue flag

In the spring, *Iris hexagona* adds a brilliant blue hue to gardens throughout the South, and also to swamps and other moist lands where it grows wild.

Swamp rose mallow

A large plant found in brackish and fresh-water swamps, *Hibiscus moscheutos* grows up to six feet tall, with petals of cream and crimson six inches across.

Cypress vine

Clusters of scarlet flowers bloom from late summer through early fall on the 10-to-20-foot-long stems of *Ipomoea quamoclit*, a type of morning-glory.

Japanese honeysuckle

Though colorful, with a strong, sweet scent, *Lonicera japonica* is also a destructive weed, smothering other plants and trees in its tight tangle of vines.

Purple passion flower

European explorers, seeing in its blossoms a resemblance to Christ's crown of thorns, named the purple *Passiflora incarnata*, the passion flower.

Longleaf pine

Clusters of needles up to 18 inches long identify *Pinus palustris*, whose hard wood is important for flooring and whose sap supplies resin and turpentine.

Loblolly pine

Pinus taeda, tallest of the Southern pines, reaches 150 feet or more in height. It frequently grows in natural depressions locally called loblollies.

Bald cypress

A wide base helps balance *Taxodium distichum* on its unstable bed in swamps, while its roots rise like stumplike "knees." It is often used for railway ties.

Southern white cedar

A dark swamp tree, *Chamaecyparis thyoides* produces wood that is very resistant to decay, making it excellent for shingles and siding.

Cabbage palmetto

Forming dense groves from Florida to South Carolina, *Sabal palmetto* has no limbs; its fanlike leaves grow directly from its 20- to-30-foot-high trunk.

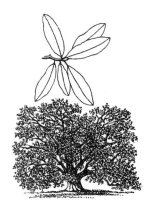

Live oak

The low, spreading *Quercus virginiana* is a symbol of the Old South, with limbs that are bigger than most tree trunks and are often hung with Spanish moss.

Southern magnolia

With rich green leaves, similar in texture to leather, and strongly scented white flowers, *Magnolia grandiflora* is perhaps the most attractive of all Southern trees.

Sassafras

Sassafras albidum can grow to 90 feet. A useful tree, its roots are boiled to make tea, its leaves are added to soup for flavor, and its oil is used in perfume.

Sweet gum

The corklike bark of *Liquidambar styraciflua* oozes a fragrant, sweet gum, good for chewing, and its fine-grained wood makes an easily stained, hard veneer.

Common persimmon

Found throughout the South, *Diospyros virginiana* bears an orange to purple fruit with a harsh, astringent flavor that turns sweet after the first frost.

Statistical information

Origin of state name, state nicknames, date of admission, capital

Alabama: Name is probably derived from Choctaw Indian words *"alba ayamule,"* best translated as "thicket clearers"; Cotton State, Yellowhammer State, Heart of Dixie; admitted 1819 (the 22nd state); Montgomery.

Florida: Named for *Pascua Florida,* as the Spanish called Easter Sunday, the time when Ponce de León may have first sighted the coast of the peninsula in 1513; Sunshine State; admitted 1845 (the 27th state); Tallahassee.

Georgia: Named for King George II of Great Britain when the land was chartered as a colony in 1732; Empire State of the South, Peach State, Cracker State, Goober State among others; 1788 (fourth of the original 13 states to ratify the Constitution); Atlanta.

Mississippi: Named after the river —from the Ojibway Indian words *"misi sipi,"* meaning "great river" or "father of the waters"— that forms most of its western boundary; Magnolia State; admitted 1817 (the 20th state); Jackson.

South Carolina: First called Carolana in honor of Charles I, became Carolina in the charter of 1663 issued by Charles II; Palmetto State; 1788 (eighth of the original 13 states to ratify the Constitution); Columbia.

Population

By state *(1968 Editor and Publisher Market Guide,* January 1, 1968, estimate): Florida: 6,352,852. Georgia: 4,589,787. Alabama: 3,619,548. South Carolina: 2,623,236. Mississippi: 2,454,765.

By city (region's 10 largest cities are listed below, followed by their population according to the January 1, 1968, estimate of the *1968 Editor and Publisher Market Guide):*

Atlanta, Georgia: 537,175.
Miami, Florida: 386,778.
Birmingham, Alabama: 362,704.
Tampa, Florida: 334,639.
Mobile, Alabama: 251,040.
St. Petersburg, Florida: 222,271.
Jacksonville, Florida: 189,370.
Jackson, Mississippi: 177,495.
Montgomery, Alabama: 154,955.
Savannah, Georgia: 149,693.

Total areas

Georgia: 58,876 square miles.
Florida: 58,560 square miles.
Alabama: 51,609 square miles.
Mississippi: 47,716 square miles.
South Carolina: 31,055 square miles.

Principal rivers (total lengths in miles)

Note: Only the states in the Old South region that these rivers flow through are named.

Mississippi (Mississippi): 2,348.

Tennessee (Mississippi, Alabama): 652.

Apalachicola-Chattahoochee (Florida, Alabama, Georgia): 500.

Pearl (Mississippi): 490.

Pee Dee-Yadkin (South Carolina): 435.

Tombigbee (Mississippi, Alabama): 409.

Big Black (Mississippi): 330.

Alabama (Alabama): 315.

Savannah (Georgia, South Carolina): 314.

Tallahatchie (Mississippi): 301.

Principal lakes and other bodies of water

Okeechobee (Florida): 700 square miles; maximum depth, 15 feet; natural.

Marion (South Carolina): 157.03 square miles; maximum depth, 35 feet; man-made.

Clark Hill (Georgia, South Carolina): 111.09 square miles; maximum depth, 109 feet; man-made.

Guntersville (Alabama): 107.97 square miles; maximum depth, 60 feet; man-made.

Wheeler (Alabama): 104.84 square miles; maximum depth, 58 feet; man-made.

Sardis (Mississippi): 91 square miles; maximum depth, 65 feet; man-made.

Sidney Lanier (Georgia): 57.96 square miles; maximum depth, 180 feet; man-made.

Principal swamps

The Everglades (Florida): About 4,000 square miles.

Big Cypress Swamp (Florida): About 2,400 square miles.

Okefenokee Swamp (Georgia, Florida): Some 660 square miles.

Some U.S. superlatives

Mississippi ranks second in the nation in the production of cotton.

South Carolina's cotton mills rank first in the nation in output of yard goods.

Florida produces 80 per cent of the nation's citrus fruits. In 1966 it produced some 6.5 million tons of oranges and more than 1.5 million tons of grapefruit. The state also ranks first in the production of watermelons, first in the production of phosphate rock and second in vegetables.

Georgia is the largest state east of the Mississippi River.

Georgia leads the U.S. in the production of peanuts—in 1966 the crop was valued at more than $90 million. The state is also first in the nation in the output of pulpwood and ranks second in the production of pecans.

Some historical firsts

South Carolina's Fort Sumter, in Charleston Harbor, was the place where the Civil War began. A federal installation, it was bombarded by the Confederates on April 12-13, 1861.

The Confederate States were organized at Montgomery, Alabama, on February 4, 1861. Jefferson Davis took the oath as their first President on the portico of the State Capitol here two weeks later, and Montgomery was the capital of the Confederacy until May 1861 when it was moved to Richmond.

Florida's Cape Kennedy was the site of the launching of the nation's first earth satellite on January 31, 1958; the first U.S. manned space flight on May 5, 1961; and the first U.S. manned orbital flight on February 20, 1962.

The first underwater park in the United States, John Pennekamp Coral Reef State Park, is located off Key Largo, Florida.

The first gold rush in the U.S. took place in Georgia around the town of Dahlonega in 1828.

The first Indian newspaper, *The Cherokee Phoenix,* was published at New Echota, Georgia, in 1828.

On March 2, 1912, the Girl Scouts of America was founded in Savannah, Georgia, by Juliette Gordon Low.

A Georgian, Dr. Crawford W. Long, first discovered and demonstrated the use of ether as an anesthetic in surgical operations in 1842 at Jefferson, Georgia.

The cotton gin was invented in 1793 by Eli Whitney near Savannah, Georgia, and placed in operation near Washington, Georgia.

St. Augustine, Florida, founded in 1565, is the oldest permanent settlement in the United States.

Agricultural statistics (1964)

	Number of farms	Acreage (in millions)	Principal crops
Mississippi	109,141	17.8	Cotton, soybeans, cottonseed, corn.
Alabama	92,530	15.2	Cotton, corn, peanuts, hay.
Georgia	83,366	17.9	Peanuts, cotton, corn, tobacco.
South Carolina	56,248	8.1	Tobacco, cotton, soybeans, corn.
Florida	40,541	15.4	Oranges, grapefruit, tomatoes, sugar cane and its seed.

Pronunciation glossary

Altamaha (AL tuh muh haw). River in southeastern Georgia formed by confluence of Oconee and Ocmulgee Rivers near Charlotteville.

Beaufort (BYOO furt). County and city in South Carolina; year-round resort and tourist center.

Chattahoochee (cha tah HOO chee). River formed by confluence of headstreams in Blue Ridge Mountains in Georgia; in its lower course it is part of state boundary between Georgia and Alabama

and between Georgia and Florida; also county in Georgia and town in Florida.

Dahlonega (da LAH neh gah). City in northern Georgia; trade center and sawmilling area.

Dothan (DOUGH thun). City in southeastern Alabama; agricultural area; trade center for livestock.

Milledgeville (MI ludge ville). City in central Georgia; trade and processing center for cotton and clay.

Natchez (NAA chiz). City in southwestern Mississippi famous for its antebellum houses.

Ocala (oh KAH luh). City in north-central Florida; trade and shipping center.

Okefenokee (OH kee fuh NOH kee). One of the most famous and primitive swamps in the U.S.; mostly in southeastern Georgia, but partly also in northeastern Florida.

Pascagoula (pas kah GOO luh). City and river in southeastern Mississippi.

Piedmont (PEED mont). Upland region bordering Older

Appalachian Mountains; extends from New Jersey to Alabama.

Savannah (suh VAN nuh). Oldest and second-largest city in Georgia.

Tallahatchie (ta luh HAA chee). County and river in northern Mississippi.

Tuskegee (tus KEE gee). City and noted Negro school in Alabama.

Yoknapatawpha (YUK na pa TAW pha). Imaginary county, patterned after the Oxford, Mississippi, area, home of William Faulkner, and used by him as setting for many of his novels and stories.

Credits and acknowledgments

Maps for front and back end papers by Jeppesen & Company, Denver, Colorado. Maps on pages 174 through 179 © by The H. M. Gousha Company, San Jose, California. Maps on pages 10 and 37 by Lothar Roth.

The sources for the illustrations and quotations that appear in this book are shown below. Credits for the pictures from left to right are separated by commas, from top to bottom by dashes. Cover—Alfred Eisenstaedt. Front end papers—Drawings by Richard Boland. Chapter 1: 8—Bill Ray. 13— Quotation © 1967, D. Van Nostrand Company, Inc., Princeton, New Jersey. 15 through 31—Alfred Eisenstaedt. Chapter 2: 32—Library of Congress. 34—From *Florida, Old and New* by Frederick Dau, Putnam's Sons, 1934. 39— *Harper's Weekly*, November 27, 1858. 41—Library of Congress. 42—National Archives, Georgia Department of Archives and History, Atlanta. 44, 45—Library of Congress, Cook Collection of the Valentine Museum, Richmond, Virginia. 46, 47— Brady Collection of the National Archives. 48, 49—Courtesy Sea Pines Plantation Company, Hilton Head Island, South Carolina. 50 —Beaufort County Library, Beaufort, South Carolina; South Carolina Historical Society. Chapter 3: 52, 53—Bruce Roberts from Rapho Guillumette. 56—The Bettmann Archive. 59

—Culver Pictures, Inc. 60, 61— Don Cravens, Burton McNeely, Mike Smith. 63 through 77— Burke Uzzle from Magnum. Chapter 4: 78—South Caroliniana Library, Columbia, South Carolina. 82—Culver Pictures, Inc. (2) 86—No credit— Bill Murphy courtesy the Georgia Department of Industry and Trade. 89—Charlie Preston (2). 91 through 99—Bruce Roberts from Rapho Guillumette. Chapter 5: 100—Jerome Drown. 102—Courtesy Atlanta Chamber of Commerce. 105—Harold J. Terhune, H & H Photo Service, Atlanta. 107—No credit. 108— Miami-Metro News Bureau. 111 —John Launois from Black Star. 112—Jack Levy courtesy McKee's Museum of Sunken Treasure, Plantation Key, Florida —Leonard McCombe. 113—Fred Ward from Black Star, drawings by Gaetano di Palma. 114, 115 —Hank Walker—Henri Dauman. 116—Leonard McCombe. 117— Alfred Eisenstaedt, Shelley Grossman—Lynn Pelham from Rapho Guillumette—Alfred Eisenstaedt. 118, 119—Drawings by Gaetano di Palma—Alfred Eisenstaedt, Mark Kauffman. 120 —Alfred Eisenstaedt. 121— Dennis Hallinan from FPG (2). 122—Alfred Eisenstaedt (2)— drawings by Gaetano di Palma. 123—Fred Ward from Black Star. 124, 125—Mark Kauffman— Edward H. Thompson from Alpha Photo Associates, Inc., Alfred Eisenstaedt. 126, 127—Alfred Eisenstaedt (2). Chapter 6: 128—Dr. Georg Gerster from Black Star. 133— Maps by Lothar Roth adapted from John Fraser Hart. 137

through 139—Leviton-Atlanta for FORTUNE. 140, 141—Map by Nicholas Fasciano, photographed by Crandall Associates. 142, 143 —Ken Kay. 144, 145—Leviton-Atlanta. 146, 147—Bruce Roberts from Rapho Guillumette, Ken Kay. Chapter 7: 148—Bruce Roberts from Rapho Guillumette. 151— Gisele Freund, Kay Bell, Carl Mydans. 153—Allan Gould, Leonard McCombe, Don Uhrbrock. 158—Drawings by Arthur Burdette Frost and quotations from *The Complete Tales of Uncle Remus* by Joel Chandler Harris, Houghton Mifflin Company. 161 through 173— From *Faulkner's County: Yoknapatawpha* by Martin J. Dain. © 1963 by Martin J. Dain. Reprinted by permission of Random House, Inc. and Martin J. Dain. Except 163 top (2), 170 left, 172 left Martin J. Dain. 182 through 185—Drawings by Rudolf Freund. Back end papers—Drawings by Richard Boland.

The editors of this book wish to thank the following persons and institutions for their assistance: Luis R. Arana, Chief Park Historian, Castillo de San Marcos and Fort Matanzas National Monuments, St. Augustine, Florida; Donald F. Blake, H. J. Porter Company, Pittsburgh, Pennsylvania; Dr. Earl D. C. Brewer, Director of Research, National Council of Churches, New York City; Donald A. Brown, Editor, *Birmingham Magazine*, Birmingham, Alabama; Grant G. Cannon, Editor, *Farm Quarterly*, Cincinnati, Ohio; Professor William Smith Clark II, Department of English, University of Cincinnati; James M. Donovan Jr., American Textile

Manufacturers Institute, Inc., New York City; Marshall Doswell, Springs Mills Inc., Fort Mill, South Carolina; Hollis L. Green, Director of Public Relations, Church of God, Cleveland, Tennessee; R. E. Hamilton, Tufted Textile Manufacturers Association, Dalton, Georgia; Professor John Fraser Hart, Department of Geography, University of Minnesota, Minneapolis; Dan Henderson, Deering Milliken Research Corporation, Spartanburg, South Carolina; Mrs. Iola O. Hessler, Department of Political Science, University of Cincinnati; Donald Hill, Riegel Textile Corporation, La France, South Carolina; Ray Moore, Director of News, WSB-Television, Atlanta; Ben M. Patrick, Miami-Metro News Bureau, Miami; Campbell Petty, West Point Pepperell Carpet and Rug Division, Cabin Crafts, Dalton, Georgia; Edna Schappert, Man-Made Fiber Producers Association, Inc., New York City; John G. Smith, Sea Pines Plantation Company, Hilton Head Island, South Carolina; Mrs. Martha Stephens, Assistant Professor, Department of English, University of Cincinnati; Rivers Stone, Stone Manufacturing Company, Greenville, South Carolina; Samuel G. Stoney, Charleston, South Carolina; Robert L. Thompson Jr., American Textile Manufacturers Institute, Inc., Greenville, South Carolina; U.S. Department of Agriculture, Office of Public Information.

Grateful acknowledgment is extended to the Estate of William Faulkner and to Random House, Inc., for permission to use the copyright quotations from the works of William Faulkner.

Bibliography

*Available also in paperback.
†Available only in paperback.

General and historical reading

Alden, John Richard, *The South in the Revolution, 1763-1789.* Louisiana State University Press, 1957.

Blair, Lewis H., *A Southern Prophecy.** Little, Brown, 1964.

Bridenbaugh, Carl, *Myths and Realities: Societies of the Colonial South.** Louisiana State University Press, 1952.

Cash, Wilbur J., *The Mind of the South.** Knopf, 1941.

Catton, Bruce, *The American Heritage Picture History of the Civil War.* American Heritage Publishing Company, 1960.

Clark, Thomas D., *The Emerging South.* Oxford University Press, 1961.

Clark, Thomas D., and Albert D. Kirwan, *The South Since Appomattox.* Oxford University Press, 1967.

Cooper, J. Wesley, *Natchez.* Southern Historical Publications, 1957.

Coulter, E. Merton:
Georgia: A Short History. University of North Carolina Press, 1960.
The South During Reconstruction, 1865-1877. Louisiana State University Press, 1947.

Craven, Wesley F., *The Southern Colonies in the Seventeenth Century, 1607-1689.* Louisiana State University Press, 1949.

Eaton, Clement:
*The Growth of Southern Civilization, 1790-1860.** Harper & Row, 1961.
A History of the Old South. Macmillan, 1966.

Ezell, John S., *The South Since 1865.* Macmillan, 1963.

Franklin, John Hope, *Reconstruction: After the Civil War.** University of Chicago Press, 1961.

Hesseltine, William B., and David L. Smiley, *The South in American History.* Prentice-Hall, 1960.

Kane, Harnett T., ed., *The Romantic South.* Coward-McCann, 1961.

Miller, Francis Trevelyan, ed., *The Photographic History of the Civil War.* Thomas Yoseloff, 1957.

Sellers, Charles G., Jr., ed., *The Southerner As American.** University of North Carolina Press, 1960.

Simkins, Francis B., *A History of the South.* Knopf, 1953.

Stampp, Kenneth M., *The Era of Reconstruction, 1865-1877.** Knopf, 1965.

Sydnor, Charles S., *The Development of Southern Sectionalism, 1819-1848.* Louisiana State University Press, 1948.

Tindall, George B., *The Emergence of the New South, 1913-1945.* Louisiana State University Press, 1967.

Wiley, Bell I., *Embattled Confederates.* Harper & Row, 1964.

Woodward, C. Vann:
*The Burden of Southern History.** Louisiana State University Press, 1960.
*Origins of the New South, 1877-1913.** Louisiana State University Press, 1951.
*Reunion and Reaction.** Little, Brown, 1951.
*Tom Watson: Agrarian Rebel.** Macmillan, 1938.

The Negro

Burns, W. Haywood, *The Voices of Negro Protest in America.** Oxford University Press, 1963.

Davis, John P., ed., *The American Negro Reference Book.* Prentice-Hall, 1966.

Du Bois, William E. B., *Black Reconstruction in America, 1860-1880.†* Meridian Books, 1964.

Franklin, John Hope, *From Slavery to Freedom.* Knopf, 1967.

Hughes, Langston, and Milton Meltzer, *A Pictorial History of the Negro in America.* Crown, 1956.

Myrdal, Gunnar, *An American Dilemma.** 2 vols. Harper, 1944.

Parsons, Talcott, and Kenneth B. Clark, eds., *The Negro American.** Houghton Mifflin, 1966.

Stampp, Kenneth M., *The Peculiar Institution: Slavery in the Ante-Bellum South.** Knopf, 1956.

Economics

Bogue, Donald J., and Calvin L. Beale, *Economic Areas of the United States.* Free Press of Glencoe, 1961.

Maddox, James G., *The Advancing South: Manpower Prospects and Problems.* Twentieth Century Fund, 1967.

Nicholls, William H., *Southern Tradition and Regional Progress.* University of North Carolina Press, 1960.

Atlanta

Hunter, Floyd, *Community Power Structure.†* University of North Carolina Press, 1953.

Jennings, M. Kent, *Community Influentials: The Elites of Atlanta.* Free Press of Glencoe, 1964.

Kahn, E. J., Jr., *The Big Drink: The Story of Coca-Cola.* Random House, 1960.

Sibley, Celestine, *Peachtree Street, U.S.A.* Doubleday, 1963.

Literature and culture

Bradbury, John M., *Renaissance in the South.* University of North Carolina Press, 1963.

Brooks, Cleanth, *William Faulkner: The Yoknapatawpha Country.* Yale University Press, 1963.

Harris, Joel Chandler, *The Complete Tales of Uncle Remus.* Houghton Mifflin, 1955.

Harris, Julia Collier, *The Life and Letters of Joel Chandler Harris.* Houghton Mifflin, 1918.

Hubbell, Jay B., ed., *The South in American Literature: 1607-1900.* Duke University Press, 1954.

Millgate, Michael, *The Achievement of William Faulkner.* Random House, 1966.

Spiller, Robert E., and others, *Literary History of the United States.* Macmillan, 1963.

Tyler, Moses Coit, *A History of American Literature: 1607-1765.** Cornell University Press, 1949.

Special topics

Hill, Samuel S., Jr., *Southern Churches in Crisis.* Holt, Rinehart and Winston, 1967.

Key, V. O., Jr., *Southern Politics.** Knopf, 1949.

McGill, Ralph, *The South and the Southerner.** Little, Brown, 1963.

McKinney, John C., and Edgar T. Thompson, eds., *The South in Continuity and Change.* Duke University Press, 1965.

Sindler, Allan P., ed., *Change in the Contemporary South.*

Duke University Press, 1963.

Thorp, Willard, ed., *A Southern Reader.* Knopf, 1955.

Natural setting and wildlife

Conant, Roger, *A Field Guide to Reptiles and Amphibians.* Houghton Mifflin, 1958.

Fenneman, Nevin M., *Physiography of Eastern United States.* McGraw-Hill, 1938.

Hamilton, William J., *The Mammals of Eastern United States.* Hafner, 1963.

Hart, John Fraser, *The Southeastern United States.** Van Nostrand, 1967.

Hausman, Leon A., *Field Book of Eastern Birds.* Putnam, 1946.

Hylander, Clarence J., and Edith Farrington Johnston, *Macmillan Wild Flower Book.* Macmillan, 1954.

Palmer, Ralph S., *The Mammal Guide.* Doubleday, 1954.

Peterson, Roger Tory, *A Field Guide to the Birds.* Houghton Mifflin, 1947.

Platt, Rutherford, *A Pocket Guide to Trees.†* Washington Square Press, 1960.

U.S. Department of Agriculture, *Land Resource Regions and Major Land Resource Areas of the United States.* Government Printing Office, 1965.

Guidebooks

Alabama Writers' Project, *Alabama: A Guide to the Deep South.* Richard R. Smith, 1941.

Federal Writers' Project:
Florida: A Guide to the Southernmost State. Oxford University Press, 1939.
Mississippi: A Guide to the Magnolia State. Hastings House, 1938.

Fodor, Eugene, ed., *Fodor Shell Travel Guides U.S.A.; Southeast.* David McKay, 1967.

Hepburn, Andrew, *Complete Guide to Florida.* Doubleday, 1961.

Leckie, George G., ed., *Georgia: A Guide to Its Towns and Countryside.* Tupper & Love, 1954.

Mobil Travel Guide, *Southeastern States.** Simon & Schuster, 1966.

Raisz, Erwin, and John R. Duncle, *Atlas of Florida.* University of Florida Press, 1964.

South Carolina Writers' Project, *South Carolina: A Guide to the Palmetto State.* Oxford University Press, 1941.

Index

Numerals in italics indicate an illustration of the subject mentioned.

Abolitionists, 57
Absalom! Absalom!, 159
Adams, Henry, 156
Adams, John, 154
Adamsville, Georgia, 109
"Agrarian revolt," 83-84
"Agrarians" (literary group), 159
Agriculture: cattle raising, *118-119*, 135; chicken farming, 135; citrus growing, *122-123;* farming in Alabama, 130; in Florida, 118, *122-123,* 126; high return of, 14; mechanization and diversification of, 14, 134-135; Mississippi farmer, *166;* peanut growing, 126; prolonged growing season, 35; rice growing, 36, 38, 39; sharecroppers, *64-69;* small farmers, 37-38, 82; soil fertility, 35; sugar-cane growing, 118; tobacco growing, 39, 126; truck farming, 118. See also "Agrarian revolt"; Cotton
Alabama: agriculture in, 130; becomes a territory, 36; "Big Jim" Folsom, *89;* cattle raising, 135; civil rights, 54-55, *60-61;* climate 12; constitution of 1901, 87; cotton in, 40, *maps* 133; Democratic Party in, 88; federal aid to, 90; growth and development in, 130-132; Indian removal, 34-35; industry in, 130; Negro colleges in, 157; Negro sheriff, 62; opportunity in the 18th Century, 37; as part of Spanish Florida, 34; physical characteristics, 11; politics in, 88, *89,* 90; school desegregation, 54-55, 62, 90; secession of, 41; settlement of, *map* 37; tournament in, *39;* writers, 160. See also Birmingham
Albertville, Alabama, 130
Allen, Mayor Ivan, Jr., 107, 110
Allen University, 157
American Missionary Society of New York, teachers in South Carolina, *50*
American Revolution, 25, 38, 153
Anderson, Maxwell, 159-160
Anderson, South Carolina, as a textile center, *141*
Angel, 160
Anti-Semitism, 85
Appalachian range, 11, 104
Architecture: of antebellum period, 15-31; Neo-Grecian style, 15, 22-23; Spanish influence in, 24, 25
Aristocracy: dominance of, 38; as a minority in the South, 37; image as upholders of the chivalric tradition, 39
Arlington Mansion, *26-27;* doll collection, *28-29*
As I Lay Dying, 159
Ashley River, 35
Atlanta Constitution, The (newspaper), 104, 107
Atlanta, Georgia, 11, 101-110, 151; becomes state capital, 104; burning of, 46, 104; Chamber of Commerce, 74; character of the citizenry, 104; citizens' pride in their city, 104, 105; climate, 103; cultural life, 103; desegregation in, 110; development in, 101-102; early names of, 103; education of Negroes, 108-109; Equitable Life Assurance Society Building, *74, 102-103;* favorable situation of, 103-104; First National Bank, *102-103;* "Forward Atlanta" program, 107; founding of, 103; Fulton

National Bank, *102-103;* Gas Tower Building, *102-103;* growth of, *102-103;* Indian lore of "The Standing Peach Tree," 103; industry in, 104, 107; leaders of, *74-77,* 104-105, 109-110; Merchandise Mart, *102-103;* Negro leaders, 74-77, 109-110; newspapers, 107-108; official symbol, 104; Peachtree Center, *100, 102-103;* population, 101; problems of, 102; proposed annexation of outlying communities, 108-109; race relations, 102, 107, 108-109, 110; Regency Hyatt House, *102-103;* Rich's department store, 106; school system, 106; slums and poverty, 102, 106; Summit Leadership Conference, 110; as the topographical and economic center of the South, 104; transportation, 103; well-known families of, 106; white control, 108-109
Atlanta Journal (newspaper), 107
Atlanta (periodical), 109
Atlanta University, 109, 157
Atlantic Ocean, 11, 34, 104
Auden, W. H., quoted, 151
Audubon, John James, prints of used in decorating, *17*
Augusta States Rights Sentinel, 155
Automation, in the textile industry, 139

Bailey, Kenneth K., quoted, 91
Bainbridge, Georgia, 12
Baldwin, D. H. (piano and organ manufacturing company), 135-136
Barnum, Mrs. Hubert, 27; doll collection of, *28-29*
Barwick (E. T.) Mills, 144
Bastard, The, 159
Basso, Hamilton, 158
Battle of Angels, 159
Beaufort, South Carolina, 34
Bilbo, Senator Theodore, 87
Bill of Rights, 57
Birmingham, Alabama, diversification of industry, 107, 131; Downtown Action Committee, 70; Fairfield Steel Works, *107;* as leading steel producer, 131, 134; race relations in, 62; revival meeting *98-99*
Biscayne Bay, *115*
Black April, 160
Black Codes, 39, 49, 59
Blues (magazine), 157
Bontemps, Arna, quoted, 62
"Bourbons" (politicians), 81, 82, 83, 84, 85
Boykins, Amelia, *70*
Bozart (magazine), 157
Bradbury, John M., 149, 157
Bradford, Roark, 158
Bray, Paul, and family, 63, *70-73*
Brite, Red, *163*
Brown, Mrs. Calvin, *163*
Brown, Governor Joseph E., 81
Brown, William Garrott, 87
Bruce, Blanche K., 60
Bull, Governor William, 152
Bull Run, Second Battle of, 45
Burlington Mills, 141
Butler, Senator Matthew C., 81

Caldwell, Erskine, *151,* 159
Calhoun, S. S., 87
Calhoun, John C., 55-57, 58, 86; writings of, 155
Caloosahatchee River, 121
Candler, Asa Griggs, *105,* 106
Cape Coral, Florida, *121*
Cape Kennedy, *128,* 132
Carmer, Carl, 83
Carolina, colony, 34, 35. See also North Carolina; South Carolina
"Carpetbaggers," 50, 59
Carpetmaking, *144-145*
Carter, Hodding, 149
Cash, Wilbur J., 11, 12, 159

Catholics. See Roman Catholics
Cattle raising, *118-119,* 135; Brahman-Angus crossbred, *diagram* 119
Chancellorsville, Battle of, 45
Charles II, King of England, 35
Charleston, South Carolina, 11, 34, 35, 37, 38, 104, 151; aristocrats, 55; Cabbage Row, *148;* development of port, 132; on the eve of the Civil War, 43; execution of rebellious slaves, 39; interest in the arts, 152-153; occupied by British, 36, 38; after Union bombardment, *46-47.* See also Fort Sumter
Chattahoochee River, 102, 103, 104
Chemical industry. See Synthetic fibers; Textile industry
Cherokee Indians, 103
Chesapeake Bay, 104
Chesnut, Mary Boykin, 55
Chicken farming, 135
Chrisman, Judge J. B., quoted, 87
"Christmas Night in the Quarters," 156
Church of England, 40
Church of God, 91
Cigarmaking, 112. See also Tobacco
Citizens' Councils, 136
Citrus growing and processing, *122-123*
Civil Rights Act of 1964, 52
Civil Rights Act of 1965, 62, 87
Civil War, *41-51,* 80, 81; beginnings of, 41, 43-45, 56; Confederate soldiers, *44-45;* first battle of, 9; halts plantation construction, 30; "march to the sea," 46; Northern strategy, 46; the South defeated, 46. See also Reconstruction
Claflin College, 157
Cleveland, President Grover, 85
Climate, Southern, 12; of Atlanta, 103
Coal, 107
Coca-Cola: advertising of, 105; bottles, *105;* invention of, 106; manufacture of in Atlanta, 105-106
Cohn, David, 149
Coldwater, Mississippi, 64
Coles, Robert, Dr., 33
College of Charleston, 154
Columbia, South Carolina, 12, 46
Columbus, Christopher, 34
Confederate States of America. See Civil War
Conner Steel Company, 70
Constitutional Convention of 1787, 39, 40
Cooper, Thomas, 154
Coral formations of the Florida Keys, *113*
Corinth, Battle of, 45
"Corn," 157
Cotton: acreage under cultivation, *maps* 133; the boll weevil, 133; in California, 135; decline in, 14, 133; dependence upon, 82; economics of, 134; in Georgia, 37, 40; growth of the industry, 40; invention of the cotton gin, 35, 40; leading cotton-producing states, 133; in Mississippi, 40, 133, 134; modern improvements in production, 133; raw cotton being prepared for ginning, *32;* and slavery, 56; in Texas, 135. See also Synthetic fibers; Textile industry
Creek Indians, 103
Cultural life in the post-Civil War period, 156-157
Cycle, The (magazine), 157

Dahlgren, Charles, 22
Dahlgren, Sarah Ann, 22
Daily News, Jackson, Mississippi, 150
Dalton, Georgia, 141, 144
Daniels, E. J., 99
Davis, George M., 19
Davis, Jefferson, President of the

Confederacy, 22, 86; inauguration of, 42
Decatur, Alabama, 130
Declaration of Independence, 40, 57, 155
Decoration and design: interiors of mansions, *17, 18-19;* imported furniture, 15, 16, *17, 18-19, 20-21, 25;* wrought-iron staircase, *25*
Deering Milliken Research Corporation, 141, *142-143*
Delta Wedding, 159
Democratic Party, 81, 88
De Soto, Hernando, 34
D'Evereux Mansion, 4, 21
Discourse on the Constitution and Government of the United States, A, 155
Disquisition on Government, 155
Do, Lord, Remember Me, 160
Dolls, Barnum collection at Arlington Mansion, Natchez, *28-29*
Dothan, Alabama, 130-131, 136
Double Dealer, The (magazine), 157
Dragon Fly, The (magazine), 157
Drayton family, 37
Drayton, William Henry, 38
Drew, George F. "Millionaire," 81
Dunleith Mansion, *22-23*

East, Charles, 160
Economy: development in the South, 129-136; poverty in the South, 80
Education: beginnings of the public school system in the South, 153-154; in Colonial times, 152-153; English influence in, 152; establishment of colleges and universities, 154; establishment of Negro colleges and universities, 157; illiteracy, 85, 86, 87, 132, 136, 150, 154, 155; intellectual blight in mid-19th Century, 154-155; of Negroes, 14, 50, 60, 109, 132, 157; poor quality of public schools, 150; as a prerogative of the rich, 152, 153; reforms under Reconstruction, 60; school segregation and desegregation, 55, 62; in South Carolina, 132, 153
Eisenhower, General Dwight D., 89
Electronics industry, 120
Elms Mansion, The, *24-25*
Emory University, 106
England: the English in Natchez, 25; English settlers, 34, 35, 37; influence of on the South, 37, 152; loyalty to during Revolution, 38; receives Florida from Spain, 38; trade with the Southern colonies, 36
Equitable Life Assurance Building, Atlanta, 74, *102*
Eskridge, W. S., 86
Evangelism. See Religion
Everglades National Park, *116-117*
Evers, Medgar, 14
Exploration of the New World in the 16th Century, 34
Ezell, John Samuel, 84, 132

Fairfield Steel Works, Birmingham, *107*
Falkner, J.W.T., II, *162*
Fall Line (geologic demarcation), 11
Faulkner, William, 12, 149, 150, 158, 159; quoted, 11; the world of, *161-173*
Faulkner's County: Yoknapatawpha, 161-173
Fauntleroy, Mrs. Frank, 16
Federal government: in Atlanta, 104; intervention in Southern government, 33, 79, 80, 88, 89
Federal Reserve Bank, 104
Fellows, Alice, 158
First Flight, 160
First National Bank of Atlanta, *102*
Fisher, Carl, 114
Fishing, *168;* shrimp fleet, *112,* 120
Flagler, Henry, 114

Flora and fauna: of the Florida panhandle, *126;* live oak trees, *124-125;* in Everglades National Park, *116, 117. See also* Coral

Florida: association with the traditional South, 9; becomes part of the U.S., 36, 112, 124, 154; Cape Kennedy, *128, 132;* cattle raising, *118-119,* 135; ceded by Spain to Great Britain, 38; cigarmaking, 112; citrus growing, *122-123;* climate, 12; cotton in, *maps* 133; early exploration and naming of, 34; elects Republican governor in 1966, 79; Everglades National Park, *116-117;* farming in, 126; fishing, 112; the Gold Coast, 114-115; Indian removal, 35; industry in, 120, 126, 132; Keys, *112-113;* land development, 120, *121;* as a major food-producing region, 118; military establishments, 126; military rule in, 59; Negro college founded, 157; Negroes in, 53, 87; northern sector of, *124-125;* occupation forces withdrawn, 81; Overseas Highway, *113;* panhandle, *126-127;* piracy and smuggling, 112; politics in, 88, 89; population, 111; retention of Southern identity, 11; as a retirement haven, 120, 121; school segregation and desegregation in, 55, 62; secession of, 41; ship salvage and treasure hunting, 112; shrimp fleet, 112, 120; slavery in, 124; under the Spanish, 35, 38, 112; special character of, 11; Sun Coast, 120; swampland, 11; textile industry in, *map* 140-141; tourism, 109, *111,* 112, 113, *114-115,* 126; writers, 160. *See also* St. Augustine

Florida Agricultural and Mechanical College, 157

Florida East Coast Railway, 113

Folsom, "Big Jim," *89*

Food and cooking, 13

Fort Lauderdale, 114

Fort Myers, Florida, 120, 121

Fort Sumter, 9, 16, 43

Fort Walton Beach, 126

Foster, Stephen, 125

France: exploration of the New World in the 16th Century, 34; settlement at Natchez, 25

Frank, Leo, lynching of, 85

Franklin, Benjamin, 152

Freedom Riders, 61

"Freedom Summer," 62

French and Indian Wars, 25

Frost, Arthur Burdette, 158

Fugitive group, 158, 159

Fugitive, The (magazine), 157, 158

Fulton National Bank, Atlanta, *102*

Gammadion, The (magazine), 157

Gardens of South Carolina, 14

Garrett, George, 160

Garrison, William Lloyd, 57

Geography: physical characteristics of the South, 11; *map* 10. *See also* Climate

George, James Z., 85

George II, King of England, establishes Georgia, 35-36

Georgia: well-known families of, 37; cattle raising, 135; chicken farming, 135; in the Civil War, 46; constitutional amendment of 1908, 87; cotton in, 37, 40, *maps* 133; Democratic Party in, 88; economy of, 132; education in, 153; established by George II of England, 36; federal aid to, 90; first settlement, 36; granite quarrying, 134; Indian removal, 34; industry in, 132; in literature, 151; military rule in, 59; Negro colleges in, 157; Negro legislators, 62; opportunity in the 18th Century, 37; physical

characteristics, 11; politics in, 86; population in 18th Century, 38; power of landowners, 36; pro-British feeling in at time of the Revolution, 38; Puritans in, 153; railroads in, 103; receives cash subsidy from Britain during Colonial times, 36; regional differences, 11; resentment over British taxation, 37; and the Revolutionary movement, 153; school segregation and desegregation in, 55, 62; secession of, 41; settlement of, *map* 37, 38, 103; slavery in, 39; small farmers in, 38; textile industry in, 139, *map* 140-141; unwillingness to accept control from London, 36; writers of, 151, 155, 156, 159, 160. *See also* Atlanta

Georgia Baptist Hospital, 106

Georgia Boy, 159

Georgia Gazette, 153

Georgia Scenes, 155

Gershwin, George, 149, 160

Gibbes, James, 79

Gibbons, Robert, 158

Glass Menagerie, The, 159

Gliddon, George R., 155

Gloucester Mansion, *20*

Gold, search for by early settlers, 35

Gold Coast, 114-115

Goldwater, Barry, 89

Gone With the Wind, 104, 160

Gordon, General John B., 81

Grady, Henry, 34, 60-61, 104-105

Graham, Billy, 99

Great Britain. *See* England

Great Depression, and the South, 129, 134

Great Salt Lake, Utah, 118

Green Thursday, 160

Greene, Mrs. Nathanael, 40

Greensboro, North Carolina, 61

Greenville, South Carolina, 137, 141; Tremont Avenue Church of God congregation, *95*

Greenwood, Mississippi, 136

Grove Plantation, South Carolina, *50-51*

Gulf Coast, 134

Gulf of Mexico, 11, 34, 104, 116, 120, 126

Hamilton, Mrs. Grace Towns, 109

Hamlet, The, 159

Hammond, Senator James H., 155

Hampton, General Wade, 81, *82,* 84, 85

Harris, Joel Chandler, 156, 158

Hartsfield, William B., 110

Hayes, Rutherford B., 81, 82

Heard, Robert Lee, and family, *63, 64-69*

Heart Is a Lonely Hunter, The, 160

Hercules Incorporated, *146-147*

Heyward, DuBose, 149, 158, 160

Highway programs, 134; Overseas Highway (Florida), *113*

History of the Old South, four periods of, 33

Hollings, Senator Ernest F., 90

Holman, Hugh, 159

Hoover, President Herbert, 88

Howell, Ronald, 155

Huguenots in the New World in the 16th Century, 34

Huie, William Bradford, 158

Huntsville, Alabama, 130, 136

I*'ll Take My Stand* (essay collection), 159

Illiteracy, 85, 86, 87, 132, 136, 150, 154, 155

Immigrants: adventurers and debtors as early settlers in the South, 35; first true Southerners, 35; religious origins of, 38; settlement of the South, *map* 37

In the Land of Cotton, 158

Indian River, 122

Indians: Cherokee, 103; cowboy, *119;* Creek, 103; elimination of Indian culture, 34, 35; enslavement of, 57; estimated population figures, 34, 35; lore of "The Standing Peachtree," 103; Muskogee, 119; Natchez, 25; Seminole, *119*

Indigo dyes, as a major export crop, 36, 38

Industry: in Atlanta, 104, 107; chemical (synthetic fibers), 126, 130, *137, map* 140-141, 141, *146-147;* citrus growing and processing, *122-123;* development and growth of, 13, 14, 101, 129-130; diversification of, 107; electronics, 120; in Florida, 120, 126, 132; industrialization of the South, 130-136, 150; iron, 107; neglect of in post-Civil War South, 105; soft-drinks manufacture, 105-106; steel, *107,* 131; textiles, 85, 132, *137-147, map,* 140-141

Intruder in the Dust, 159

Ireland: Irish literary tradition compared to the Southern literary renaissance, 151

Iron industry, 107

Izard family, 37

Jackson, Mississippi, 150

Jackson College, 157

Jacksonville, Florida, 124

Jacob's Ladder, 160

James River, 35

Jamestown, Virginia, 35

Jarrell, Randall, 158

Jefferson, Thomas, 40, 56, 154

Jennison, Private Edwin, *41*

Johnson, Paul, 90

Johnson, President Andrew, 49, 58

Johnson, President Lyndon B., 89, 90

Johnson, Samuel, 153

Johnson, Senator Leroy, 109, 110

Jones, Boisfeuillet, 106

Jones, Hugh, quoted, 152

Journey, The, 160

Joyce, James, 151

Kentucky: attitude to slavery, 57; politics in, 88

Key West, Florida, *112,* 113

Killers of the Dream, 160

King, Reverend Martin Luther, Jr., 55, 74

King, Reverend Martin Luther, Sr., 109

Knoxville, Georgia, 106

Koch, Professor Frederick Henry, 158

Ku Klux Klan, 59, 84, 107, 136

Ladd, Dr. Joseph Brown, quoted, 153

LaFayette, Georgia, 144

Lafayette County, Mississippi, *161-173*

Lakeland, Florida, 97

Lamar, Lucius Quintus Cincinnatus, 81, *82,* 84, 85, 86

Lane, Mills B., Jr., 103, 105

Lanier, Sidney, 156-157

Laurens, Henry, 38

Leckie, George, 104

Lee, Harper, *153*

Lee, General Robert E., 44, 156

Lee, Rooney, 156

Leesburg, Florida, 122

Lewis, Sinclair, 157

Light in August, 159

Limestone, mining of, 107

Lincoln, President Abraham, 42-43, 57, 58

Linden Mansion, *16*

Literature: the "Agrarians," 159; antebellum life as a favorite subject in Southern literature, 156; awards to Southern authors, 149; the "Fugitive Group," 158, 159; influence of Bible on, 151-152; Irish literary movement compared with the South's, 151; literary

centers, 158; literary magazines, 157; "The Lost Cause," 156; meager literary heritage, 157; "new freedom" movement, 150; periods of regional creativity, 150-151; poetry renaissance, 157; regional writing, 156; renaissance, 149-150, 157-160; of slavery, 155; of states' rights, 155; sterility of until the '20s, 150

Live Oak Plantation, Florida, *124-125*

Logging. *See* Lumbering

Longstreet, Augustus Baldwin, 155

Longwood ("Nutt's Folly") Mansion, 15, *30, 31*

Louisiana: impact of French and Spanish in, 34; occupation forces withdrawn, 81; original territory, 34; politics in, 88

Louisville & Nashville Railroad, 81

Lowe, Ed, *163*

Lowe, Eph, *163*

Lowery, T. F., 99

Lowndes County, 62

Lumbering, 126, 134

Lynching, 61, 84, 85

Maddox, Lester, 110

Main Street, 157

Mamba's Daughters, 160

Mansions: Mulberry Grove, Savannah, 40; of Natchez, Mississippi, *15-31;* restoration of, 27; Shipp Mansion, Oxford, Mississippi, *172-173*

Marble Faun, The, 159

"March to the Sea, The," 46

Marion, General Francis ("The Swamp Fox"), 38

Marshall (George C.) Space Flight Center, 130

"Marshes of Glynn, The," 157

Marthasville (later Atlanta). *See* Atlanta

Maryland: free Negroes in, 57; statute on miscegenation of 1664, 40

Master William Mitten, 155

McComb, Mississippi, 54

McCullers, Carson, *153,* 160

McGill, Ralph, 107-108

McKee, Art, 112

McKinney, John C., 157

McMurran, John T., 19

McNair, Governor Robert E., 90

McRea, James, 50, *51*

Mellichampe, 155

Melrose Mansion, *18-19*

Member of the Wedding, The, 160

Mencken, H. L., 150

Meredith, James, *61*

Miami, Florida, 113, 114, *115;* development of, 109; International Airport, *108;* population, 109; as second largest metropolitan area in the Old South, 109

Miami Beach, Florida, *111, 114-115,* 120

Midwest, literary renaissance, 150-151

Military installations, 126, 129, 130

Milledgeville, Georgia, 104

Mind of the South, The, 11

Mining, 107

Mississippi: becomes a territory, 36; Civil War in, 46; climate, 12; constitution of, 85, 86, 87; cotton growing in, 40, *map* 133, 134; Democratic Party in, 88; economy of, 135; "Freedom Summer," 62; illiteracy in, 85, 86, 87; Indians moved from, 35; industry in, 14, 135; literacy test, 87, 88; livestock raising, 135; "Mississippi Plans," 85, 87; Negro colleges in, 157; Negroes in, 53, 57, 62, 79, 80, 86-87; opportunity in the 18th Century, 37; physical characteristics, 11; politics in, 82, 85-87; as poorest of the Southern states, 132; regional differences, 11; rise in urban population, 14; school segregation and

desegregation, 55, 62; secession
of, 41; settlement of, *map* 37, 103;
state university desegregated, 61-
62; threatened racial warfare in,
59; white reaction to Negro
assertiveness, 61; white supremacy
in, 85, 87; the world of William
Faulkner, *161-173;* writers of, 151,
156, 159, 160. *See also* Natchez
Mississippi River, 15, 24, 25, 35, 37,
104, 135
Mississippi Valley, 104
Missouri Compromise, 56
Mitchell, Margaret, 160
Mobile, Alabama, 34, 37
Montgomery, Alabama: bus boycott,
55, 60; fire, 12; Jefferson Davis
inaugurated at, *42;* slave market,
56
Moses, Franklin, *78*
Mosquitoes, 159
Mulberry Grove (Savannah plantation),
40
Murphy, Reverend Edgar Gardiner, 87-
88
Muskogee Indians, 119

Nashville, Tennessee, 158
Natchez, Mississippi: as birthplace of
Richard Wright, 159; in the 18th
Century, 21; history of, 24-25;
mansions of, 14, *15-31;* as a social
center in the antebellum period, 26,
27
Natchez Indians, massacre of by
French, 25
National Association for the
Advancement of Colored People
(NAACP), 70
National Book Awards, Southern
recipients of, 149
Native Son, 159
Natural resources of the South, *map*
10
Negro Voters League, 110
Negroes: and "the agrarian revolt,"
83-84; in Atlanta, *74-77,* 108-
109; attitude to the South, 9;
"Black Codes," 39, 49, 59; class
structure among, 63; Constitutional
rights of enforced, 37; deprived of
new-found political rights in the
1880s, 50; economic plight of, 82;
education of, 14, 50, 60, 109, 132,
157; the fight for rights, 12-13, 54-
55, *60-61*, 61-62; in Florida, 53,
87; free Negroes in 1860, 57;
Freedom Riders, 61; heavy
concentration of in urban centers,
108; ill-treatment of, 86, 87;
leaders in Atlanta, 109-110; in
literature, 151, 156, 158, 160;
lynching of, 61, 82; in Maryland,
40, 57; middle-class, 54, *70-72;*
migration from the countryside, 82;
migration to the North, 53, 133;
miscegenation, 40, 59; Negro
colleges and universities
established, 157; and the North,
60; as pawns in the struggle for
governmental control, 83-87;
population of in the South, 53, 83;
postbellum freedom to choose jobs,
50-51; in the Reconstruction
period, 50-51, 58, 59-60, 80;
relations with whites in the South,
54-55, 61; the rich minority, *74-
77;* run for public office in
Mississippi in 1967, 79;
sharecropper's life, *64-69;* sit-ins,
54, 61; skilled worker, *70-73;* in
Southern industry, 13, *70-71;*
supported by liberal editor in
Atlanta, 107-108; unemployment,
135; U.S. Supreme Court ruling of
1954, 54, 55; voting rights, 57, 58,
62, 79, 80, 85-88, 110; writers,
159. *See also* Slavery
New Deal, and the South, 129, 135
New England, 19th Century literary
creativity, 151

New Orleans, 15, *37,* 158
New York City, draft riots of 1863,
57
New York Drama Critics' Circle,
awards to Southern playwrights,
149
Newspapers: in the 18th Century,
152; racist attitudes of, 155-156
Nigger, 160
"Nirvâna," 156
Nobel Prize, awarded to Southern
author, 149
Noble Jones family, 37
Nomad, The (magazine), 157
Nombre de Dios Mission, St.
Augustine, *124*
North Carolina: attitude to slavery in,
57; boundary problems, 35;
settlement of, 35, 37
Nott, Dr. Josiah C., 155
Nutt, Haller, 30
Nutt's Folly. *See* Longwood

O'Casey, Sean, 151
Oconee River, 37
O'Connor, Flannery, 160; quoted, 151
Odum, Howard W., quoted, 150
Office of Economic Opportunity, 70
Oglethorpe, General James, founds
Savannah, 36
Ohio Valley, 104
Okeechobee, Lake, 116, 117, *map*
118, 119
O'Reilly, John, quoted, 116
Oxford, Mississippi, *8,* 12, *161-173*

Palm Beach, Florida, 114
Peachtree Street, U.S.A., 104, 106
Peanut growing, 126
Pemberton, John Styth, 106
Pensacola, Florida, 127
Pentecostal Holiness church, 91
People's Party (Populist movement),
83-84, 85, 86
Perry, Benjamin F., provisional
Governor of South Carolina, 58
Peterkin, Julia, 158, 160
Phillips, Rubel, 90
Phosphate, 120
Pickens County, Georgia, 105
Piedmont, 11, 103
Pinckney, Charles Cotesworth, 38
Pinckney, Thomas, 38
Pinckney family, 37
Plantations. *See* Mansions
Plumes, 159
Poe, Edgar Allan, 155
Politics, 79-90; agrarian movement,
83-85; in Alabama, 81, 87, 88, 89,
90; "Bourbons," 81, 82, 83, 84,
85, 86, 87; demagogues, 84;
Democratic Party in the South, 58,
79, 81, 88, 89; "Dixiecrat" ticket
in 1948 Presidential election, 88-
89; emergence of two-party
politics in the South, 79, 89;
exploitation of nostalgia for
antebellum South, 81-82; federal
intervention, 33, 79, 80, 88, 89;
importance of primaries, 88; low
level of political concern and
performance, 88; in Mississippi, 82,
85-87; post-Civil War politics, 58,
59, 78, *82;* post-Reconstruction
politics, 80-87; Negro issue in, 79,
80, 82-89; radicals, 58, *78;*
reapportionment of election
districts, 79; during the
Reconstruction period, 50, 59-60,
78, 80, 81; "Redeemers," 81, *82;*
Republican Party in the South, 58,
79-81, 88, 89; revolution in, 79-
80; self-government returns to the
South, 82; the "solid South," 88;
states' rights as a major issue in, 36
Pollution, of Chattahoochee River, 102
Ponce de León, 34, 122
Poor Fool, 159
Poor whites, 37-38, 82, 85
Populist movement. *See* People's
Party

Porgy, 149, 160
Porgy and Bess, 149, 160
Pulitzer Prizes, awarded to Southern
authors, 149, 160
Puritans, 35

Quartering Act of 1765, 36

Race struggle. *See* Negroes; White
supremacy
Railroads: in Atlanta, 103; in Georgia,
103; Louisville & Nashville, 81;
Western & Atlantic, 103
Ransom, John Crowe, 158, 159
Rawlings, Marjorie Kinnan, 160
Reconstruction, 33, 41, 49, 50, 59-
60, *78,* 80, 81, 82, 83, 85
"Redeemers" (politicians), 81, 82. *See
also* "Bourbons"
Reed, Senator Thomas B., 16
Reflections in a Golden Eye, 160
Regionalism, in the South, 33-34
Register, Larry, 131
Religion, *91-99;* baptism by total
immersion, *96-97;* belief in the
literal interpretation of the Bible,
97; emotionalism in Southern
religion, *91, 94-95;* evangelical
Protestantism, *91-99;* fellowship
and warmth of Southern services,
92-93; varieties of, 38; revival
meetings, *98-99;* "speaking in
tongues," *94*
Republican Party, 58, 79-81, 88, 89
Revels, Hiram R., 60
Reviewer, The (magazine), 157
Rice growing, 36, 38, 39
Rich, Morris, 106
Rich, Richard B., 107
Rich Foundation, 106-107
Rich's department store, 106, 107
Riverboats, 15
Robber Bridegroom, The, 159
Roman Catholics, prejudice against,
85
Rony, Vera, quoted, 84
Roosevelt, President Franklin D., 129,
132; quoted, 129
Routh family, 22
Russell, Herman J., 63; and family,
74-77
Russell, Irwin, 156
Rutledge, Edward, 38
Rutledge, John, 38
Rutledge family, 37

St. Augustine, Florida, 34; Nombre
de Dios Mission, *124*
St. Joseph's Infirmary, 106
St. Petersburg, old people in, *120*
Salisbury, North Carolina, 134
Sandburg, Carl, 160
Sandy Springs, Georgia, 109
Sargent, George Washington, 21
Sargent, Winthrop (first territorial
governor of Mississippi), 21
Sartoris, 159
Savannah, Georgia, 37, 104, 151; as
a cultural center, 153; falls to
Sherman, 46; founding of, 36;
occupied by British, 38
"Scalawags," 50, 59
Scarborough, Dorothy, 158
Scarlet Sister Mary, 160
Schaw, Janet, 40
Schools. *See* Education
Scientific research, 120
Scott, Sir Walter, 156
Scout, The, 155
Scribner's Monthly, 156
Sebring, Florida, 122
Secession, 41, 42, 43
Segregation. *See* Education; Negroes
Selma, Alabama, 62
Selma University, 157
Seminole Indian, *119*
Separatism, 33, 35
Settlers. *See* Immigrants
Shards (magazine), 157
Sharecroppers. *See* Agriculture
Shaw, George Bernard, 151

Sherman, General William T., 104;
"march to the sea," 46
Shrimp fishing, *112,* 120
Sibley, Celestine, 106
Simkins, Francis Butler, 152
Simms, William Gilmore, 155
Slavery: abolition of, 80; "Black
Codes," 39, 49, 59; defense of
during the 1820s, 33; dependence
of Old South on, 41; duties of
slaves on the plantations, 16, 27;
effect of the invention of the cotton
gin on, 35, 40; effect on Southern
culture of, 12; importation of slaves
forbidden, 40; John C. Calhoun on,
55-57, 155; literature of, 155, 156;
miscegenation, 39-40; moral basis
questioned after the Revolution,
153; origins and early history in the
South, 36, 39-40; in plantation
building, 30; preparing cotton, *32;*
price of slaves, 56; as a settled
institution, 33; slave auction, *56;*
rebellions, 39; in South Carolina,
33, 39; spreads to the new
territories of the South, 36; use of
slaves in cotton growing, 35; white
Southerners' belief in, 55-57, 154.
See also Negroes
Sleeping Gypsy, 160
Sloan, Samuel, 30
Sloane, Frank, 90
Smalls, Robert, 60
Smith, Alfred E., 88
Smith, Captain John, 35
Smith, Lillian, 160
Social life and customs: in antebellum
Natchez, 26-27; courting and
chaperonage, 19; influence of
English customs in Southern
colonies, 37
Soldiers' Pay, 159
"Song of the Chattahoochee," 157
Sound and the Fury, The, 159
South, in Continuity and Change, The,
157
South Carolina: aristocratic families
of, 37; boundary problems, 35;
Civil War in, 46; constitution of
1895, 87; cotton growing in, 40,
maps 10, 133; Democratic Party
in, 88; economy of, 36, 38, 132;
education in, 132, 153;
establishment of, 35, 36; fur
trading, 38; indigo as a leading
crop, 36; industry in, 132, 138-
139; John C. Calhoun and the tariff
issue, 56; major exports of, 38;
military rule in, 59; Negro colleges
in, 157; Negro vote in, 80;
occupation forces withdrawn, 81;
physical characteristics, *map* 10,
11; politics in, 38, 81, 82, 84, 85,
88, 89; population in 18th Century,
38; power of landowners, 36; pro-
British feeling in at time of the
Revolution, 38; regional
differences, 11; Republican
legislature in the Reconstruction
period, 59, *78,* 79, 80; rice
growing, 36; school segregation
and desegregation in, 55, 62;
secession of, 41; segregation in,
52-53; settlement of, 35, *map* 37,
38; as site of first battle of the Civil
War, 9; slavery in, 39; small
farmers in, 38; society in the 18th
Century, 37; textile industry in,
132, *138-139;* unwillingness to
accept control from London, 36;
writers, 160. *See also* Charleston,
South Carolina
South Carolina College, 154
South-Carolina Gazette, 39, 152-153
Southern attitudes: on land
ownership, 36; love of comfort and
opulence, 16; love of the past and
its institutions and traditions, 9, 14,
81-82, 101; of planters, 152; of
poor whites, 38; sense of alienation

from rest of country, 11, 38; the "Southern experience" as a way of life, 33-40; unwillingness to accept central authority over local affairs, 36

South Moon Under, 160

"Southern experience," the: origins and growth of a way of life, 32-40

Space program, 129, 130, 132. *See also* Cape Kennedy

Spain: cedes Florida to Great Britain, 38; loss of the "Plate Fleet," 112; New World discoveries, 34; settlement at Natchez, 25; settlement at St. Augustine, *34;* the Spanish in Florida, 112; Spanish treasure found in Florida, 112; territorial claims in the New World, 35

Spartanburg, South Carolina, 141, 142, 146

Speech patterns: of Charleston, 11; origin of Southern speech, 36

Sports and pastimes: fishing and hunting, *168, 169;* tournaments, *39*

Stallings, Laurence, 159-160

Star Spangled Virgin, 160

Stars Fell on Alabama, 83

States' rights, 36, 39, 56, 59; literature of, 155

Steel industry: at Birmingham, 107, 131; Fairfield Works, *107*

Stevens, J. P., & Company, 137, *138-139,* 141

Stevens, Representative Thaddeus, 58

Stevens, William Bacon, quoted, 153

Stone, Phil, *163*

Stories with a Moral Humorous and Descriptive of Southern Life a Century Ago, 155

Strange Fruit, 100

Streetcar Named Desire, A, 159

Sugar-cane growing, 118

Sulfur, 134

Sumner, Senator Charles, 82

Sumter County, 42

Sumter Light Guards, *42-43*

Surget, Pierre, 26

Suwannee River, *125*

"Symphony, The," 157

Synthetic fibers industry, 126, 130, *137,* 141, *map* 140-141, *146-147. See also* Textile industry

Tallahassee, Florida, 124

Tampa, Florida, 61, 120

Tate, Allen, 158, 159

Taxation, resentment over British taxes in the Southern colonies, 37

Tennessee: attitude to slavery, 57; early settlers in, 37; politics in, 88

Tennessee River, 130

Tennessee Valley Authority, 130

Texas as leading cotton-producing state, 133, 135

Textile industry, 85, *137-147;* automation in, 139; carpetmaking, *144-145;* in Georgia, 139; *map* 140-141; research and development, *142-143;* in South Carolina, 132, 138-139; tufting process, 140, 141, 144; woolen goods, 140. *See also* Cotton; Synthetic fibers

Thompson, Basil, 157

Thompson, Edgar T., 157

Thompson, Lieutenant P. F., *45*

Thurmond, Senator Strom, 89, 90

Tillery, Carlyle, 158

Tillman, Benjamin R. ("Pitchfork Ben"), 84, 85, 86-87

Tillotson, Frances, 158

To Kill a Mockingbird, 153

Tobacco growing, 39, 126

Tobacco Road, 151, 159

Tombigbee River, 37

Tougaloo College, 157

Tournaments, *39*

Treasure hunting, in Florida, 112

Trouble in July, 159

Truck farming, 118

Truman, President Harry, 88

Tuskegee Normal and Industrial Institute, 157

Twentieth Century Fund, Study of the South, 14

Types of Mankind, 155

Uncle Cap Interviewed," 156

Uncle Remus stories, 156, *158*

Uncle Tom's Children, 159

U.S. Steel, 107

University of Alabama, 154, 158

University of Georgia, 154

University of Mississippi, *61,* 62, 81, 154

University of South Carolina, 154

Unvanquished, The, 159

Vardaman, Senator James K., 54

Verse Craft (magazine), 157

Violent Bear It Away, The, 160

Virginia: attitude toward slavery, 57; settlers in, 34, 35, 37; tobacco growing in, 39

Waddel, Moses, 55

Walden, A. T., 110

Wallace, George Corley, Jr., 90

Wallace, Lurleen, 90

Walthall, Edward C., 85

Warren, Robert Penn, 158, 159

Washington, Booker T., 157

Washington, George, 56

Watson, Thomas Edward, 84-85, *86,* 87

Welty, Eudora, 149, *151,* 159

West Indies: English settlers from, 35; slave trade with South Carolina, 57

West Point, Georgia, 141

Western & Atlantic Railroad, 103

What Price Glory?, 159

Where the Music Was, 160

White, Captain James Hampton, 26

White, Jane Surget, 26

White supremacy, 12, 33, 49, 50, 62, 80-81, 82, 85, 86, 88, 90, 108-109

Whitefield, George, 39

Whitmarsh, Thomas, 152

Whitney, Eli, 40

Wide Net, The, 159

Wildlife. *See* Flora and fauna

Williams, Ben Ames, 149

Williams, Maria McIntosh, 21

Williams, Tennessee, 149, *153,* 159

Wire Lake Church of God, baptism, *96-97*

Wise Blood, 160

Wolfe, Thomas, 159

Wood, Clement, 160

Woodruff, Ernest, 106

Woodruff, Robert, 106

Woodruff Foundation, 106

Woodward, C. Vann, 33

World War I, 150

Wright, Sir James, Governor of Georgia, 37

Wright, Richard, 149, *151,* 159

Yearling, The, 160

Yeats, William Butler, 151

Yoknapatawpha County, 12, 159, *161-173*

Young, Stark, 149

Young, Whitney M., Jr., 62

X

PRODUCTION STAFF FOR TIME INCORPORATED

John L. Hallenbeck (Vice President and Director of Production), Robert E. Foy and Caroline Ferri

Text photocomposed under the direction of Albert J. Dunn and Arthur J. Dunn